MOST
requested
RECIPES

p. 154

390+ RECIPES READERS
LOVE MOST!

All good home cooks face the conundrum of creating nutritionally balanced meals that are a cinch to prepare and offer all the flavor and fulfillment they know their families love. But with so many recipes out there, many are left wondering just where to start.

Look no further! It's never been easier to impress your gang when you rely on the best-loved recipes from *Taste of Home*. We made it our mission to sift through all the letters and online comments on *TasteofHome.com* to collect those dishes our readers have proclaimed the best of the best—those trusted standbys they can't live without—and feature them in the third edition of our popular series, *Most Requested Recipes.*

From cover to cover, this treasure trove of reader and staff favorites is packed with delectable homemade creations and expert kitchen tips. Find more than 390 top-rated recipes, from golden casseroles and fresh-baked pies to crowd-pleasing sandwiches and quick pasta dinners. You'll also find munchable appetizers, sensational salads and sides, breakfast delights, luscious desserts, seasonal specialties, hearty main entrees of every kind and so much more!

What sets these gems apart? Each delicious dish is a time-tested favorite of a family just like yours. So you can trust they're all easy to prepare and made with affordable everyday ingredients. They also feature handy kitchen tips, easy-to-follow instructions, convenient prep/cook times and helpful comments from *TasteofHome.com* community members. You can also quickly spot slow-cooker recipes and those that prep in 30 minutes or less, thanks to at-a-glance icons that accompany them.

Whether you're looking for a new spin on a traditional weeknight supper or planning a special-occasion feast, you know you'll find a winner when you have *Most Requested Recipes* at your fingertips. Each and every mouthwatering specialty inside this cream-of-the-crop collection will have your family saying, "More, please!"

MOST
requested
RECIPES

EDITORIAL

Editor-in-Chief	Catherine Cassidy
Creative Director	Howard Greenberg
Editorial Operations Director	Kerri Balliet
Managing Editor/Print and Digital Books	Mark Hagen
Associate Creative Director	Edwin Robles Jr.
Editor	Amy Glander
Art Directors	Jessie Sharon; Jennifer Ruetz
Layout Designer	Nancy Novak
Editorial Production Manager	Dena Ahlers
Copy Chief	Deb Warlaumont Mulvey
Copy Editor	Alysse Gear
Chief Food Editor	Karen Berner
Food Editors	James Schend; Peggy Woodward, RD
Associate Food Editor	Krista Lanphier
Associate Editor/Food Content	Annie Rundle
Recipe Editors	Mary King; Jenni Sharp, RD; Irene Yeh
Content Operations Manager	Colleen King
Content Operations Assistant	Shannon Stroud
Executive Assistant	Marie Brannon
Test Kitchen And Food Styling Manager	Sarah Thompson
Test Cooks	Nicholas Iverson (Lead), Matthew Hass, Lauren Knoelke
Food Stylists	Kathryn Conrad (Senior), Shannon Roum, Leah Rekau
Prep Cooks	Megumi Garcia, Melissa Hansen, Nicole Spohrleder, Bethany VanOpdorp
Photography Director	Stephanie Marchese
Photographers	Dan Roberts, Jim Wieland
Photographer/Set Stylist	Grace Natoli Sheldon
Set Stylists	Stacey Genaw, Melissa Haberman, Dee Dee Jacq
Business Analyst	Kristy Martin
Billing Specialist	Mary Ann Koebernik
Editor, *Taste of Home*	Jeanne Ambrose
Associate Creative Director, *Taste of Home*	Erin Burns
Art Director, *Taste of Home*	Kristin Bowker

BUSINESS

General Manager, Taste of Home Cooking Schools	Erin Puariea
Vice President, Brand Marketing	Jennifer Smith
Vice President, Circulation and Continuity Marketing	Dave Fiegel

READER'S DIGEST NORTH AMERICA

Vice President, Business Development and Marketing	Alain Begun
President, Books and Home Entertainment	Harold Clarke
General Manager, Canada	Philippe Cloutier
Vice President, Operations	Mitch Cooper
Chief Operating Officer	Howard Halligan
Vice President, Chief Sales Officer	Mark Josephson
Vice President, General Manager, Milwaukee	Frank Quigley
Vice President, Digital Sales	Steve Sottile
Vice President, Chief Content Officer	Liz Vaccariello
Vice President, Global Financial Planning and Analysis	Devin White

THE READER'S DIGEST ASSOCIATION, INC.

President and Chief Executive Officer	Robert E. Guth

©2013 Reiman Media Group, Inc.
5400 S. 60th St., Greendale WI 53129

International Standard Book Number: 978-1-61765-230-1
International Standard Serial Number: 2166-0522
Component Number: 119200008H

Cover Photography: Taste of Home Photo Studio
Pictured on front cover: Mexican Lasagna (p. 128); Chocolate Almond Cheesecake (p. 182); Barbecued Beef Sandwiches (p. 63)

Pictured on back cover: Hearty Chipotle Chicken Soup (p. 62); Mixed Berry French Toast Bake (p. 43)

TABLE OF CONTENTS

32

78

131

PORCUPINE MEATBALLS, PAGE 19

BUFFALO CHICKEN DIP, 8

TORTELLINI APPETIZERS, 12

STRAWBERRY SPRITZER, 21

APPETIZERS, SNACKS & BEVERAGES

Need some tasty tidbits for a special occasion or simply craving some fun-to-eat finger food? Family and friends will waste no time grabbing a plate when you dish up any of the hot nibblers, delicious dips, juicy chicken wings, pop-in-your-mouth appetizer cups, munchable snack mixes, sweet sippers and more in this chapter. From casual fare to fancy food, these sensational party starters will have everyone's taste buds reeling!

Critter Crunch

I make a big batch of this fun sweet snack throughout the year to keep on hand for hungry kids of all ages. Once you get started eating, it's hard to stop. Plus, it makes a great take-along treat.
—**WILMA MILLER** PORT ANGELES, WASHINGTON

PREP: 10 MIN. • **BAKE:** 30 MIN. • **MAKES:** ABOUT 8 CUPS

- ¼ cup butter, cubed
- 3 tablespoons brown sugar
- 1 teaspoon ground cinnamon
- 1½ cups Crispix
- 1½ cups Cherrios
- 1½ cups animal crackers
- 1½ cups honey bear-shaped crackers
- 1 cup bite-sized Shredded Wheat
- 1 cup miniature pretzels

1. In a saucepan or microwave-safe bowl, heat the butter, brown sugar and cinnamon until butter is melted; stir until blended. In a large bowl, combine the remaining ingredients. Add butter mixture and toss to thoroughly coat.

2. Place in a greased 15x10x1-in. baking pan. Bake, uncovered, at 300° for 30 minutes, stirring every 10 minutes. Store in an airtight container.

❝Wow! Just enough salty flavor and just enough sweet flavor. I will definitely make this again.❞

—**THECAMPINGLADY** FROM TASTEOFHOME.COM

FAST FIX

Beer Cheese in a Bread Bowl

My entire family loves this cheese dip, and my friends always request I bring it to gatherings. It's also quite attractive thanks to the bread bowl. Serve with bread cubes, tortilla chips, crackers or chopped veggies.
—**JULIE KOCH** DELAWARE, OHIO

PREP/TOTAL TIME: 15 MIN. • **MAKES:** 2½ CUPS

- 1 round loaf (1 pound) pumpernickel bread
- 2 jars (5 ounces each) sharp American cheese spread
- 1 package (8 ounces) cream cheese, softened
- ¼ cup beer or nonalcoholic beer
- ½ cup real bacon bits

1. Cut top fourth off loaf of bread; carefully hollow out bottom, leaving a ½-in. shell. Cut removed bread into cubes; set aside.

2. In a microwave-safe bowl, combine cheese spread and cream cheese. Microwave, uncovered, on high for 2 minutes, stirring every 30 seconds. Stir in beer. Microwave, uncovered, for an additional 20 seconds. Stir in bacon bits.

3. Fill bread shell with cheese dip. Serve with reserved bread cubes.

NOTE *This recipe was tested in a 1,100-watt microwave.*

Cucumber-Stuffed Cherry Tomatoes

I love this recipe because it's one that I can make the night before a party. I often triple the recipe because these little bites disappear fast.
—**CHRISTI MARTIN** ELKO, NEVADA

PREP/TOTAL TIME: 25 MIN. • **MAKES:** 2 DOZEN

> 24 cherry tomatoes
> 1 package (3 ounces) cream cheese, softened
> 2 tablespoons mayonnaise
> ¼ cup finely chopped peeled cucumber
> 1 tablespoon finely chopped green onion
> 2 teaspoons minced fresh dill

1. Cut a thin slice off the top of each tomato. Scoop out and discard pulp; invert tomatoes onto paper towels to drain.

2. In a small bowl, combine cream cheese and mayonnaise until smooth; stir in the cucumber, onion and dill. Spoon or pipe into tomatoes. Refrigerate until serving. Add an additional sprig of dill to each if desired.

Deviled Eggs Extraordinaire

These creamy, mild deviled eggs boast a pleasant mustard flavor. They're perfect for summertime picnics but could also work for formal occasions when garnished with tiny amounts of red or black caviar.

—**CAROL ROSS** ANCHORAGE, ALASKA

PREP: 40 MIN. • **MAKES:** 4 DOZEN

- 24 **hard-cooked eggs, peeled**
- 4 **ounces cream cheese, softened**
- ½ **cup mayonnaise**
- 2 **tablespoons prepared mustard**
- 1 **teaspoon cider vinegar**
- ¼ **teaspoon salt**
- ¼ **teaspoon onion powder**

Cut eggs in half lengthwise. Remove yolks; set whites aside. In a small bowl, mash yolks. Add the cream cheese, mayonnaise, mustard, vinegar, salt and onion powder; mix well. Stuff or pipe into egg whites. Refrigerate until serving.

FAST FIX Tender Chicken Nuggets

Four ingredients are all it takes to create these moist golden bites that are healthier than fast food. I serve them with ranch dressing and barbecue sauce for dipping.

—**LYNNE HAHN** WINCHESTER, CALIFORNIA

PREP/TOTAL TIME: 25 MIN.
MAKES: 4 SERVINGS

- ½ **cup seasoned bread crumbs**
- 2 **tablespoons grated Parmesan cheese**
- 1 **egg white**
- 1 **pound boneless skinless chicken breasts, cut into 1-inch cubes**

1. In a large resealable plastic bag, combine bread crumbs and cheese. In a shallow bowl, beat the egg white. Dip chicken pieces in egg white, then place in bag and shake to coat.
2. Place chicken in a 15x10x1-in. baking pan coated with cooking spray. Bake, uncovered, at 400° for 12-15 minutes or until no longer pink, turning once.

FAST FIX Buffalo Chicken Dip

Family members always request my zippy baked dip for football parties and holidays. Serve it warm from the oven with a bowl of tortilla chips.

—**PEGGY FOSTER** FLORENCE, KENTUCKY

PREP/TOTAL TIME: 30 MIN.
MAKES: ABOUT 2 CUPS

- 1 **package (8 ounces) cream cheese, softened**
- 1 **can (10 ounces) chunk white chicken, drained**
- ½ **cup buffalo wing sauce**
- ½ **cup ranch salad dressing**
- 2 **cups (8 ounces) shredded Colby-Monterey Jack cheese French bread baguette slices, celery ribs or tortilla chips, optional**

1. Preheat oven to 350°. Spread cream cheese in an ungreased shallow 1-qt. baking dish. Layer with chicken, wing sauce and salad dressing. Sprinkle with cheese.
2. Bake, uncovered, 20-25 minutes or until cheese is melted. If desired, serve with baguette slices.

FAST FIX
Crisp Cucumber Salsa

Here's a twist on typical salsa and a fantastic way to use up a bounty of cucumbers. You'll love the creamy and crunchy texture and fresh flavors.
—CHARLENE SKJERVEN
HOOPLE, NORTH DAKOTA

PREP/TOTAL TIME: 20 MIN.
MAKES: 2½ CUPS

- 2 cups finely chopped seeded peeled cucumber
- ½ cup finely chopped seeded tomato
- ¼ cup chopped red onion
- 2 tablespoons minced fresh parsley
- 1 jalapeno pepper, seeded and chopped
- 4½ teaspoons minced fresh cilantro
- 1 garlic clove, minced
- ¼ cup reduced-fat sour cream
- 1½ teaspoons lemon juice
- 1½ teaspoons lime juice
- ¼ teaspoon ground cumin
- ¼ teaspoon seasoned salt
  Baked tortilla chip scoops

In a small bowl, combine the first seven ingredients. In another bowl, combine the sour cream, lemon juice, lime juice, cumin and seasoned salt. Pour over cucumber mixture and toss gently to coat. Serve immediately with chips.
NOTE *Wear disposable gloves when cutting hot peppers; the oils can burn skin. Avoid touching your face.*

SPEEDY SEEDED CUCUMBER
To easily remove seeds from a cucumber, cut it in half lengthwise, then run a melon baller down the length of both halves to scoop out the seeds. This method is quicker than using a knife and wastes little of the cucumber.

FAST FIX Cinnamon Baked Pretzels

Create your favorite mall treat in the comfort of your own kitchen with this easy breezy recipe. It's a great brunch starter or perfect for the morning after the kids have a slumber party.
—MARINA HEPPNER
ORCHARD PARK, NEW YORK

PREP/TOTAL TIME: 15 MIN.
MAKES: 6 SERVINGS

- 3 tablespoons cinnamon-sugar
- 2 tablespoons butter
- ¼ teaspoon ground nutmeg
- 1 package (13 ounces) frozen baked soft pretzels
- ½ cup red raspberry preserves, warmed

1. In a small microwave-safe bowl, combine the cinnamon-sugar, butter and nutmeg. Microwave, uncovered, on high for 30-45 seconds or until butter is melted; brush over pretzels. Transfer to an ungreased baking sheet.
2. Bake at 400° for 3-4 minutes or until heated through. Serve with raspberry preserves.

Sausage-Stuffed Mushrooms

A perennial favorite, stuffed mushrooms are what most guests look forward to at a party. This Italian adaptation, done in less than an hour, will have company begging for more. Add sliced green onions on top for a pretty garnish.

—BEATRICE VETRANO
LANDENBERG, PENNSYLVANIA

PREP: 25 MIN. • **BAKE:** 20 MIN.
MAKES: 12-15 SERVINGS

- **12 to 15 large fresh mushrooms**
- **2 tablespoons butter, divided**
- **2 tablespoons chopped onion**
- **1 tablespoon lemon juice**
- **¼ teaspoon dried basil**
- **Salt and pepper to taste**
- **4 ounces bulk Italian sausage**
- **1 tablespoon chopped fresh parsley**
- **2 tablespoons dry bread crumbs**
- **2 tablespoons grated Parmesan cheese**

1. Remove stems from the mushrooms. Chop stems finely; set mushroom caps aside. Place stems in paper towels and squeeze to remove any liquid.

2. In a large skillet, heat 1½ tablespoons butter. Cook stems and onion until tender. Add the lemon juice, basil, salt and pepper; cook until almost all the liquid has evaporated. Cool.

3. In a large bowl, combine the mushroom mixture, sausage and parsley; stuff reserved mushroom caps. Combine crumbs and cheese; sprinkle over tops. Dot each mushroom with remaining butter.

4. Place in a greased baking pan. Bake at 400° for 20 minutes or until sausage is no longer pink, basting occasionally with pan juices. Serve mushrooms hot.

Reuben Rolls

I wanted the flavor of a classic Reuben in a fun-to-eat appetizer. The empty plate at my party signaled these rolls were a hit!

—**DARLENE ABNEY** MUENSTER, TEXAS

PREP: 30 MIN. + CHILLING • **MAKES:** ABOUT 8 DOZEN

- 1 package (8 ounces) cream cheese, softened
- 3 tablespoons spicy brown mustard
- ¼ teaspoon prepared horseradish
- 5 flour tortillas (10 inches), room temperature
- 7 packages (2 ounces each) thinly sliced deli corned beef
- 15 thin slices Swiss cheese
- 1 can (14 ounces) sauerkraut, rinsed and well drained

1. In a small bowl, beat the cream cheese, mustard and horseradish until blended. Spread a heaping tablespoonful of cream cheese mixture over each tortilla.
2. Layer each tortilla with eight slices of corned beef, three slices of cheese, another heaping tablespoonful of cream cheese mixture and ½ cup sauerkraut. Roll up each tortilla tightly. Chill for 1 hour. Cut each roll-up into ½-in. slices.

Refrigerator Dill Pickles

Looking for a homemade appetizer that's economical and easy? Give these tangy and crispy pickles a try. No one will believe you made them yourself!

—**JAKE HAEN** OCALA, FLORIDA

PREP: 40 MIN. + CHILLING • **MAKES:** 100 PICKLE SPEARS

- 6 to 8 pounds pickling cucumbers
- 40 fresh dill sprigs
- 2 large onions, thinly sliced
- 5 garlic cloves, sliced
- 1 quart water
- 1 quart white vinegar
- ¾ cup sugar
- ½ cup canning salt

1. Cut each cucumber lengthwise into four spears. In a large bowl, combine the cucumbers, dill, onions and garlic; set aside. In a Dutch oven, combine the remaining ingredients. Bring to a boil; cook and stir just until salt is dissolved. Pour over cucumber mixture; cool.
2. Cover tightly and refrigerate for at least 24 hours. Store in the refrigerator for up to 2 months.

Cola Hot Wings

These delectable wings are so easy to make and they offer year-round versatility, from summer cookouts to autumn tailgates. My husband likes them so much he'll stand out in the snow to grill them!

—**LISA LINVILLE** RANDOLPH, NEBRASKA

PREP: 15 MIN. • **GRILL:** 40 MIN. • **MAKES:** ABOUT 2½ DOZEN

- 3 pounds chicken wings
- 1 cup Louisiana-style hot sauce
- 1 can (12 ounces) cola
- 1 tablespoon soy sauce
- ¼ teaspoon cayenne pepper
- ¼ teaspoon pepper
  Blue cheese salad dressing

1. Cut chicken wings into three sections; discard wing tip sections. In a small bowl, combine the hot sauce, cola, soy sauce, cayenne and pepper.
2. Prepare grill for indirect heat, using a drip pan. Moisten a paper towel with cooking oil; using long-handled tongs, lightly coat the grill rack. Grill chicken wings, covered, over indirect medium heat for 10 minutes. Grill 30-40 minutes longer, turning occasionally and basting frequently with sauce until wings are nicely glazed. Serve with salad dressing.
NOTE *Uncooked chicken wing sections (wingettes) may be substituted for whole chicken wings.*

Tortellini Appetizers

These cute, lighter kabobs will lend a little Italian flavor to any get-together. Cheese tortellini is marinated in salad dressing, then skewered onto toothpicks along with stuffed olives, salami and cheese.
—**PATRICIA SCHMIDT** STERLING HEIGHTS, MICHIGAN

PREP: 25 MIN. + MARINATING • **MAKES:** 1½ DOZEN

- 18 **refrigerated cheese tortellini**
- ¼ **cup fat-free Italian salad dressing**
- 6 **thin slices (4 ounces) reduced-fat provolone cheese**
- 6 **thin slices (2 ounces) Genoa salami**
- 18 **large pimiento-stuffed olives**

1. Cook tortellini according to package directions; drain and rinse in cold water. In a resealable plastic bag, combine the tortellini and salad dressing. Seal bag and refrigerate for 4 hours.
2. Place a slice of cheese on each slice of salami; roll up tightly. Cut into thirds. Drain tortellini and discard dressing. For each appetizer, thread a tortellini, salami roll-up and olive on a toothpick.

FAST FIX ▶ Three-Cheese Quesadillas

I turn to this tasty appetizer when I'm short on time because it comes together in a snap. Serve alongside your favorite salsa or as dippers with chili for a simple meal.
—**SANDY SMITH** SAUGERTIES, NEW YORK

PREP/TOTAL TIME: 20 MIN. • **MAKES:** 2 SERVINGS

- 1 **tablespoon butter**
- 4 **flour tortillas (8 inches)**
- 2 **ounces cream cheese, softened**
- ¼ **cup shredded sharp cheddar cheese**
- ¼ **cup shredded Monterey Jack cheese**
- 2 **tablespoons thinly sliced green onion**
- 1 **tablespoon minced fresh cilantro**

- 2 **teaspoons chopped ripe olives**
- ¼ **cup salsa**
  Sour cream, optional

1. Spread butter over one side of each tortilla. Spread cream cheese over unbuttered side on half the tortillas. Sprinkle with cheeses, onion, cilantro and olives. Top with remaining tortillas, buttered side up.
2. Cook on a griddle over medium heat for 1-2 minutes on each side or until cheese is melted. Cut into wedges. Serve with salsa and sour cream if desired.

FAST FIX ▶ Shrimp Spread

This colorful and tasty appetizer is always a crowd-pleaser. People will never know you've used lighter ingredients.
—**NORENE WRIGHT** MANILLA, INDIANA

PREP/TOTAL TIME: 15 MIN. • **MAKES:** 20 SERVINGS

- 1 **package (8 ounces) reduced-fat cream cheese**
- ½ **cup reduced-fat sour cream**
- ¼ **cup reduced-fat mayonnaise**
- 1 **cup seafood cocktail sauce**
- 2 **cups (8 ounces) shredded part-skim mozzarella cheese**
- 1 **can (6 ounces) small shrimp, rinsed and drained**
- 3 **green onions, sliced**
- 1 **medium tomato, finely chopped**
  Sliced Italian bread or assorted crackers

1. In a small bowl, beat the cream cheese, sour cream and mayonnaise until smooth. Spread onto a 12-in. round serving plate; top with seafood sauce. Sprinkle with cheese, shrimp, onions and tomato.
2. Chill until serving. Serve with bread or crackers.

Zucchini Fritters

You will not believe how fast these fritters disappear. Even confirmed veggie-haters devour these tasty snacks as fast as I can make them!

—**TRISHA KRUSE** EAGLE, IDAHO

PREP: 20 MIN. • **BAKE:** 20 MIN.
MAKES: 10 SERVINGS (¾ CUP SAUCE)

- ¼ **cup buttermilk**
- ¼ **cup egg substitute**
- ½ **cup panko (Japanese) bread crumbs**
- ½ **cup seasoned bread crumbs**
- ¼ **cup grated Parmesan cheese**
- 1½ **teaspoons taco seasoning**
- ¼ **teaspoon garlic salt**
- 3 **medium zucchini, cut into ¼-inch slices**
- ¼ **cup fat-free sour cream**
- ¼ **cup fat-free ranch salad dressing**
- ¼ **cup salsa**

1. In a shallow bowl, combine buttermilk and egg substitute. In another shallow bowl, combine the bread crumbs, cheese, taco seasoning and garlic salt. Dip zucchini in buttermilk mixture, then bread crumb mixture.

2. Place on baking sheets coated with cooking spray. Bake at 400° for 20-25 minutes or until golden brown, turning once.

3. In a small bowl, combine the sour cream, ranch dressing and salsa. Serve with zucchini.

> **ZUCCHINI 101**
>
> Handle zucchini carefully; they're thin-skinned and easily damaged. To pick the freshest zucchini, look for a firm heavy squash with a moist stem end and a shiny skin. Smaller squash are generally sweeter and more tender than larger ones. One medium zucchini yields about 2 cups sliced.

Bacon Quiche Tarts

Flavored with vegetables, cheese and bacon, these memorable morsels are bound to be winners at any party or celebration. The tarts look impressive but are actually quite easy to make.

—KENDRA SCHERTZ NAPPANEE, INDIANA

PREP: 15 MIN. • **BAKE:** 20 MIN. • **MAKES:** 8 SERVINGS

  2 **packages (3 ounces each) cream cheese, softened**
  5 **teaspoons 2% milk**
  2 **eggs**
  ½ **cup shredded Colby cheese**
  2 **tablespoons chopped green pepper**
  1 **tablespoon finely chopped onion**
  1 **tube (8 ounces) refrigerated crescent rolls**
  5 **bacon strips, cooked and crumbled**

1. In a small bowl, beat cream cheese and milk until smooth. Add the eggs, cheese, green pepper and onion.
2. Separate dough into eight triangles; press onto the bottom and up the sides of greased muffin cups. Sprinkle half of the bacon into cups. Pour egg mixture over bacon; top with remaining bacon.
3. Bake, uncovered, at 375° for 18-22 minutes or until a knife inserted near the center comes out clean. Serve warm.

Mexican Cheesecake

People will rave over this super-easy cheesecake appetizer. I've made this recipe several times at parties, and people were so surprised it was low-fat. Make it a day ahead for convenience, adding salsa just before serving.

—SANDY BURKETT GALENA, OHIO

PREP: 20 MIN. • **BAKE:** 30 MIN. + CHILLING
MAKES: 24 SERVINGS

- 2 packages (8 ounces each) reduced-fat cream cheese
- 1¼ cups reduced-fat sour cream, divided
- 1 envelope taco seasoning
- 3 eggs, lightly beaten
- 1½ cups (6 ounces) shredded sharp cheddar cheese
- 1 can (4 ounces) chopped green chilies
- 1 cup chunky salsa, drained
  Tortilla chips or fresh vegetables

1. In a large bowl, beat cream cheese, ½ cup sour cream and taco seasoning until smooth. Add eggs; beat on low speed just until combined. Stir in cheddar cheese and chilies.

2. Transfer to a greased 9-in. springform pan. Place on a baking sheet. Bake at 350° for 25-30 minutes or until center is almost set. Spread remaining sour cream evenly over top. Bake 5-8 minutes longer or until topping is set.

3. Cool on a wire rack for 10 minutes. Carefully run a knife around edge of pan to loosen; cool 1 hour longer. Refrigerate overnight.

4. Just before serving, spread salsa over cheesecake. Serve with tortilla chips or vegetables.

🍲 SLOW COOKER Chili Cheese Dip

After trying to create a Mexican soup, I ended up with this outstanding dip that eats like a meal. My husband and two young children love it! Now it's popular for football game days or family gatherings.

—SANDRA FICK LINCOLN, NEBRASKA

PREP: 20 MIN. • **COOK:** 4½ HOURS • **MAKES:** 8 CUPS

- 1 pound lean ground beef (90% lean)
- 1 cup chopped onion
- 1 can (16 ounces) kidney beans, rinsed and drained
- 1 can (15 ounces) black beans, rinsed and drained
- 1 can (14½ ounces) diced tomatoes in sauce
- 1 cup frozen corn
- ¾ cup water
- 1 can (2¼ ounces) sliced ripe olives, drained
- 3 teaspoons chili powder
- ½ teaspoon dried oregano
- ½ teaspoon chipotle hot pepper sauce
- ¼ teaspoon garlic powder
- ¼ teaspoon ground cumin
- 1 package (16 ounces) reduced-fat process cheese (Velveeta), cubed
  Corn chips

1. In a large skillet, cook the beef and onion over medium heat until no longer pink; drain. Transfer to a 5-qt. slow cooker. Stir in the beans, tomatoes, corn, water, olives, chili powder, oregano, pepper sauce, garlic powder and cumin.

2. Cover and cook on low for 4-5 hours or until heated through; stir in cheese. Cover and cook for 30 minutes or until cheese is melted. Serve with corn chips.

Simple Marinated Shrimp

Seafood is a staple here in Florida. This recipe is quick and easy to make and can be prepared well in advance. I always seem to get a lot of requests for the recipe when I make it for a party or special occasion.

—MARGARET DELONG LAKE BUTLER, FLORIDA

PREP: 10 MIN. + MARINATING • **MAKES:** 14 SERVINGS

- 2 **pounds cooked medium shrimp, peeled and deveined**
- 1 **medium red onion, sliced and separated into rings**
- 2 **medium lemons, cut into slices**
- 1 **cup pitted ripe olives, drained**
- ½ **cup olive oil**
- ⅓ **cup minced fresh parsley**
- 3 **tablespoons lemon juice**
- 3 **tablespoons red wine vinegar**
- 1 **garlic clove, minced**
- 1 **bay leaf**
- 1 **tablespoon minced fresh basil or 1 teaspoon dried basil**
- 1 **teaspoon salt**
- 1 **teaspoon ground mustard**
- ¼ **teaspoon pepper**

1. In a 3-qt. glass serving bowl, combine the shrimp, onion, lemons and olives. In a jar with a tight-fitting lid, combine the remaining ingredients; shake well. Pour over shrimp mixture and stir gently to coat.
2. Cover and refrigerate for 24 hours, stirring occasionally. Discard bay leaf before serving.

Blue Cheese-Stuffed Strawberries

I was enjoying a salad with strawberries and blue cheese when the idea hit me to stuff the strawberries and serve them as an appetizer. It worked out great, and the flavors blend so nicely.

—DIANE NEMITZ LUDINGTON, MICHIGAN

PREP/TOTAL TIME: 25 MIN. • **MAKES:** 16 APPETIZERS

- ½ **cup balsamic vinegar**
- 3 **ounces fat-free cream cheese**
- 2 **ounces crumbled blue cheese**
- 16 **fresh strawberries**
- 3 **tablespoons finely chopped pecans, toasted**

1. Place vinegar in a small saucepan. Bring to a boil; cook until liquid is reduced by half. Cool to room temperature.
2. Meanwhile, in a small bowl, beat cream cheese until smooth. Beat in blue cheese. Remove stems and scoop out centers from strawberries; fill each with about 2 teaspoons cheese mixture. Sprinkle pecans over filling, pressing lightly. Chill until serving. Drizzle with balsamic vinegar.

> "Mmm...so good. I love the balsamic vinegar reduction with the blue cheese and strawberries."
>
> **—DYNAGIRL99** FROM TASTEOFHOME.COM

Antipasto Platter

We entertain often, and antipasto is one of our favorite crowd-pleasers. Everyone loves that there are so many salty, fresh and savory treats to nibble on. It's a satisfying change of pace from the usual chips and dip.
—**TERI LINDQUIST** GURNEE, ILLINOIS

PREP: 10 MIN. + CHILLING • **MAKES:** 14-16 SERVINGS

- 1 jar (24 ounces) pepperoncini, drained
- 1 can (15 ounces) garbanzo beans or chickpeas, rinsed and drained
- 2 cups halved fresh mushrooms
- 2 cups halved cherry tomatoes
- ½ pound provolone cheese, cubed
- 1 can (6 ounces) pitted ripe olives, drained
- 1 package (3½ ounces) sliced pepperoni
- 1 bottle (8 ounces) Italian vinaigrette dressing
  Lettuce leaves

1. In a large bowl, combine the pepperoncini, beans, mushrooms, tomatoes, cheese, olives and pepperoni. Pour vinaigrette over mixture; toss to coat.
2. Refrigerate for at least 30 minutes or overnight. Arrange ingredients on a lettuce-lined platter. Serve with toothpicks.

FAST FIX ▶ Fresh Peach Lemonade

Looking for a new twist on lemonade? Fresh peaches lend a fruity flavor to this summertime must-have.
—**JOAN HALLFORD** NORTH RICHLAND HILLS, TEXAS

PREP/TOTAL TIME: 20 MIN. • **MAKES:** 5 SERVINGS

- 4 cups water, divided
- 2 medium peaches, chopped
- 1 cup sugar
- ¾ cup lemon juice
- 1 medium lemon, sliced
  Mint sprigs, optional

1. In a small saucepan, bring 2 cups water, peaches and sugar to a boil. Reduce heat; cover and simmer for 5-7 minutes or until peaches are tender. Remove from the heat. Cool. Strain, discarding peach skins.
2. In a large pitcher, combine the peach mixture, lemon juice and remaining water. Add lemon slices and mint if desired. Serve over ice.

PRETTY PRESENTATION

Make lemonade or iced tea special by dipping the rims of glasses in a little fresh lemon juice, then twisting the glasses slightly in a saucer of sugar. Set trays of glasses in the refrigerator until ready to serve.

FAST FIX

Old-Fashioned Ice Cream Sodas

I keep the ingredients for these ice cream sodas on hand so I can enjoy a treat any time I want. You can easily make more when feeding a crowd.
—**ANNA ERICKSON** SILVERDALE, WASHINGTON

PREP/TOTAL TIME: 15 MIN. • **MAKES:** 4 SERVINGS

- ¾ cup chocolate syrup
- 1 cup milk
- 4 cups carbonated water, chilled
- 8 scoops chocolate ice cream (about 2⅔ cups), divided
  Whipped cream in a can, optional

Place 3 tablespoons chocolate syrup in each of four 16-oz. glasses. Add ¼ cup milk and 1 cup carbonated water to each; stir until foamy. Add two scoops of ice cream to each glass. Top with whipped cream if desired.

MAKE-AHEAD MARVEL

Ice cream sodas can be an easy and fun make-ahead dessert. Prior to the party or meal, place two scoops of ice cream into eight 8-ounce clear plastic drink cups. Set them on cookie sheets, cover with plastic wrap and freeze. At dessert time, mix the liquid ingredients in a pitcher, then pour ⅛ of the mixture over each cup. Kids of all ages enjoy this treat!

Mini Sausage Quiches

These bite-size quiches are loaded with sausage and cheese, plus their crescent roll base makes preparation a breeze. Serve the cute "muffinettes" at any brunch or potluck gathering.
—**JAN MEAD** MILFORD, CONNECTICUT

PREP: 25 MIN. • **BAKE:** 20 MIN. • **MAKES:** 4 DOZEN

- ½ pound bulk hot Italian sausage
- 2 tablespoons dried minced onion
- 2 tablespoons minced chives
- 1 tube (8 ounces) refrigerated crescent rolls
- 4 eggs, lightly beaten
- 2 cups (8 ounces) shredded Swiss cheese
- 1 cup (8 ounces) 4% cottage cheese
- ⅓ cup grated Parmesan cheese
  Paprika

1. In a large skillet, brown sausage and onion over medium heat for 4-5 minutes or until meat is no longer pink; drain. Stir in chives.

2. On a lightly floured surface, unroll crescent dough into one long rectangle; seal seams and perforations. Cut into 48 pieces. Press onto the bottom and up the sides of greased miniature muffin cups.

3. Fill each cup with about 2 teaspoons of sausage mixture. In a large bowl, combine the eggs and cheeses. Spoon 2 teaspoonfuls over sausage mixture. Sprinkle with paprika.

4. Bake at 375° for 20-25 minutes or until a knife inserted in the center comes out clean. Cool for 5 minutes before removing from pans to wire racks. Serve warm.

Mexican Salsa

I love to make this zippy, blood-red salsa with fresh tomatoes and peppers from my garden. It's not only great served as a snack with tortilla chips, but also as a topping for a baked potato or over fish or chicken.

—ROGER STENMAN BATAVIA, ILLINOIS

PREP: 40 MIN. • **MAKES:** 3½ CUPS

- 3 jalapeno peppers
- 1 medium onion, quartered
- 1 garlic clove, halved
- 2 cans (one 28 ounces, one 14½ ounces) whole tomatoes, drained
- 4 fresh cilantro sprigs
- ½ teaspoon salt
  Tortilla chips

1. Heat a small ungreased cast-iron skillet over high heat. With a small sharp knife, pierce jalapenos; add to hot skillet. Cook for 15-20 minutes or until peppers are blistered and blackened, turning occasionally.

2. Immediately place jalapenos in a small bowl; cover and let stand for 20 minutes. Peel off and discard charred skins. Remove the stems and seeds.

3. Place onion and garlic in a food processor; cover and pulse four times. Add the tomatoes, cilantro, salt and jalapenos. Cover and process until desired consistency. Chill until serving. Serve with chips.
NOTE *Wear disposable gloves when cutting hot peppers; the oils can burn skin. Avoid touching your face.*

Porcupine Meatballs

These well-seasoned meatballs smothered in rich tomato sauce are one of my mom's best main dishes. I used to love this meal when I was growing up. I made them at home for our children, and now my daughters make them as an appetizer!

—DARLIS WILFER WEST BEND, WISCONSIN

PREP: 20 MIN. • **COOK:** 1 HOUR
MAKES: 4-6 SERVINGS

- ½ cup uncooked long grain rice
- ½ cup water
- ⅓ cup chopped onion
- 1 teaspoon salt
- ½ teaspoon celery salt
- ⅛ teaspoon pepper
- ⅛ teaspoon garlic powder
- 1 pound ground beef
- 2 tablespoons canola oil
- 1 can (15 ounces) tomato sauce
- 1 cup water
- 2 tablespoons brown sugar
- 2 teaspoons Worcestershire sauce

In a bowl, combine the first seven ingredients. Add beef and mix well. Shape into 1½-in. balls. In a large skillet, brown meatballs in oil; drain. Combine tomato sauce, water, brown sugar and Worcestershire sauce; pour over meatballs. Reduce heat; cover and simmer for 1 hour.

Chicken Salad in Baskets

These little cups were a big hit the first time I made them. My husband asks me to fix them for every party... or whenever he has a hankering!

—GWENDOLYN FAE TRAPP
STRONGSVILLE, OHIO

PREP: 15 MIN. • **BAKE:** 15 MIN. + CHILLING
MAKES: 20 APPETIZERS

- 1 **cup diced cooked chicken**
- 3 **bacon strips, cooked and crumbled**
- ⅓ **cup chopped mushrooms**
- 2 **tablespoons chopped pecans**
- 2 **tablespoons diced peeled apple**
- ¼ **cup mayonnaise**
- ⅛ **teaspoon salt**
  Dash pepper
- 20 **slices bread**
- 6 **tablespoons butter, melted**
- 2 **tablespoons minced fresh parsley**

1. In a small bowl, combine the first five ingredients. Combine the mayonnaise, salt and pepper; add to chicken mixture and stir to coat. Cover and refrigerate until serving.
2. Preheat oven to 350°. Cut each slice of bread with a 3-in. round cookie cutter; brush both sides with butter. Press into ungreased mini muffin cups. Bake 11-13 minutes or until cups are golden brown and crisp.
3. Cool 3 minutes before removing from pans to wire racks to cool completely. Spoon 1 tablespoonful chicken salad into each bread basket. Cover and refrigerate up to 2 hours. Just before serving, sprinkle with parsley.

FAST FIX ▶ Creamy Black Bean Salsa

I love the way sour cream tempers the heat on spicy dishes, so I decided to add it to my favorite salsa. This always goes fast at parties and get-togethers, so you may want to double the recipe.

—DARLENE BRENDEN
SALEM, OREGON

PREP/TOTAL TIME: 20 MIN.
MAKES: 4 CUPS

- 1 **can (15 ounces) black beans, rinsed and drained**
- 1½ **cups frozen corn, thawed**
- 1 **cup finely chopped sweet red pepper**
- ¾ **cup finely chopped green pepper**
- ½ **cup finely chopped red onion**
- 1 **tablespoon minced fresh parsley**
- ½ **cup sour cream**
- ¼ **cup mayonnaise**
- 2 **tablespoons red wine vinegar**
- 1 **teaspoon ground cumin**
- 1 **teaspoon chili powder**
- ½ **teaspoon salt**
- ¼ **teaspoon garlic powder**
- ⅛ **teaspoon pepper**
  Tortilla chips

In a large bowl, combine the beans, corn, peppers, onion and parsley. Combine the sour cream, mayonnaise, vinegar and seasonings; pour over corn mixture and toss gently to coat. Serve with tortilla chips. Refrigerate leftovers.

FAST FIX ▶ Strawberry Spritzer

Three simple ingredients are all you need to create this fresh and fruity summer beverage. It's bound to become a warm-weather favorite.
—**KRISTA COLLINS** CONCORD, NORTH CAROLINA

PREP/TOTAL TIME: 10 MIN. • **MAKES:** 2½ QUARTS

- 1 package (10 ounces) frozen sweetened sliced strawberries, thawed
- 2 liters lemon-lime soda, chilled
- 1 can (12 ounces) frozen pink lemonade concentrate, thawed

Place the strawberries in a blender; cover and process until pureed. Pour into a large pitcher; stir in the soda and lemonade concentrate. Serve immediately.

Southwest Egg Rolls

Moderately crispy with a rich and creamy filling, these semi-spicy appetizers taste like they've been fried.
—**DANIELLE BOOTH** MINNEAPOLIS, MINNESOTA

PREP: 45 MIN. • **BAKE:** 10 MIN. • **MAKES:** 2½ DOZEN

- 1 cup fresh baby spinach, chopped
- 2 tablespoons finely chopped red onion
- 2 tablespoons finely chopped sweet red pepper
- 1 jalapeno pepper, seeded and minced
- 1 tablespoon canola oil
- ⅓ cup frozen corn, thawed
- ¼ cup black beans, rinsed and drained
- ⅛ teaspoon salt
  Dash cayenne pepper
  Dash ground cumin
- ¾ cup shredded reduced-fat Monterey Jack cheese or reduced-fat Mexican cheese blend
- 4 ounces reduced-fat cream cheese
- 30 wonton wrappers
  Cooking spray

1. In a large skillet, saute the spinach, onion, red pepper and jalapeno in oil until tender. Stir in the corn, beans and seasonings; heat through. Remove from the heat. Stir in shredded cheese and cream cheese until melted.

2. Position a wonton wrapper with one point toward you. (Keep remaining wrappers covered with a damp paper towel until ready to use.) Place 2 teaspoons of filling in the center of wrapper. Fold bottom corner over filling; fold sides toward center over filling. Roll toward the remaining point. Moisten top corner with water; press to seal. Repeat with remaining wrappers and filling.

3. Place in a 15x10x1-in. baking pan coated with cooking spray; lightly coat egg rolls with additional cooking spray. Bake at 425° for 8-10 minutes or until golden brown, turning once.

NOTE *Wear disposable gloves when cutting hot peppers; the oils can burn skin. Avoid touching your face.*

Candied Pecans

I packed these crispy pecans in jars tied with pretty ribbon for family and friends. My granddaughter gave some to a doctor at the hospital where she works, and he said they were too good to be true!

—OPAL TURNER HUGHES SPRINGS, TEXAS

PREP: 20 MIN. • **BAKE:** 40 MIN. • **MAKES:** ABOUT 1 POUND

- 2¾ cups pecan halves
- 2 tablespoons butter, softened, divided
- 1 cup sugar
- ½ cup water
- ½ teaspoon salt
- ½ teaspoon ground cinnamon
- 1 teaspoon vanilla extract

1. Place pecans in a shallow baking pan in a 250° oven for 10 minutes or until warmed. Grease a 15x10x1-in. baking pan with 1 tablespoon butter; set aside.

2. Grease the sides of a large heavy saucepan with remaining butter; add sugar, water, salt and cinnamon. Cook and stir over low heat until sugar is dissolved. Cook and stir over medium heat until mixture comes to a boil. Cover and cook for 2 minutes to dissolve sugar crystals.

3. Cook, without stirring, until a candy thermometer reads 236° (soft-ball stage). Remove from the heat; add vanilla. Stir in warm pecans until evenly coated.

4. Spread onto prepared baking pan. Bake at 250° for 30 minutes, stirring every 10 minutes. Spread on a waxed paper-lined baking sheet to cool.

NOTE *We recommend that you test your candy thermometer before each use by bringing water to a boil; the thermometer should read 212°. Adjust your recipe temperature up or down based on your test.*

FAST FIX # Mozzarella Sticks

You won't believe something this easy could taste so fantastic! Crunchy on the outside, gooey cheese on the inside...this is a treat all ages will love. Kids could help wrap them, too.

—SHIRLEY WARREN THIENSVILLE, WISCONSIN

PREP/TOTAL TIME: 20 MIN. • **MAKES:** 1 DOZEN

- 12 pieces string cheese
- 12 egg roll wrappers
  Oil for deep-fat frying
  Marinara or spaghetti sauce

1. Place a piece of string cheese near the bottom corner of one egg roll wrapper (keep remaining wrappers covered with a damp paper towel until ready to use). Fold bottom corner over cheese. Roll up halfway; fold sides toward center over cheese. Moisten remaining corner with water; roll up tightly to seal. Repeat with remaining wrappers and cheese.

2. In an electric skillet, heat ½ in. of oil to 375°. Fry sticks, a few at a time, for 30-60 seconds on each side or until golden brown. Drain on paper towels. Serve with marinara sauce.

FLAVOR BOOST

To take the flavor of these mozzarella sticks up a notch, try adding a dash of Italian seasoning or minced garlic to each egg roll wrapper. You can also add chopped pepperoni or chicken for extra heartiness.

Mini Pizza Cups

These little pizzas are wonderful served hot or cold. Their small size makes them ideal for an after-school snack or kid-friendly party. Plus, they're so easy to make, little ones can help you in the kitchen!
—**JANE JONES** CEDAR, MINNESOTA

PREP: 25 MIN. • **BAKE:** 15 MIN. • **MAKES:** 32 APPETIZERS

- 1 tube (11.3 ounces) refrigerated dinner rolls
- 1 can (8 ounces) pizza sauce
- ¼ cup finely chopped onion
- ⅓ cup finely chopped green pepper
- 2 ounces sliced turkey pepperoni, chopped
- 1 cup (4 ounces) shredded part-skim mozzarella cheese

1. Separate dough into eight rolls; cut each into quarters. Press dough onto the bottom and up the sides of miniature muffin cups coated with cooking spray.
2. Spoon pizza sauce into each cup. Sprinkle with onion, green pepper, pepperoni and cheese. Bake at 375° for 15-18 minutes or until crusts are browned and cheese is melted.

Baked Reuben Dip

I love me a good Reuben sandwich, and this recipe combines all of the classic flavors into a great party dip.
—**JEFFREY METZLER** CHILLICOTHE, OHIO

PREP: 10 MIN. • **BAKE:** 25 MIN. • **MAKES:** 8 CUPS

- 1 jar (32 ounces) sauerkraut, rinsed and well drained
- 10 ounces sliced deli corned beef, chopped
- 2 cups (8 ounces) shredded sharp cheddar cheese
- 2 cups (8 ounces) shredded Swiss cheese
- 1 cup mayonnaise
- ¼ cup Russian salad dressing
- 1 teaspoon caraway seeds, optional
  Rye crackers

In a large bowl, mix the first six ingredients; stir in caraway seeds, if desired. Transfer mixture to a greased 13x9-in. baking dish. Bake at 350° for 25-30 minutes or until bubbly. Serve with crackers.

Garden Salsa

I'm proud to say that I grow most of the ingredients for this salsa in my garden. The recipe makes a large batch, but it's always gone in no time!
—**BARBARA MUNDY** RADFORD, VIRGINIA

PREP/TOTAL TIME: 30 MIN. • **MAKES:** 7 CUPS

- 4 to 5 medium tomatoes, chopped
- 1 medium onion, chopped
- 1 medium green pepper, chopped
- 2 jalapeno peppers, seeded and chopped
- 2 to 3 tablespoons chopped pimiento-stuffed olives
- 2 tablespoons minced fresh basil
- 2 tablespoons minced fresh parsley
- 1 can (8 ounces) tomato sauce
- 2 tablespoons olive oil
- 4 teaspoons lime juice
- 1½ teaspoons garlic salt
- ½ teaspoon pepper
  Tortilla chips

In a large bowl, combine the first seven ingredients. In another bowl, combine the tomato sauce, oil, lime juice, garlic salt and pepper. Pour over vegetable mixture; toss to coat. Cover and refrigerate until serving. Serve with tortilla chips.
NOTE *Wear disposable gloves when cutting hot peppers; the oils can burn skin. Avoid touching your face.*

FAST FIX ▶ Banana-Pear Caterpillar

I like being creative with food so I took an ordinary banana and a red pear and transformed them into this creepy crawler. My little brother was too young to help prepare the salads, but he sure enjoyed eating them! Not only are they fun, they're a healthy snack, too.
—**KENDRA PAIGE-WRISCHNIK** CINCINNATI, OHIO

PREP/TOTAL TIME: 15 MIN. • **MAKES:** 1 SERVING

- 1 **lettuce leaf**
- 1 **medium banana, peeled**
- ½ **medium red pear, cut into ¼-inch slices**
- 2 **raisins**

Place lettuce on a salad plate; top with the banana. Cut ¼-in. V-shaped slices halfway through the banana, spacing cuts 1 in. apart. Place a pear slice, peel side up, in each cut. For eyes, gently press raisins into one end of banana. Serve immediately.

Sun-Dried Tomato Spread

This creamy, bubbly spread is sure to please. Baked to a golden brown, cream cheese and mayonnaise give this appetizer a mild flavor.
—**VALERIE ELKINTON** GARDNER, KANSAS

PREP: 15 MIN. • **BAKE:** 20 MIN.
MAKES: 28 SERVINGS (¼ CUP EACH)

- 2 **packages (8 ounces each) cream cheese, softened**
- 2 **cups mayonnaise**
- ¼ **cup finely chopped onion**
- 4 **garlic cloves, minced**
- 1 **jar (7 ounces) oil-packed sun-dried tomatoes, drained and chopped**

- ⅔ **cup chopped roasted sweet red peppers**
- 2 **cups (8 ounces) shredded part-skim mozzarella cheese**
- 2 **cups (8 ounces) shredded Italian cheese blend**
- 1 **cup shredded Parmesan cheese, divided**
  Assorted crackers

1. In a large bowl, combine the cream cheese, mayonnaise, onion and garlic until blended. Stir in tomatoes and red peppers. Stir in the mozzarella cheese, Italian cheese blend and ¾ cup Parmesan cheese.

2. Transfer to a greased 13x9-in. baking dish. Sprinkle with the remaining Parmesan cheese. Bake, uncovered, at 350° for 18-22 minutes or until edges are bubbly and lightly browned. Serve with crackers.

FAST FIX ▶ BLT Dip

Fans of bacon, lettuce and tomato sandwiches will fall for this creamy dip. It's easy to transport to fun functions and always draws recipe requests.
—**EMALEE PAYNE** EAU CLAIRE, WISCONSIN

PREP/TOTAL TIME: 10 MIN. • **MAKES:** 6 CUPS

- 2 **cups (16 ounces) sour cream**
- 2 **cups mayonnaise**
- 2 **pound sliced bacon, cooked and crumbled**
- 6 **plum tomatoes, chopped**
- 3 **green onions, chopped**
  Crumbled cooked bacon or thinly sliced green onions, optional
  Assorted crackers or chips

In a large bowl, combine the sour cream, mayonnaise, bacon, tomatoes and onions. Refrigerate until serving. Garnish with bacon and green onions if desired. Serve with crackers or chips.

Frosty Orange Smoothie

This is a refreshing treat for warm-weather months, and a festive drink to serve around the holidays. It's a healthier alternative to sugared soft drinks, too—and tastes way better!

—RITA SWANSON
THREE HILLS, ALBERTA

PREP/TOTAL TIME: 10 MIN.
MAKES: 4-5 SERVINGS

- 1 can (6 ounces) frozen orange juice concentrate, thawed
- 1 cup milk
- 1 cup water
- ¼ cup sugar
- 1 teaspoon vanilla extract
- 10 to 12 ice cubes

In a blender, combine the orange juice, milk, water, sugar and vanilla. Cover and blend until smooth. With blender running, add ice cubes, one at a time, through the opening in lid. Blend until smooth. Serve immediately.

Chewy Energy Bars

My husband and I take these in our lunches, and they're also a portable breakfast or snack. How quick, simple to store and handy to have on hand!

—SHARON RAST SHOW LOW, ARIZONA

PREP: 20 MIN. + COOLING
MAKES: 1½ DOZEN

- 2½ cups crisp rice cereal
- 2 cups old-fashioned oats
- ¼ cup toasted wheat germ
- 1 cup corn syrup
- 1 cup peanut butter
- ½ cup packed brown sugar
- 1 teaspoon vanilla extract

1. In a large bowl, combine the cereal, oats and wheat germ. In a small saucepan, combine the corn syrup, peanut butter and brown sugar. Cook over medium heat until peanut butter is melted, stirring occasionally. Remove from the heat. Stir in vanilla. Pour over cereal mixture; mix well.
2. Transfer to a greased 9-in. square pan. Gently press cereal mixture evenly into pan. Cool completely. Cut into bars.

FAST FIX ## Crab Spread

We have fond memories of traveling to my parents' house for Christmas. After a 12-hour drive, we worked up a big appetite! This seafood spread was one of our favorites when we arrived.

—BARBARA BIDDLE
HARRISBURG, PENNSYLVANIA

PREP/TOTAL TIME: 20 MIN.
MAKES: 2 CUPS

- 1 package (8 ounces) cream cheese, softened
- 1 can (6 ounces) crabmeat, drained, flaked and cartilage removed
- 2 tablespoons mayonnaise
- 1 teaspoon Dijon mustard
- ½ teaspoon lemon-pepper seasoning
- ¼ teaspoon minced garlic
  Paprika
  Assorted crackers or vegetables

1. In a small bowl, combine the first six ingredients. To serve chilled, cover and refrigerate until serving. Sprinkle with paprika.
2. To serve warm, spoon mixture into a greased 3-cup baking dish. Bake, uncovered, at 375° for 15 minutes or until heated through. Serve with crackers or vegetables.

**TRUE BELGIAN
WAFFLES, PAGE 30**

OLD-TIME CAKE DOUGHNUTS, 42

BREAKFAST CREPES WITH BERRIES, 40

SPINACH SWISS QUICHE, 47

BREAKFAST &
BRUNCH

Wake up sleepyheads that are nestled in bed with a rise-and-shine bounty of breakfast delights. From hearty egg bakes and fluffy pancakes to fruit-filled crepes and sugar-dusted doughnuts (and everything in between), these sunrise specialties are a great way to greet the day. Whether you're feeding just a few or an entire crowd, there's an eye-opening recipe for every palate and every occasion.

FAST FIX ▶ Nutmeg Waffles

Bake an extra batch of these tender, golden waffles on the weekend. Eat one, then freeze the other to reheat on hurried mornings. Nutmeg adds to their warm, feel-good flavor!

—JAMES CHRISTENSEN
ST. ANTHONY, IDAHO

PREP/TOTAL TIME: 15 MIN.
MAKES: 8 WAFFLES

1¼ cups all-purpose flour
1 teaspoon baking powder
1 teaspoon ground cinnamon
½ teaspoon salt
½ teaspoon ground nutmeg
¼ teaspoon baking soda
1 egg, lightly beaten
1 cup fat-free milk
1 teaspoon canola oil
1 teaspoon vanilla extract
Butter and maple syrup, optional

1. In a small bowl, combine the flour, baking powder, cinnamon, salt, nutmeg and baking soda. In another bowl, combine the egg, milk, oil and vanilla; stir into dry ingredients until smooth.
2. Bake in a preheated waffle iron according to manufacturer's directions until golden brown. Serve with butter and syrup if desired.

Spiced Bacon Twists

Whenever I share this recipe, I have to issue a caveat that bacon might become even more addictive after your first bite. Don't say I didn't warn you!

—GLENDA EVANS WITTNER
JOPLIN, MISSOURI

PREP: 10 MIN. • **BAKE:** 25 MIN.
MAKES: 5 SERVINGS

¼ cup packed brown sugar
1½ teaspoons ground mustard
⅛ teaspoon ground cinnamon
⅛ teaspoon ground nutmeg
Dash cayenne pepper
10 center-cut bacon strips

1. In a small bowl, combine the first five ingredients; rub over bacon on both sides. Twist bacon; place on a rack in a 15x10x1-in. baking pan.
2. Bake at 350° for 25-30 minutes or until firm; bake longer if desired.

FAST FIX

Cherry-Granola French Toast Sticks

The warm aroma of cinnamon and brown sugar helps wake my family. Convenient toast sticks topped with granola, banana and whipped cream carry them through busy days.

—TERRI MCKITRICK
DELAFIELD, WISCONSIN

PREP/TOTAL TIME: 20 MIN.
MAKES: 4 SERVINGS

¼ cup heavy whipping cream
3 tablespoons brown sugar
2 tablespoons butter
1 tablespoon dried cherries
¼ teaspoon ground cinnamon
¼ teaspoon vanilla extract
1 package (12.7 ounces) frozen French toast sticks
1 medium banana, sliced
¼ cup granola without raisins

1. For syrup, in a small saucepan, combine the cream, brown sugar, butter, cherries and cinnamon. Bring to a boil over medium heat, stirring constantly. Cook and stir for 2 minutes. Remove from the heat; stir in vanilla.
2. Prepare French toast sticks according to package directions. Serve sticks with banana, granola and syrup.
NOTE *This recipe was tested with Eggo French Toaster Sticks.*

▶ FRENCH TOAST REDUX

Are the kids craving French toast sticks, but you're out of bread? Improvise with leftover hot dog buns. Simply split each bun and cut each side in half lengthwise. Then dip each "stick" into the egg batter and cook as normal.

Zucchini Crescent Pie

This is one of my mother's many recipes designed to take advantage of bountiful zucchini. Refrigerated crescent rolls and cooked ham cut prep time but not taste. My family loves it!

—SUSAN DAVIS
ANN ARBOR, MICHIGAN

PREP: 25 MIN. • **BAKE:** 20 MIN.
MAKES: 6 SERVINGS

- 1 package (8 ounces) refrigerated crescent rolls
- 2 medium zucchini, sliced lengthwise and quartered
- ½ cup chopped onion
- ¼ cup butter, cubed
- 2 teaspoons minced fresh parsley
- ½ teaspoon salt
- ½ teaspoon garlic powder
- ½ teaspoon pepper
- ¼ teaspoon dried basil
- ¼ teaspoon dried oregano
- 2 eggs, lightly beaten
- 2 cups (8 ounces) shredded part-skim mozzarella cheese
- ¾ cup cubed fully cooked ham
- 1 medium Roma tomato, thinly sliced

1. Separate crescent dough into eight triangles; place in a greased 9-in. pie plate with points toward the center. Press onto the bottom and up the sides to form a crust; seal seams and perforations. Bake at 375° for 5-8 minutes or until lightly browned.

2. Meanwhile, in a large skillet, saute zucchini and onion in butter until tender; stir in seasonings. Spoon into crust. Combine the eggs, cheese and ham; pour over zucchini mixture. Top with slices of tomato.

3. Bake at 375° for 20-25 minutes or until a knife inserted near the center comes out clean. Let stand for 5 minutes before cutting.

FAST FIX ▶ ## Breakfast Pizza

Pizza for breakfast? Yes, please! I used to make this for my morning drivers when I worked at a pizza delivery place. It's a quick and easy eye-opener that appeals to all.

—CATHY SHORTALL
EASTON, MARYLAND

PREP/TOTAL TIME: 25 MIN.
MAKES: 8 SLICES

- 1 tube (13.8 ounces) refrigerated pizza crust
- 2 tablespoons olive oil, divided
- 6 eggs
- 2 tablespoons water
- 1 package (3 ounces) real bacon bits
- 1 cup (4 ounces) shredded Monterey Jack cheese
- 1 cup (4 ounces) shredded cheddar cheese

1. Unroll the crust into a greased 15x10x1-in. baking pan; flatten dough and build up edges slightly. Brush with 1 tablespoon oil. Prick dough thoroughly with a fork. Bake at 400° for 7-8 minutes or until lightly browned.

2. Meanwhile, in a small bowl, whisk eggs and water. In a small skillet, heat remaining oil until hot. Add eggs; cook and stir over medium heat until completely set.

3. Spoon eggs over crust. Sprinkle with bacon and cheeses. Bake 5-7 minutes longer or until cheese is melted.

FAST FIX ▶ True Belgian Waffles

I received this recipe while my husband and I were visiting his relatives in Belgium. Back in the U.S., I served the waffles to his Belgian-born grandmother. She said they tasted just like home.
—**ROSE DELEMEESTER** ST. CHARLES, MICHIGAN

PREP/TOTAL TIME: 20 MIN.
MAKES: 10 WAFFLES (ABOUT 4½ INCHES)

- 2 **cups all-purpose flour**
- ¾ **cup sugar**
- 3½ **teaspoons baking powder**
- 2 **eggs, separated**
- 1½ **cups milk**
- 1 **cup butter, melted**
- 1 **teaspoon vanilla extract**
  Sliced fresh strawberries or syrup

1. In a bowl, combine flour, sugar and baking powder. In another bowl, lightly beat egg yolks. Add milk, butter and vanilla; mix well. Stir into dry ingredients just until combined. Beat egg whites until stiff peaks form; fold into batter.
2. Bake in a preheated waffle iron according to manufacturer's directions until golden brown. Serve with strawberries or syrup.

FAST FIX ▶ Berry-Filled Doughnuts

Just four ingredients are all you'll need for this sure-to-be-popular treat. Friends and family will never guess that refrigerated buttermilk biscuits are the base for these golden, jelly-filled doughnuts.
—**GINNY WATSON** BROKEN ARROW, OKLAHOMA

PREP/TOTAL TIME: 25 MIN. • **MAKES:** 10 SERVINGS

- 4 **cups canola oil**
- 1 **tube (7½ ounces) refrigerated buttermilk biscuits, separated into 10 biscuits**
- ¾ **cup seedless strawberry jam**
- 1 **cup confectioners' sugar**

1. In an electric skillet or deep-fat fryer, heat oil to 375°. Fry biscuits, a few at a time, for 1-2 minutes on each side or until golden brown. Drain on paper towels.
2. Cut a small hole in the corner of a pastry or plastic bag; insert a very small tip. Fill bag with jam. Push the tip through the side of each doughnut to fill with jam. Dust with confectioners' sugar while warm. Serve immediately.

FAST FIX ▶ Bird's Nest Breakfast Cups

This is a lightened-up version of an original recipe that called for regular bacon and eggs. Everyone loves it! I have them convinced that I fussed, but it's actually quite easy.
—**ARIS GONZALEZ** DELTONA, FLORIDA

PREP/TOTAL TIME: 30 MIN. • **MAKES:** 6 SERVINGS

- 12 **turkey bacon strips**
- 1½ **cups egg substitute**
- 6 **tablespoons shredded reduced-fat Mexican cheese blend**
- 1 **tablespoon minced fresh parsley**

1. In a large skillet, cook bacon over medium heat for 2 minutes on each side or until partially set but not crisp. Coat six muffin cups with cooking spray; wrap two bacon strips around the inside of each cup. Fill each with ¼ cup egg substitute; top with cheese.
2. Bake at 350° for 18-20 minutes or until set. Cool for 5 minutes before removing from pan. Sprinkle with parsley.

Potato Egg Bake

No one will ever guess that this nutritious, mouthwatering breakfast bake is lighter than its original counterpart. Potatoes give it a hearty base while cheese and veggies pile on color and wonderful flavor.

—RENA CHARBONEAU GANSEVOORT, NEW YORK

PREP: 20 MIN. • **BAKE:** 35 MIN. • **MAKES:** 8 SERVINGS

- **2 pounds Yukon Gold potatoes (about 6 medium), peeled and diced**
- **½ cup water**
- **1 cup frozen chopped broccoli, thawed**
- **6 green onions, thinly sliced**
- **1 small sweet red pepper, chopped**
- **6 eggs**
- **8 egg whites**
- **1 cup (8 ounces) 1% cottage cheese**
- **1 cup (4 ounces) shredded reduced-fat cheddar cheese**
- **½ cup grated Parmesan cheese**
- **½ cup fat-free milk**
- **2 tablespoons dried parsley flakes**
- **½ teaspoon salt**
- **¼ teaspoon pepper**

1. Place potatoes and water in a microwave-safe dish. Cover and microwave on high for 7 minutes or until tender; drain.

2. Spread potatoes in a 13x9-in. baking dish coated with cooking spray. Top with the broccoli, onions and red pepper.

3. In a large bowl, whisk the remaining ingredients until blended. Pour over vegetables. Bake, uncovered, at 350° for 35-40 minutes or until center is set.

❝Very easy, simple and yummy. I sprinkled in some crushed red pepper flakes. My family enjoyed this egg bake, and it was perfect for a last-minute meal.❞

—1275 FROM TASTEOFHOME.COM

yolk, milk, orange juice and peel. Stir into the dry ingredients just until blended. Fold in the chopped cranberries.

4. Drop batter by ¼ cupfuls onto a greased hot griddle; turn when bubbles form on top. Cook until second side is golden brown. Serve with syrup. Garnish with orange peel strips if desired.

Potato & Bacon Frittata

This filling frittata is so versatile. You can serve it with pesto or fresh salsa, and it's tasty with almost any type of cheese.
—MARIELA PETROSKI HELENA, MONTANA

PREP: 30 MIN. • **BAKE:** 20 MIN. + STANDING
MAKES: 8 SERVINGS

- 10 **eggs**
- ¼ **cup minced fresh parsley**
- 3 **tablespoons 2% milk**
- ¼ **teaspoon salt**
- ⅛ **teaspoon pepper**
- 8 **bacon strips, chopped**
- 2 **medium potatoes, peeled and thinly sliced**
- 2 **green onions, finely chopped**
- 4 **fresh sage leaves, thinly sliced**
- 1 **cup (4 ounces) shredded pepper jack cheese**
- 2 **plum tomatoes, sliced**

1. In a large bowl, whisk the eggs, parsley, milk, salt and pepper; set aside. In a 10-in. ovenproof skillet, cook the bacon over medium heat until partially cooked but not crisp.

2. Add the potatoes, onions and sage; cook until potatoes are tender. Reduce heat; sprinkle with cheese. Top with egg mixture and tomato slices.

3. Bake, uncovered, at 400° for 20-25 minutes or until eggs are completely set. Let stand for 15 minutes. Cut into wedges.

Cranberry Orange Pancakes

As special as Christmas morning itself, these fluffy pancakes are drop-dead gorgeous, ready in just minutes and brimming with sweet, tart and tangy flavor. Seconds, anyone?

—NANCY ZIMMERMAN
CAPE MAY COURT HOUSE, NEW JERSEY

PREP: 20 MIN. • **COOK:** 5 MIN./BATCH
MAKES: 12 PANCAKES (1¼ CUPS SYRUP)

SYRUP
- 1 **cup fresh or frozen cranberries**
- ⅔ **cup orange juice**
- ½ **cup sugar**
- 3 **tablespoons maple syrup**

PANCAKES
- 2 **cups biscuit/baking mix**
- 2 **tablespoons sugar**
- 2 **teaspoons baking powder**
- 2 **eggs**
- 1 **egg yolk**
- 1 **cup evaporated milk**
- 2 **tablespoons orange juice**
- 1 **teaspoon grated orange peel**
- ½ **cup chopped fresh or frozen cranberries**
  Orange peel strips, optional

1. In a small saucepan, bring the cranberries, orange juice and sugar to a boil. Reduce heat; simmer, uncovered, for 5 minutes. Cool slightly. With a slotted spoon, remove ¼ cup cranberries; set aside.

2. In a blender, process cranberry mixture until smooth. Transfer to a small bowl; stir in maple syrup and reserved cranberries. Keep warm.

3. In a large bowl, combine the biscuit mix, sugar and baking powder. In another bowl, whisk the eggs, egg

FAST FIX ▶ Eggs in Muffin Cups

My mother used to make these delicious egg cups for us all the time while I was growing up, and now I carry on the tradition with my own family. They are quick to put together, and I like that I can walk away to get ready for the day while they bake in the oven.

—**LISA WALDER** URBANA, ILLINOIS

PREP/TOTAL TIME: 30 MIN. • **MAKES:** 6 SERVINGS (2 EACH)

- 12 **thin slices deli roast beef**
- 6 **slices process American cheese, quartered**
- 12 **eggs**

1. Press one slice of beef onto the bottom and up the sides of each greased muffin cup, forming a shell. Arrange two cheese pieces in each shell. Break one egg into each cup.

2. Bake, uncovered, at 350° for 20-25 minutes or until eggs are completely set.

FAST FIX ▶ Morning Fruit Salad

My best friend made this refreshing fruit salad for lunch one sultry summer day. It was so good, I just had to have the recipe. Now I make it every chance I get. It's always a hit at picnics and church brunches.

—**NIKKI GAINES** COVINGTON, GEORGIA

PREP/TOTAL TIME: 25 MIN. • **MAKES:** 6-8 SERVINGS

- 1 **can (11 ounces) mandarin oranges**
- ¼ **cup plus 2 tablespoons mayonnaise**
- 1½ **cups seedless grapes, halved**
- 2 **small apples, chopped**
- 2 **small bananas, sliced**
- ⅓ **cup flaked coconut**
- ⅓ **cup chopped walnuts**
- ¼ **cup maraschino cherries, halved**
- ¼ **cup raisins**

1. Drain oranges, reserving 4½ teaspoons juice (discard remaining juice or save for another use). In a small bowl, combine mayonnaise and reserved juice.

2. In a large bowl, combine the oranges, grapes, apples, bananas, coconut, walnuts, cherries and raisins. Divide among serving dishes; drizzle with mayonnaise mixture. Serve immediately.

FAST FIX ▶ Breakfast on the Grill

I thought having breakfast in our backyard would be a nice way to soak up the morning sunshine on our new patio, so I came up with this combination to cook on the grill. It's a fun idea for camping, too.

—**SHIRLEY ELLUL** REDFORD TOWNSHIP, MICHIGAN

PREP/TOTAL TIME: 30 MIN. • **MAKES:** 4 SERVINGS

- 1 **can (8 ounces) pineapple chunks**
- 3 **cups cubed French bread (1-inch cubes)**
- ¼ **cup butter, melted**
- ⅓ **cup sugar**
- 1½ **teaspoons ground cinnamon**
- 8 **slices Canadian bacon, quartered**

1. Drain the pineapple, reserving 2 tablespoons juice; set aside. Place bread in a large bowl; drizzle with butter and toss to coat. Combine sugar and cinnamon; sprinkle over bread mixture and toss to coat.

2. Transfer bread mixture to a double thickness of greased heavy-duty foil (about 28x18 in.). Add Canadian bacon and pineapple; drizzle with reserved pineapple juice.

3. Fold foil around bread mixture and seal tightly. Grill, covered, over medium heat for 4-5 minutes on each side or until heated through. Open foil carefully to allow steam to escape.

Baked Apple French Toast

This is a simply wonderful brunch recipe that tastes special and will have your guests asking for seconds. I serve it with whipped topping, maple syrup and additional nuts.

—BEVERLY JOHNSTON RUBICON, WISCONSIN

PREP: 20 MIN. + CHILLING • **BAKE:** 35 MIN.
MAKES: 10 SERVINGS

20 slices French bread (1 inch thick)
1 can (21 ounces) apple pie filling
8 eggs, lightly beaten
2 cups 2% milk
2 teaspoons vanilla extract
½ teaspoon ground cinnamon
½ teaspoon ground nutmeg

TOPPING
1 cup packed brown sugar
½ cup cold butter, cubed
1 cup chopped pecans
2 tablespoons corn syrup

1. Arrange 10 slices of bread in a greased 13x9-in. baking dish. Spread with pie filling; top with remaining bread. In a large bowl, whisk the eggs, milk, vanilla, cinnamon and nutmeg. Pour over bread. Cover and refrigerate overnight.
2. Remove from the refrigerator 30 minutes before baking. Meanwhile, place brown sugar in a small bowl. Cut in butter until mixture resembles coarse crumbs. Stir in pecans and corn syrup. Sprinkle over French toast.
3. Bake, uncovered, at 350° for 35-40 minutes or until a knife inserted near the center comes out clean.

Peaches & Cream French Toast

Wake up your tired clan with the wonderfully warm aroma of peaches and brown sugar in this delectable breakfast French toast bake.

—SUSAN WESTERFIELD ALBUQUERQUE, NEW MEXICO

PREP: 20 MIN. + CHILLING • **BAKE:** 50 MIN.
MAKES: 12 SERVINGS

- 1 cup packed brown sugar
- ½ cup butter, cubed
- 2 tablespoons corn syrup
- 1 can (29 ounces) sliced peaches, drained
- 1 loaf (1 pound) day-old French bread, cubed
- 1 package (8 ounces) cream cheese, cubed
- 12 eggs
- 1½ cups half-and-half cream
- 1 teaspoon vanilla extract

1. In a small saucepan, combine the brown sugar, butter and corn syrup. Cook and stir over medium heat until the sugar is dissolved; pour mixture into a greased 13x9-in. baking dish.

2. Arrange peaches in dish. Place half of the bread cubes over peaches. Layer with cream cheese and remaining bread. Place the eggs, cream and vanilla in a blender; cover and process until smooth. Pour over top. Cover and refrigerate overnight.

3. Remove from the refrigerator 30 minutes before baking. Bake, uncovered, at 350° for 50-60 minutes or until a knife inserted near the center comes out clean.

Hash Brown Breakfast Casserole

This savory, scrumptious recipe uses egg substitute to cut down on fat and cholesterol. Serve with your favorite fresh fruit for a morning meal that will keep your family satisfied until lunch.

—CINDY SCHNEIDER SARASOTA, FLORIDA

PREP: 10 MIN. • **BAKE:** 40 MIN. • **MAKES:** 4 SERVINGS

- 4 cups frozen shredded hash brown potatoes, thawed
- 1½ cups egg substitute
- 1 cup finely chopped cooked chicken breast
- ½ teaspoon garlic powder
- ½ teaspoon pepper
- ¾ cup shredded reduced-fat cheddar cheese

1. In a large bowl, combine the hash browns, egg substitute, chicken, garlic powder and pepper. Transfer to an 8-in. square baking dish coated with cooking spray; sprinkle with cheese.

2. Bake, uncovered, at 350° for 40-45 minutes or until a knife inserted near the center comes out clean. Let stand for 5 minutes before serving.

❝I expanded this recipe to include vegetables, like bell peppers, onions and spinach. It is delicious!❞

—GISSELL FROM TASTEOFHOME.COM

FAST FIX Gingerbread Pancakes

The cinnamon-ginger aroma of these puffy pancakes is how I wake up my gang on Christmas morning. I like to top them with warm apple pie filling and dried fruit.
—**MICHELLE SMITH** SYKESVILLE, MARYLAND

PREP/TOTAL TIME: 20 MIN. • **MAKES:** 3 SERVINGS

- 1 cup all-purpose flour
- 2 tablespoons sugar
- 1 teaspoon baking powder
- ½ teaspoon ground cinnamon
- ¼ teaspoon ground ginger
- ¼ teaspoon ground allspice
- 1 egg
- ¾ cup 2% milk
- 2 tablespoons molasses
- 1 tablespoon canola oil
- 6 tablespoons maple pancake syrup
- ¾ cup apple pie filling, warmed
- 3 tablespoons dried cranberries

1. In a large bowl, combine the first six ingredients. Combine the egg, milk, molasses and oil; stir into dry ingredients just until moistened.
2. Pour batter by ¼ cupfuls onto a greased hot griddle; turn when bubbles form on top. Cook until the second side is golden brown.
3. To serve, place two pancakes on each plate; drizzle with 2 tablespoons syrup. Top with ¼ cup apple pie filling; sprinkle with cranberries.

FAST FIX Italian Garden Frittata

I like to serve this pretty frittata with melon wedges for a delicious breakfast or brunch.
—**SALLY MALONEY** DALLAS, GEORGIA

PREP/TOTAL TIME: 30 MIN. • **MAKES:** 4 SERVINGS

- 6 egg whites
- 4 eggs
- ½ cup grated Romano cheese, divided
- 1 tablespoon minced fresh sage
- ½ teaspoon salt
- ¼ teaspoon pepper
- 1 small zucchini, sliced
- 2 green onions, sliced
- 1 teaspoon olive oil
- 2 plum tomatoes, thinly sliced

1. In a large bowl, whisk the egg whites, eggs, ¼ cup Romano cheese, sage, salt and pepper; set aside.
2. In a 10-in. ovenproof skillet coated with cooking spray, saute zucchini and onions in oil for 2 minutes. Add egg mixture; cover and cook for 4-6 minutes or until eggs are nearly set.
3. Uncover; top with tomato slices and remaining cheese. Broil 3-4 in. from the heat for 2-3 minutes or until eggs are completely set. Let stand for 5 minutes. Cut into wedges.

Baked Oatmeal

You may think you're biting into a warm-from-the-oven oatmeal cookie when you taste this breakfast treat. Just add milk to get your morning off to the perfect start.

—**ARLENE RIEHL** DUNDEE, NEW YORK

PREP: 10 MIN. • **BAKE:** 40 MIN. • **MAKES:** 9 SERVINGS

- 3 cups quick-cooking oats
- 1 cup packed brown sugar
- 2 teaspoons baking powder
- 1 teaspoon salt
- 1 teaspoon ground cinnamon
- 2 eggs
- 1 cup milk
- ½ cup butter, melted
  Additional milk

1. In a large bowl, combine the oats, brown sugar, baking powder, salt and cinnamon. In another bowl, whisk the eggs, milk and butter. Stir into oat mixture until blended.

2. Spoon into a greased 9-in. square baking pan. Bake at 350° for 40-45 minutes or until set. Serve warm.

❝**This is delicious and moist, and the house smelled wonderful while it was baking. I even ate cold slices as a snack.**❞

—**KMCCORQU** FROM TASTEOFHOME.COM

Hearty Breakfast Egg Bake

I whip up this casserole in advance whenever we're expecting overnight guests. I pop it into the oven the next morning, and then I simply add some toast or biscuits and fresh fruit for a complete meal that everyone loves.

—**PAMELA NORRIS** FENTON, MISSOURI

PREP: 10 MIN. + CHILLING • **BAKE:** 45 MIN. + STANDING
MAKES: 8 SERVINGS

- 1½ pounds bulk pork sausage
- 3 cups frozen shredded hash brown potatoes, thawed
- 2 cups (8 ounces) shredded cheddar cheese
- 8 eggs, lightly beaten
- 1 can (10¾ ounces) condensed cream of mushroom soup, undiluted
- ¾ cup evaporated milk

1. Crumble sausage into a large skillet. Cook over medium heat until no longer pink; drain. Transfer to a greased 13x9-in. baking dish. Sprinkle with hash browns and cheese.

2. In a large bowl, whisk the remaining ingredients; pour over the top. Cover and refrigerate overnight.

3. Remove from the refrigerator 30 minutes before baking. Bake, uncovered, at 350° for 45-50 minutes or until a knife inserted near the center comes out clean. Let stand for 10 minutes before cutting.

FAST FIX ▶

Breakfast Wraps

We like quick and simple morning meals during the week, and these wraps are great when prepared ahead of time. After just one speedy minute in the microwave, breakfast is ready!

—**BETTY KLEBERGER**
FLORISSANT, MISSOURI

PREP/TOTAL TIME: 15 MIN.
MAKES: 4 SERVINGS

- 6 **eggs**
- 2 **tablespoons milk**
- ¼ **teaspoon pepper**
- 1 **tablespoon canola oil**
- 1 **cup (4 ounces) shredded cheddar cheese**
- ¾ **cup diced fully cooked ham**
- 4 **flour tortillas (8 inches), warmed**

1. In a small bowl, whisk the eggs, milk and pepper. In a large skillet, heat oil. Add egg mixture; cook and stir over medium heat until eggs are completely set. Stir in cheese and ham.

2. Spoon egg mixture down the center of each tortilla; roll up. Serve immediately, or wrap in plastic wrap and freeze in a resealable plastic bag.

TO USE FROZEN WRAPS *Thaw in the refrigerator overnight. Remove plastic wrap; wrap tortilla in a moist paper towel. Microwave on high for 30-60 seconds or until heated through. Serve immediately.*

Eggs Benedict Casserole

Here's a casserole as tasty as classic eggs Benedict, but without the hassle. Simply assemble the ingredients the night before, and pop it into the oven the next morning for an elegant breakfast or brunch dish.

—**SANDIE HEINDEL** LIBERTY, MISSOURI

PREP: 25 MIN. + CHILLING
BAKE: 45 MIN.
MAKES: 12 SERVINGS (1⅔ CUPS SAUCE)

- ¾ **pound Canadian bacon, chopped**
- 6 **English muffins, split and cut into 1-inch pieces**
- 8 **eggs**
- 2 **cups 2% milk**
- 1 **teaspoon onion powder**
- ¼ **teaspoon paprika**

HOLLANDAISE SAUCE
- 4 **egg yolks**
- ½ **cup heavy whipping cream**
- 2 **tablespoons lemon juice**
- 1 **teaspoon Dijon mustard**
- ½ **cup butter, melted**

1. Place half of the bacon in a greased 13x9-in. baking dish; top with English muffins and remaining bacon. In a large bowl, whisk the eggs, milk and onion powder; pour over the top. Cover and refrigerate overnight.

2. Remove from the refrigerator 30 minutes before baking. Sprinkle with paprika. Cover and bake at 375° for 35 minutes. Uncover; bake 10-15 minutes longer or until a knife inserted near the center comes out clean.

3. In a double boiler or metal bowl over simmering water, constantly whisk the egg yolks, cream, lemon juice and mustard until mixture reaches 160° or is thick enough to coat the back of a spoon. Reduce heat to low. Slowly drizzle in warm melted butter, whisking constantly. Serve immediately with casserole.

HOLLANDAISE SAUCE

Egg-rich sauces are fully cooked when the mixture is thickened and coats the back of a spoon. To determine doneness, dip a spoon into the mixture and run your finger across the back of the spoon. The cooked mixture will hold a firm line and not run down onto the stripe you've made. A mixture that's not fully cooked will be too thin to hold the line.

Benedict Eggs in Pastry

Here's a new twist on an old favorite. Inside these puffy golden bundles is an omelet-like filling of eggs, ham, cheese and a rich, lemony hollandaise sauce.
—CATHY SLUSSLER MAGNOLIA, TEXAS

PREP: 30 MIN. • **BAKE:** 20 MIN. • **MAKES:** 4 SERVINGS

- 2 **egg yolks**
- 2 **tablespoons lemon juice**
- 1 **teaspoon Dijon mustard**
- ½ **cup butter, melted**
  Dash cayenne pepper
- 2 **cups cubed fully cooked ham**
- 2 **green onions, chopped**
- 1 **tablespoon butter**
- 6 **eggs, lightly beaten**
- 2 **tablespoons 2% milk**
- 1 **package (17.3 ounces) frozen puff pastry, thawed**
- 1 **cup (4 ounces) shredded cheddar cheese**
- 1 **egg**
- 1 **tablespoon water**
  Minced fresh tarragon, optional

1. In a double boiler over simmering water or a small heavy saucepan, constantly whisk the egg yolks, lemon juice and mustard until mixture begins to thicken and reaches 160°. Reduce heat to low. Slowly drizzle in warm melted butter, whisking constantly. Whisk in cayenne.

2. Transfer to a small bowl if necessary. Place bowl in a larger bowl of warm water. Keep warm, stirring occasionally, until ready to use.

3. In a large skillet over medium heat, cook and stir ham and onions in butter until onions are tender. In a large bowl, whisk six eggs and milk. Add egg mixture to the pan; cook and stir until set. Remove from the heat; stir in ⅓ cup reserved hollandaise sauce. Set aside.

4. On a lightly floured surface, unfold puff pastry. Roll each sheet into a 12x9½-in. rectangle; cut each in half widthwise. Place 1 cup egg mixture on half of each rectangle; sprinkle with cheese.

5. Beat egg and water; brush over pastry edges. Bring an opposite corner of pastry over the egg mixture; pinch seams to seal. With a small sharp knife, cut several slits in the top.

6. Transfer to a greased baking sheet; brush with remaining egg mixture. Bake at 400° for 18-22 minutes or until golden brown. Serve with remaining hollandaise sauce. Sprinkle with tarragon if desired.

FAST FIX

Savory Apple-Chicken Sausage

These easy, healthy sausages taste great, and they make an elegant brunch dish. The recipe is also very versatile. It can be doubled or tripled for a crowd, and the sausage freezes well either cooked or raw.

—**ANGELA BUCHANAN** LONGMONT, COLORADO

PREP/TOTAL TIME: 25 MIN. • **MAKES:** 8 PATTIES

- 1 **large tart apple, peeled and diced**
- 2 **teaspoons poultry seasoning**
- 1 **teaspoon salt**
- ¼ **teaspoon pepper**
- 1 **pound ground chicken**

1. In a large bowl, combine the apple, poultry seasoning, salt and pepper. Crumble chicken over mixture and mix well. Shape into eight 3-in. patties.

2. In a large skillet coated with cooking spray, cook patties over medium heat for 5-6 minutes on each side or until no longer pink.

❝I made this for my family for Christmas breakfast last year, and they all raved. You can also use ground turkey instead of chicken.❞

—**NYXRIZZI** FROM TASTEOFHOME.COM

FAST FIX

Breakfast Crepes with Berries

After a long day of blackberry picking, I whipped up a sauce to dress up some crepes I had on hand. This speedy dish hit the spot! The crepes make an elegant addition to any brunch, and the sauce is delectable over waffles, pancakes and French toast.

—**JENNIFER WEISBRODT** OCONOMOWOC, WISCONSIN

PREP/TOTAL TIME: 20 MIN. • **MAKES:** 8 SERVINGS

- 1½ **cups fresh raspberries**
- 1½ **cups fresh blackberries**
- 1 **cup (8 ounces) sour cream**
- ½ **cup confectioners' sugar**
- 1 **carton (6 ounces) orange creme yogurt**
- 1 **tablespoon lime juice**
- 1½ **teaspoons grated lime peel**
- ½ **teaspoon vanilla extract**
- ⅛ **teaspoon salt**
- 8 **prepared crepes (9 inches)**

1. In a large bowl, combine raspberries and blackberries; set aside. In a small bowl, combine sour cream and confectioners' sugar until smooth. Stir in the yogurt, lime juice, lime peel, vanilla and salt.

2. Spread 2 tablespoons sour cream mixture over each crepe; top with about ⅓ cup berries. Roll up; drizzle with remaining sour cream mixture. Serve crepes immediately.

Raspberry-Cinnamon French Toast

Our staff came up with this moist French toast bake that's a snap to assemble the night before and bake in the morning. While it's pleasantly sweet as is, let guests drizzle raspberry syrup over the top for a finishing touch.
—TASTE OF HOME TEST KITCHEN

PREP: 10 MIN. + CHILLING • **BAKE:** 35 MIN.
MAKES: 6-8 SERVINGS

- 12 slices cinnamon bread, cubed
- 5 eggs, beaten
- 1¾ cups milk
- 1 cup packed brown sugar, divided
- ¼ teaspoon ground cinnamon
- ¼ teaspoon ground nutmeg
- ½ cup slivered almonds
- ¼ cup butter, melted
- 2 cups fresh raspberries

1. Place bread cubes in a greased 13x9-in. baking dish. In a bowl, combine the eggs, milk, ¾ cup brown sugar, cinnamon and nutmeg; pour over bread. Cover and refrigerate for 8 hours or overnight.
2. Remove from the refrigerator 30 minutes before baking. Sprinkle almonds over the egg mixture. Combine butter and remaining brown sugar; drizzle over the top.
3. Bake, uncovered, at 400° for 25 minutes. Sprinkle with raspberries. Bake 10 minutes longer or until a knife inserted near the center comes out clean.

Pear-Pecan Sausage Quiche

This distinctive quiche combines the savory flavor of sausage with the sweetness of pear slices. It makes a wonderful appetizer or brunch dish, especially during the holiday season.
—PATRICIA HARMON
BADEN, PENNSYLVANIA

PREP: 15 MIN. • **BAKE:** 35 MIN.
MAKES: 8 SERVINGS

- 1 sheet refrigerated pie pastry
- ½ pound bulk hot Italian sausage
- ⅓ cup chopped sweet onion
- 1 medium pear, sliced
- ⅓ cup chopped pecans
- 4 eggs
- 1½ cups half-and-half cream
- ½ teaspoon salt
- ½ teaspoon dried thyme
- ⅛ teaspoon ground nutmeg
- 1 cup (4 ounces) shredded cheddar cheese
- 8 pecan halves

1. Line a 9-in. pie plate with pastry. Trim pastry to ½ in. beyond edge of pie plate; flute edges.
2. In a large skillet, cook sausage and onion over medium heat for 4-5 minutes or until meat is no longer pink; drain. Arrange pear slices in crust; top with sausage. Sprinkle with pecans. In a large bowl, whisk the eggs, cream, salt, thyme and nutmeg. Stir in cheese. Pour over sausage.
3. Bake at 350° for 35-40 minutes or until a knife inserted near the center comes out clean and crust is golden brown. Cover edges with foil during the last 15 minutes to prevent overbrowning if necessary. Garnish with pecan halves. Let stand for 5 minutes before slicing.

Old-Time Cake Doughnuts

This tender cake doughnut is a little piece of heaven. To bump up the richness and flavor, add a little rum extract or 1 tablespoon dark rum.

—ALISSA STEHR
GAU-ODERNHEIM, GERMANY

PREP: 30 MIN. + CHILLING
COOK: 5 MIN./BATCH
MAKES: ABOUT 2 DOZEN

- 2 tablespoons unsalted butter, softened
- 1½ cups sugar, divided
- 3 eggs
- 4 cups all-purpose flour
- 1 tablespoon baking powder
- 3 teaspoons ground cinnamon, divided
- ½ teaspoon salt
- ⅛ teaspoon ground nutmeg
- ¾ cup 2% milk
  Oil for deep-fat frying

1. In a large bowl, beat butter and 1 cup sugar until crumbly, about 2 minutes. Add eggs, one at a time, beating well after each addition.
2. Combine the flour, baking powder, 1 teaspoon cinnamon, salt and nutmeg; add to butter mixture alternately with milk, beating well after each addition. Cover and refrigerate for 2 hours.
3. Turn onto a heavily floured surface; pat dough to ¼-in. thickness. Cut with a floured 2½-in. doughnut cutter. In an electric skillet or deep fryer, heat oil to 375°.
4. Fry doughnuts, a few at a time, until golden brown on both sides. Drain on paper towels.
5. Combine remaining sugar and cinnamon; roll warm doughnuts in mixture.

Bacon Quiche

Light and fluffy, this scrumptious quiche is ideal for breakfast or brunch but can also be served at dinnertime. Serve with chilled grapes or other fresh fruit on the side.

—COLLEEN BELBEY
WARWICK, RHODE ISLAND

PREP: 15 MIN. • **BAKE:** 40 MIN. + STANDING
MAKES: 6 SERVINGS

- 1 sheet refrigerated pie pastry
- ¼ cup sliced green onions
- 1 tablespoon butter
- 6 eggs
- 1½ cups heavy whipping cream
- ¼ cup unsweetened apple juice
- 1 pound sliced bacon, cooked and crumbled
- ⅛ teaspoon salt
- ⅛ teaspoon pepper
- 2 cups (8 ounces) shredded Swiss cheese

1. Line a 9-in. pie plate with pastry; trim and flute edges. Set aside. In a small skillet, saute green onions in butter until tender.
2. In a large bowl, whisk the eggs, cream and juice. Stir in the bacon, salt, pepper and green onions. Pour into pastry; sprinkle with cheese.
3. Bake at 350° for 40-45 minutes or until a knife inserted near the center comes out clean. Let stand for 10 minutes before cutting.
HAM QUICHE *Omit apple juice. Increase heavy whipping cream to 1¾ cup. Substitute 3 cups diced cooked ham for the bacon and cheddar cheese for the Swiss cheese. Proceed as directed.* **HAM BROCCOLI QUICHE** *Follow directions for Ham Quiche. Add 1 cup chopped broccoli florets to the egg mixture.*

AVOID WATERY QUICHE

To avoid water on the bottom of the pie when making a quiche, use an oven thermometer to check your oven temperature. Then, to avoid overbaking, do the "knife test" when the quiche appears to have set around the edges but still seems a little soft in the very center. The quiche is done if the knife inserted near the center comes out clean.

Bacon & Cheddar Strata

We love this for Christmas, but I prepare this sunrise specialty whenever we want a warm, hearty meal. It's a no-fuss delicious breakfast that's ready to pop into the oven in the morning.
—**DEB HEALEY** COLD LAKE, ALBERTA

PREP: 20 MIN. + CHILLING • **BAKE:** 45 MIN. • **MAKES:** 10 SERVINGS

- 1 pound bacon strips
- 1 medium sweet red pepper, finely chopped
- 8 green onions, thinly sliced
- ½ cup chopped oil-packed sun-dried tomatoes
- 8 slices white bread, cubed
- 2 cups (8 ounces) shredded cheddar cheese
- 6 eggs, lightly beaten
- 1½ cups 2% milk
- ¼ cup mayonnaise
- ½ teaspoon salt
- ¼ teaspoon ground mustard
- ⅛ teaspoon pepper

1. In a large skillet, cook the bacon in batches until crisp; drain on paper towels. Crumble into a small bowl. Add the red pepper, onions and tomatoes. In a greased 13x9-in. baking dish, layer half of the bread, bacon mixture and cheese. Top with remaining bread and bacon mixture.

2. In another bowl, combine the eggs, milk, mayonnaise and seasonings. Pour over top. Sprinkle with remaining cheese. Cover and refrigerate overnight.

3. Remove from the refrigerator 30 minutes before baking. Bake, covered, at 350° for 40 minutes. Uncover and bake 5-10 minutes longer or until a knife inserted near the center comes out clean. Let stand for 5 minutes before cutting.

Mixed Berry French Toast Bake

I love this recipe! Perfect for fuss-free holiday breakfasts or company, it's scrumptious and so easy to put together the night before.
—**AMY BERRY** POLAND, MAINE

PREP: 20 MIN. + CHILLING • **BAKE:** 45 MIN. • **MAKES:** 8 SERVINGS

- 1 loaf (1 pound) French bread, cubed
- 6 egg whites
- 3 eggs
- 1¾ cups fat-free milk
- 1 teaspoon sugar
- 1 teaspoon ground cinnamon
- 1 teaspoon vanilla extract
- ¼ teaspoon salt
- 1 package (12 ounces) frozen unsweetened mixed berries
- 2 tablespoons cold butter
- ⅓ cup packed brown sugar

1. Place bread cubes in a 13x9-in. baking dish coated with cooking spray. In a large bowl, combine the egg whites, eggs, milk, sugar, cinnamon, vanilla and salt; pour mixture over bread. Cover and refrigerate for 8 hours or overnight.

2. Thirty minutes before baking, remove berries from the freezer and set aside; remove the baking dish from the refrigerator. Bake, covered, at 350° for 30 minutes.

3. In a small bowl, cut butter into brown sugar until crumbly. Sprinkle berries and brown sugar mixture over French toast. Bake, uncovered, for an additional 15-20 minutes or until a knife inserted near the center comes out clean.

Sunday Brunch Casserole

My hearty brunch casserole is a lighter take on a traditional favorite. It's so decadent, your guests won't even know that it's light!

—ALICE HOFMANN SUSSEX, WISCONSIN

PREP: 20 MIN. • **BAKE:** 30 MIN. • **MAKES:** 8 SERVINGS

- 6 bacon strips
- 1 small onion, chopped
- 1 small green pepper, chopped
- 1 teaspoon canola oil
- 2 cartons (8 ounces each) egg substitute
- 4 eggs
- 1 cup fat-free milk
- 4 cups frozen shredded hash brown potatoes, thawed
- 1 cup (4 ounces) shredded reduced-fat cheddar cheese
- ¾ teaspoon salt
- ½ teaspoon pepper
- ¼ teaspoon dill weed

1. In a large skillet, cook bacon over medium heat until crisp. Remove to paper towels; drain. Crumble bacon and set aside. In the same skillet, saute onion and green pepper in oil until tender; remove with a slotted spoon.
2. In a large bowl, whisk the egg substitute, eggs and milk. Stir in the hash browns, cheese, salt, pepper, dill, onion mixture and reserved bacon.
3. Transfer to a 13x9-in. baking dish coated with cooking spray. Bake, uncovered, at 350° for 30-35 minutes or until a knife inserted near the center comes out clean.

Mushroom Quiche Lorraine

Family and friends will delight in this savory quiche. Mushrooms and green onions bring fresh flavor, while cheese and bacon lend a touch of heartiness.

—MICHELLE FINCHER LYMAN, SOUTH CAROLINA

PREP: 15 MIN. • **BAKE:** 30 MIN. • **MAKES:** 6 SERVINGS

- 1 unbaked pastry shell (9 inches)
- 1 cup sliced fresh mushrooms
- ½ cup chopped green onions
- 2 tablespoons butter
- 4 eggs
- 1¼ cups half-and-half cream
- ⅛ teaspoon pepper
- 1 cup (4 ounces) shredded Swiss cheese
- 4 bacon strips, cooked and crumbled

1. Line unpricked pastry shell with a double thickness of heavy-duty foil. Bake at 450° for 8 minutes. Remove foil; bake 5 minutes longer. Remove from the oven; reduce heat to 375°.
2. Meanwhile, in a small skillet, saute mushrooms and onions in butter until tender. In a large bowl, beat the eggs, cream and pepper. Using a slotted spoon, transfer mushrooms and onions to egg mixture. Stir in cheese and bacon.
3. Pour into crust. Cover edges loosely with foil. Bake for 30-35 minutes or until a knife inserted near the center comes out clean. Let quiche stand for 5 minutes before cutting.

Sour Cream Bundt Coffee Cake

This yummy cake is so moist, you won't even need the cup of coffee! Make it for your next get-together—your guests will thank you.

—**KATHLEEN LARIMER** DAYTON, OHIO

PREP: 40 MIN. • **BAKE:** 45 MIN. + COOLING
MAKES: 16 SERVINGS

- ⅔ cup chopped pecans
- 2 tablespoons brown sugar
- 1½ teaspoons ground cinnamon

BATTER

- 1 cup butter, softened
- 2 cups sugar
- 2 eggs
- ½ teaspoon vanilla extract
- 2 cups all-purpose flour
- 1 teaspoon baking powder
- ¼ teaspoon baking soda
- ¼ teaspoon salt
- 1 cup (8 ounces) sour cream
  Confectioners' sugar

1. In a small bowl, combine the pecans, brown sugar and cinnamon; set aside. In a large bowl, cream butter and sugar until light and fluffy. Add eggs, one at a time, beating well after each addition. Beat in vanilla. Combine the flour, baking powder, baking soda and salt; add to creamed mixture alternately with sour cream, beating well after each addition.

2. Pour half of the batter into a greased and floured 10-in. fluted tube pan; sprinkle with half of the pecan mixture. Gently top with remaining batter and pecan mixture.

3. Bake at 350° for 45-50 minutes or until a toothpick inserted near the center comes out clean. Cool for 10 minutes before removing from pan to a wire rack to cool completely. Sprinkle with confectioners' sugar.

Cherry Yogurt

Serve wholesome granola over this thick, rich yogurt for a quick breakfast. Or layer it in a parfait glass with granola and fruit for something special. It will keep in the refrigerator for one week. If you're watching your sugar intake, use 100% cherry juice; avoid the cocktail blends that have added sugar.

—TASTE OF HOME TEST KITCHEN

PREP: 10 MIN. + CHILLING • **MAKES:** 3 CUPS

- 4 cups (32 ounces) reduced-fat plain yogurt
- 1 cup frozen pitted dark sweet cherries, thawed and quartered
- ½ cup cherry juice blend
- 3 tablespoons confectioners' sugar
- 1½ teaspoons vanilla extract

1. Line a strainer with four layers of cheesecloth or one coffee filter and place over a bowl. Place yogurt in prepared strainer; cover yogurt with edges of cheesecloth. Refrigerate for 8 hours or overnight.
2. Remove yogurt from cheesecloth and discard the liquid from the bowl. Place yogurt in a small bowl; stir in the remaining ingredients. Cover and refrigerate until serving.

FAST FIX ▶ Vanilla French Toast

We discovered this recipe in Mexico. We couldn't figure out what made this French toast so delicious until we learned the secret was vanilla—one of Mexico's most popular flavorings. Since then, we've added a touch of vanilla to our waffle and pancake recipes. It makes them all very tasty.

—JOE AND BOBBI SCHOTT CASTROVILLE, TEXAS

PREP/TOTAL TIME: 10 MIN. • **MAKES:** 2 SERVINGS

- 2 eggs
- ½ cup 2% milk
- 1 tablespoon sugar
- 1 teaspoon vanilla extract
  Pinch salt
- 6 slices day-old bread
  Maple syrup or cinnamon-sugar

In a shallow bowl, beat eggs; add the milk, sugar, vanilla and salt. Soak bread for 30 seconds on each side. Cook on a greased hot griddle until golden brown on both sides and cooked through. Serve with syrup or cinnamon-sugar.

FAST FIX ▶ Crunchy Apple Salad

With fiber-rich fruit, light dressing and crunchy walnuts, this is a great snack. Try it with low-fat granola.

—KATHY ARMSTRONG POST FALLS, IDAHO

PREP/TOTAL TIME: 15 MIN. • **MAKES:** 5 SERVINGS

- 6 tablespoons fat-free sugar-free vanilla yogurt
- 6 tablespoons reduced-fat whipped topping
- ¼ teaspoon plus ⅛ teaspoon ground cinnamon, divided
- 2 medium red apples, chopped
- 1 large Granny Smith apple, chopped
- ¼ cup dried cranberries
- 2 tablespoons chopped walnuts

In a large bowl, combine the yogurt, whipped topping and ¼ teaspoon cinnamon. Add apples and cranberries; toss to coat. Refrigerate until serving. Sprinkle salad with walnuts and remaining cinnamon before serving.

Spinach Swiss Quiche

Warm wedges of this tasty quiche are packed with convenient frozen spinach, sweet red pepper and Swiss cheese. My family requests this dish year-round. You can saute the bacon mixture the night before to reduce morning prep time.

—APRIL MILNER
DEARBORN HEIGHTS, MICHIGAN

PREP: 25 MIN. • **BAKE:** 35 MIN. + STANDING
MAKES: 6 SERVINGS

- 1 refrigerated pie pastry
- 4 turkey bacon strips, diced
- ¼ cup chopped onion
- ¼ cup chopped sweet red pepper
- 1 package (10 ounces) frozen chopped spinach, thawed and squeezed dry
- 2 cups egg substitute
- ½ cup fat-free cottage cheese
- ¼ cup shredded reduced-fat Swiss cheese
- ½ teaspoon dried oregano
- ¼ teaspoon dried parsley flakes
- ¼ teaspoon each salt, pepper and paprika
- 6 tablespoons fat-free sour cream

1. On a lightly floured surface, unroll pastry. Transfer to a 9-in. pie plate. Trim pastry to ½ in. beyond edge of plate; flute edges. Line unpricked pastry with a double thickness of heavy-duty foil.

2. Bake at 450° for 8 minutes. Remove foil; bake 5 minutes longer. Cool on a wire rack. Reduce heat to 350°.

3. In a small skillet, cook the bacon, onion and red pepper until vegetables are tender; drain. Stir in spinach. Spoon spinach mixture into pastry.

4. In a small bowl, combine the egg substitute, cottage cheese, Swiss cheese and seasonings; pour over spinach mixture.

5. Bake for 35-40 minutes or until a knife inserted near the center comes out clean. Let stand for 10 minutes before cutting. Serve with sour cream.

FAST FIX ▸ Too-Yummy-To-Share Scramble

Pamper yourself some sunny morning with this scrumptious, single-serving egg dish—you're worth it! Basil gives it a fresh flavor.

—VICKEY ABATE
GREEN ISLAND, NEW YORK

PREP/TOTAL TIME: 15 MIN.
MAKES: 1 SERVING

- ¼ cup chopped sweet onion
- ¼ cup chopped tomato
- ⅛ teaspoon dried basil
  Dash salt and pepper
- 1 egg
- 1 tablespoon water
- 2 tablespoons shredded reduced-fat cheddar cheese

1. In a small nonstick skillet coated with cooking spray, cook and stir onion over medium heat until tender. Add the tomato, basil, salt and pepper; cook 1 minute longer.

2. In a small bowl, whisk egg and water. Add egg mixture to the pan; cook and stir until egg is completely set. Remove from the heat. Sprinkle with cheese; cover and let stand until cheese is melted.

FAST FIX ▶ Drop Doughnuts

I use leftover mashed potatoes from our Thanksgiving and Christmas dinners to make these light and fluffy doughnuts as a next-day breakfast treat. My neighbor's mother-in-law came up with the recipe, and I was one of many lucky recipients. My family can't get enough!

—MARILYN KLEINFALL ELK GROVE VILLAGE, ILLINOIS

PREP/TOTAL TIME: 25 MIN. • **MAKES:** 3 TO 3½ DOZEN

- ½ cup mashed potatoes (mashed with milk and butter)
- ¼ cup sugar
- 1 egg, lightly beaten
- ½ cup sour cream
- ½ teaspoon vanilla extract
- 1½ cups all-purpose flour
- ½ teaspoon baking soda
- ¼ teaspoon baking powder
- Oil for deep-fat frying
- Additional sugar or confectioners' sugar, optional

1. In a large bowl, combine the potatoes, sugar, egg, sour cream and vanilla. Combine dry ingredients; stir in potato mixture.

2. Heat oil in an electric skillet or deep-fat fryer to 375°. Drop teaspoonfuls of batter, a few at a time, into hot oil. Fry until golden brown on both sides. Drain on paper towels; roll in sugar while warm.

> ❝We love this recipe!
> Very quick and easy. I rolled the drop doughnuts in cinnamon and sugar.❞
>
> —CRAFTYGRANDMA1951 FROM TASTEOFHOME.COM

Paradise Granola

Even our 4-year-old, who isn't fond of dried fruit, enjoys this granola. It's low fat, full of fiber and just plain delicious.

—ROBYN LARABEE LUCKNOW, ONTARIO

PREP: 20 MIN. • **BAKE:** 20 MIN. + COOLING • **MAKES:** 7 CUPS

- 2 cups old-fashioned oats
- ½ cup flaked coconut
- ½ cup toasted wheat germ
- ¼ cup oat bran
- ¼ cup sunflower kernels
- ¼ cup slivered almonds
- ¼ cup chopped pecans
- 2 tablespoons sesame seeds
- ¼ cup honey
- 2 tablespoons canola oil
- 2 tablespoons grated orange peel
- 1 teaspoon vanilla extract
- ½ teaspoon salt
- 1 cup dried cranberries
- ¾ cup chopped dates
- ½ cup chopped dried figs
- ½ cup chopped dried apricots
- 3 tablespoons raisins

1. In a large bowl, combine the first eight ingredients. In a small bowl, whisk the honey, oil, orange peel, vanilla and salt; pour over the oat mixture and mix well. Spread evenly into an ungreased 15x10x1-in. baking pan.

2. Bake at 350° for 20-25 minutes or until golden brown, stirring once. Cool completely on a wire rack. Stir in dried fruits. Store in an airtight container.

Orange-Cheesecake Breakfast Rolls

These yummy rolls are a nice change of pace from the typical brown sugar and cinnamon kind. They make a nice treat for breakfast or brunch.

—HANNAH COBB OWINGS MILLS, MARYLAND

PREP: 50 MIN. + RISING • **BAKE:** 25 MIN.
MAKES: 2 DOZEN

- 2 **packages (¼ ounce each) active dry yeast**
- ¾ **cup warm water (110° to 115°)**
- 1¾ **cups warm 2% milk (110° to 115°)**
- 1 **cup sugar**
- 2 **eggs**
- 3 **tablespoons butter, melted**
- 1½ **teaspoons salt**
- 7 **to 8 cups all-purpose flour**

FILLING
- 1 **package (8 ounces) cream cheese, softened**
- ½ **cup sugar**
- 1 **tablespoon orange juice concentrate**
- ½ **teaspoon vanilla extract**

GLAZE
- 2 **cups confectioners' sugar**
- 3 **tablespoons orange juice**
- 1 **teaspoon grated orange peel**

1. In a large bowl, dissolve yeast in warm water. Add the milk, sugar, eggs, butter, salt and 5 cups flour. Beat until smooth. Stir in enough remaining flour to form a firm dough.

2. Turn onto a floured surface; knead until smooth and elastic, about 6-8 minutes. Place in a greased bowl, turning once to grease the top. Cover and let rise in a warm place until doubled, about 1 hour.

3. In a small bowl, beat the cream cheese, sugar, orange juice concentrate and vanilla until smooth. Punch dough down. Turn onto a lightly floured surface; divide in half. Roll one portion into an 18x7-in. rectangle. Spread half of the filling to within ½ in. of edges. Roll up jelly-roll style, starting with a long side; pinch seam to seal. Cut into 12 slices; place cut side down in a greased 13x9-in. baking pan. Repeat with remaining dough and filling. Cover and let rise until doubled, about 30 minutes.

4. Bake at 350° for 25-30 minutes or until golden brown. Combine the confectioners' sugar, orange juice and peel; drizzle over warm rolls. Refrigerate leftovers.

TO MAKE AHEAD *Prepare, shape and place rolls in baking pans as directed. Cover and refrigerate overnight. Remove rolls from the refrigerator and let stand for 30 minutes. Bake and glaze as directed.*

JUICY TURKEY BURGERS, PAGE 52

HOME-STYLE STEW, 61

ASIAN TURKEY LETTUCE WRAPS, 59

HEARTY CHICKEN NOODLE SOUP, 65

SOUPS & SANDWICHES

Now it's easier than ever to dish up savory soups, hearty chilis and cozy chowders. Some whip up in mere minutes for a quick meal while others slowly simmer for hours to welcome you home after a long day at work. And nothing hits the spot like a piled-high sandwich. Classic melts, burgers and wraps are just a few of the handheld wonders featured here. So turn to these standout recipes the next time you're craving the ultimate comfort-food combo!

🍲 SLOW COOKER Potato Soup

I added some fiery character to a basic potato chowder by tossing in a few roasted red peppers. The extra flavor gives a deliciously unique twist to an otherwise ordinary soup.
—**MARY SHIVERS** ADA, OKLAHOMA

PREP: 20 MIN. • **COOK:** 5½ HOURS
MAKES: 12 SERVINGS (3 QUARTS)

- 8 **medium potatoes, peeled and cut into ½-inch cubes**
- 6 **cups chicken broth**
- 1 **large onion, chopped**
- 1 **jar (7 ounces) roasted sweet red peppers, drained and chopped**
- 1 **small celery rib, chopped**
- ½ **teaspoon garlic powder**
- ½ **teaspoon seasoned salt**
- ½ **teaspoon pepper**
- ⅛ **teaspoon rubbed sage**
- ⅓ **cup all-purpose flour**
- 2 **cups heavy whipping cream, divided**
- 1 **cup grated Parmesan cheese, divided**
- 8 **bacon strips, cooked and crumbled**
- 2 **tablespoons minced fresh cilantro**

1. In a 5- or 6-qt. slow cooker, combine the first nine ingredients. Cover and cook on low for 5-6 hours or until vegetables are tender.
2. In a small bowl, combine flour and ½ cup cream until smooth; add to slow cooker. Stir in ¾ cup cheese, bacon, cilantro and remaining cream. Cover and cook for 30 minutes or until slightly thickened. Ladle into bowls; sprinkle with remaining cheese.

FAST FIX ▶ Juicy Turkey Burgers

The way to a healthy heart for my husband is through great-tasting low-fat recipes. He enjoys these grilled turkey burgers with their herb flavor and garden-fresh garnish. They make an ideal summer sandwich or in-hand meal.
—**TRINA HOPSECGER** ELKHART, INDIANA

PREP/TOTAL TIME: 25 MIN. • **MAKES:** 6 SERVINGS

- 1 **medium apple, peeled and finely shredded**
- ½ **cup cooked brown rice**
- 2 **tablespoons grated onion**
- 2 **garlic cloves, minced**
- 1½ **teaspoons rubbed sage**
- 1 **teaspoon salt**
- ½ **teaspoon pepper**
- ½ **teaspoon dried thyme**
- ¼ **teaspoon ground allspice**
- ¼ **teaspoon cayenne pepper**
- 1 **pound lean ground turkey**
- 2 **tablespoons minced fresh parsley**
- 6 **whole wheat hamburger buns, split**
- 6 **lettuce leaves**
- 6 **tomato slices**

1. In a large bowl, combine the first 10 ingredients. Crumble turkey over mixture and mix well. Shape into six ½-in.-thick patties.
2. Moisten a paper towel with cooking oil; using long-handled tongs, lightly coat the grill rack. Prepare grill for indirect heat using a grill pan.
3. Place burgers over drip pan and grill, covered, over indirect medium heat or broil 4 in. from the heat for 6-7 minutes on each side or until a thermometer reads 165° and juices run clear. Sprinkle with parsley. Serve on buns with lettuce and tomato.

White Bean Chicken Chili

My sister shared this chili recipe with me. My hungry clan eats it up fast, so I usually double the recipe and add one extra can of beans. The jalapeno adds just the right amount of heat.
—**KRISTINE BOWLES** RIO RANCHO, NEW MEXICO

PREP: 35 MIN. • **COOK:** 3 HOURS • **MAKES:** 6 SERVINGS

- ¾ **pound boneless skinless chicken breasts, cubed**
- ½ **teaspoon salt**
- ¼ **teaspoon pepper**
- 2 **tablespoons olive oil**
- 1 **medium onion, chopped**
- 4 **garlic cloves, minced**
- 1 **jalapeno pepper, seeded and chopped**
- 2 **teaspoons dried oregano**
- 1 **teaspoon ground cumin**
- 2 **cans (15 ounces each) white kidney or cannellini beans, rinsed and drained, divided**
- 3 **cups chicken broth, divided**
- 1½ **cups (6 ounces) shredded cheddar cheese**
  Sour cream and minced fresh cilantro, optional

1. Sprinkle chicken with salt and pepper. In a large skillet over medium heat, brown chicken in oil.
2. Stir in the onion, garlic and jalapeno; cook 2 minutes longer. Sprinkle with oregano and cumin; cook 1 minute longer or until chicken is browned and the vegetables are tender. Transfer to a 3-qt. slow cooker.
3. In a small bowl, mash 1 cup of beans; add ½ cup broth and stir until blended. Add to the slow cooker with the remaining beans and broth.
4. Cover and cook on low for 3 to 3½ hours or until chicken is tender. Stir before serving. Sprinkle with cheese. Garnish with sour cream and cilantro if desired.

CHICKEN CORN CHILI *Add 2 cups thawed frozen corn and ½ teaspoon ground coriander to the slow cooker along with the broth. Proceed as directed.*

NOTE *Wear disposable gloves when cutting hot peppers; the oils can burn skin. Avoid touching your face.*

Rootin'-Tootin' Cincinnati Chili

Yep, there's root beer in this spicy chili, and it adds a nice touch of sweetness. Serve over spaghetti and let everyone add their own favorite toppings to this Cincy classic!

—HOLLY GOMEZ
SEABROOK, NEW HAMPSHIRE

PREP: 25 MIN. • **COOK:** 30 MIN.
MAKES: 4 SERVINGS

- 1 **pound ground beef**
- 1 **small onion, chopped**
- 1 **small green pepper, chopped**
- 1 **garlic clove, minced**
- 1 **can (14½ ounces) fire-roasted diced tomatoes, undrained**
- 1 **cup root beer**
- 2 **tablespoons chili powder**
- 2 **tablespoons tomato paste**
- 2 **tablespoons minced chipotle peppers in adobo sauce**
- 1 **tablespoon ground cumin**
- 1 **beef bouillon cube**
  Hot cooked spaghetti
  Optional toppings: crushed tortilla chips, chopped green onions, and shredded cheddar and Parmesan cheeses

1. In a large saucepan, cook the beef, onions and green pepper over medium heat until meat is no longer pink. Add garlic; cook 1 minute longer. Drain. Add the tomatoes, root beer, chili powder, tomato paste, chipotle peppers, cumin and bouillon. Bring to a boil.
2. Reduce heat; cover and simmer for 20-30 minutes to allow flavors to blend. Serve with spaghetti. Garnish with chips, green onions and cheeses if desired.

Turkey Focaccia Club

This sandwich is pure heaven thanks to the cranberry-pecan mayo. It's a great way to use up Thanksgiving leftovers, but I guarantee you'll want to eat it all year long!

—JUDY WILSON
SUN CITY WEST, ARIZONA

PREP/TOTAL TIME: 20 MIN.
MAKES: 4 SERVINGS

- ½ **cup mayonnaise**
- ½ **cup whole-berry cranberry sauce**
- 2 **tablespoons chopped pecans, toasted**
- 2 **tablespoons Dijon mustard**
- 1 **tablespoon honey**
- 1 **loaf (8 ounces) focaccia bread**
- 3 **lettuce leaves**
- ½ **pound thinly sliced cooked turkey**
- ¼ **pound sliced Gouda cheese**
- 8 **slices tomato**
- 6 **bacon strips, cooked**

In a small bowl, mix the first five ingredients until blended. Using a long serrated knife, cut focaccia horizontally in half. Spread cut sides with mayonnaise mixture. Layer bottom half with lettuce, turkey, cheese, tomato and bacon; replace bread top. Cut into wedges.
NOTE *To toast nuts, spread in a 15x 10x1-in. baking pan. Bake at 350° for 5-10 minutes or until lightly browned, stirring occasionally.*

Grilled Pizza Burgers

Pizza burgers are usually a kid's favorite. But when served on English muffins with spices and provolone cheese, they become a favorite for adults as well.

—MITZI SENTIFF
ANNAPOLIS, MARYLAND

PREP: 20 MIN. • **GRILL:** 15 MIN.
MAKES: 4 SERVINGS

- 1 egg, lightly beaten
- ¾ cup grated Parmesan cheese
- ½ cup chopped onion
- ¼ cup minced fresh parsley
- ¾ teaspoon dried basil
- ¾ teaspoon dried oregano
- ¾ teaspoon dried rosemary, crushed
- ¾ teaspoon pepper
- 1 pound ground beef
- 4 slices provolone cheese
- 4 English muffins, split and toasted
- ½ cup pizza sauce

1. In a large bowl, combine the first eight ingredients. Crumble beef over mixture and mix well. Shape into four patties.

2. Grill burgers, covered, over medium heat for 5-7 minutes on each side or until a thermometer reads 160° and juices run clear. Top burgers with cheese; cover and grill 2-3 minutes longer or until cheese is melted. Serve on muffins with pizza sauce.

Moroccan Vegetarian Stew

This fragrant, spicy stew can also be served over couscous or with warm pita bread. Try topping it with a dollop of plain Greek yogurt or sour cream to temper the heat.

—SONYA LABBE
WEST HOLLYWOOD, CALIFORNIA

PREP: 20 MIN. • **COOK:** 30 MIN.
MAKES: 8 SERVINGS (3 QUARTS)

- 1 large onion, chopped
- 1 tablespoon olive oil
- 2 teaspoons ground cinnamon
- 2 teaspoons ground cumin
- 1 teaspoon ground coriander
- ½ teaspoon cayenne pepper
- ½ teaspoon ground allspice
- ¼ teaspoon salt
- 3 cups water
- 1 small butternut squash, peeled and cubed
- 2 medium potatoes, peeled and cubed
- 4 medium carrots, sliced
- 3 plum tomatoes, chopped
- 2 small zucchini, cut into 1-inch pieces
- 1 can (15 ounces) garbanzo beans or chickpeas, rinsed and drained

1. In a Dutch oven, saute onion in oil until tender. Add spices and salt; cook 1 minute longer.

2. Stir in the water, squash, potatoes, carrots and tomatoes. Bring to a boil. Reduce heat; simmer, uncovered, for 15-20 minutes or until potatoes and squash are almost tender.

3. Add zucchini and chickpeas; return to a boil. Reduce heat; simmer, uncovered, for 5-8 minutes or until vegetables are tender.

BOUNTY OF BEANS

If you want to serve more meatless meals, consider recipes that call for beans. They are protein-rich substitutes for the meat and poultry found in many dishes—particularly soups and stews. Feel free to experiment and get creative with beans that you're not familiar with.

FAST FIX Taco Burgers

My family loves the taste of tacos, but I dislike the mess. So I developed these burgers as a tasty but "tidy" alternative.
—**LINDA LOGAN** WARREN, OHIO

PREP/TOTAL TIME: 25 MIN. • **MAKES:** 6 SERVINGS

- 1 cup finely crushed corn chips
- 1 envelope taco seasoning
- 1 tablespoon dried minced onion
- 1 egg, lightly beaten
- 1½ pounds ground beef
- 6 slices cheddar cheese
  Sandwich buns, split
  Lettuce leaves
  Tomato slices
  Salsa, optional

1. In a large bowl, combine the corn chips, taco seasoning, onion and egg. Crumble beef over mixture and mix well. Shape into six patties.

2. Grill, covered, over medium heat or broil 4 in. from the heat for 7-8 minutes on each side or until a thermometer reads 160° and juices run clear.

3. Top each burger with a cheese slice; cook just until cheese begins to melt. Serve on buns with lettuce, tomato and salsa if desired.

FAST FIX Baked Potato Soup

I discovered this recipe in a children's cookbook. It's delicious, easy to prepare and makes the perfect amount for a hungry twosome—my husband and me.
—**LINDA MUMM** DAVENPORT, IOWA

PREP/TOTAL TIME: 20 MIN. • **MAKES:** 2 SERVINGS

- 2 medium potatoes, baked and cooled
- 1 can (14½ ounces) chicken broth
- 2 tablespoons sour cream
- ⅛ teaspoon pepper
- ¼ cup shredded cheddar cheese
- 1 tablespoon crumbled cooked bacon or bacon bits
- 1 green onion, sliced

Peel potatoes and cut into ½-in. cubes; place half in a blender. Add broth; cover and process until smooth. Pour into a saucepan. Stir in sour cream, pepper and remaining potatoes. Cook over low heat until heated through (do not boil). Garnish with cheese, bacon and onion.

Tomato Seafood Soup

We love this hearty soup on Sundays during football season. For a little extra zip, add red pepper flakes or use jalapeno-flavored tomatoes.
—**MARY ADAMS** FAIRPORT, NEW YORK

PREP: 10 MIN. • **COOK:** 35 MIN. • **MAKES:** 8 SERVINGS (2 QUARTS)

- ½ cup chopped onion
- ½ cup chopped green pepper
- 1 tablespoon olive oil
- ½ teaspoon minced garlic
- 1 can (14 ounces) diced tomatoes, undrained
- 1 jar (14 ounces) spaghetti sauce
- 1 cup salsa
- ¾ cup chicken broth
- ½ cup white wine or additional chicken broth
- 3 teaspoons dried parsley flakes
- ¼ teaspoon dried oregano
- ¼ teaspoon dried basil
- ⅛ to ¼ teaspoon pepper
- 1 package (12 ounces) frozen uncooked shrimp, thawed, peeled and deveined
- 1 package (8 ounces) imitation crabmeat, chopped, or 2 cans (6 ounces each) crabmeat, drained, flaked and cartilage removed
- 1 can (6½ ounces) minced clams, undrained

1. In a Dutch oven, saute onion and green pepper in oil until onion is tender. Add garlic; cook 1 minute longer. Stir in the tomatoes, spaghetti sauce, salsa, broth, wine and seasonings. Bring to a boil. Reduce heat; cover and simmer for 20 minutes.

2. Add the shrimp, crab and clams. Cover and simmer for 5-7 minutes or until shrimp turn pink.

Flank Steak Sandwiches

My sister and I found this recipe 15 years ago and changed a few ingredients to make it our own. Now, when family and friends hear we're making these sandwiches, they come running!

—ELIZABETH HINER CHICO, CALIFORNIA

PREP: 25 MIN. + MARINATING • **GRILL:** 25 MIN.
MAKES: 6 SERVINGS

- 1 cup chopped onion
- 1 cup dry red wine or beef broth
- ¾ cup reduced-sodium soy sauce
- ½ cup olive oil, divided
- 4½ teaspoons minced garlic, divided
- 1½ teaspoons ground mustard
- 1½ teaspoons ground ginger
- 1 beef flank steak (1½ pounds)
- 1 medium sweet red pepper, cut into 1-inch strips
- 1 medium sweet yellow pepper, cut into 1-inch strips
- 1 medium red onion, thickly sliced
- ¼ teaspoon pepper
- 6 French rolls, split

1. In a small bowl, combine the onion, wine, soy sauce, ¼ cup olive oil, 2½ teaspoons garlic, mustard and ginger. Pour 1¾ cups into a large resealable plastic bag; add steak. Pour remaining marinade into another resealable plastic bag; add the peppers and onion. Seal bags and turn to coat; refrigerate for 3 hours or overnight, turning occasionally.

2. Drain and discard marinade from steak. Dip a paper towel in cooking oil; using long-handled tongs, lightly coat the grill rack. Grill, covered, over medium heat for 6-7 minutes on each side or until meat reaches desired doneness (for medium-rare, a thermometer should read 145°; medium, 160°; well-done, 170°).

3. Drain and discard marinade from vegetables. Place in a grill basket. Grill, uncovered, over medium-hot heat for 9-11 minutes or until vegetables are tender, stirring frequently.

4. In a small bowl, combine the pepper, and remaining oil and garlic; brush over cut sides of rolls. Place cut side down on grill for 2-3 minutes or until golden brown.

5. Thinly slice steak across the grain; place on bun bottoms. Top with vegetables and bun tops. Serve immediately.

NOTE *If you do not have a grill wok or basket, use a disposable foil pan. Poke holes in the bottom of the pan with a meat fork to allow liquid to drain.*

Potato-Bar Chili

Everyone will love this mild chili, especially when it's ladled over a steamy baked potato. This sauce is so thick and hearty, it's almost a meal in itself.

—ALCY THORNE LOS MOLINOS, CALIFORNIA

PREP: 10 MIN. • **COOK:** 30 MIN. • **MAKES:** 7 CUPS

- 1½ pounds ground beef
- 2 medium onions, chopped
- 1 medium green pepper, chopped
- 1 can (28 ounces) diced tomatoes, undrained
- 1 can (16 ounces) chili beans, undrained
- 2 tablespoons sugar
- 2 teaspoons chili powder
- ¼ teaspoon salt
- ¼ teaspoon pepper
  Baked potatoes

1. In a Dutch oven, cook the beef, onions and green pepper over medium heat until meat is no longer pink; drain. Add the tomatoes, beans, sugar and seasonings.

2. Bring to a boil. Reduce heat; simmer, uncovered, for 20 minutes. Serve with potatoes.

Open-Faced Chicken Avocado Burgers

A creamy avocado spread and thick slices of fresh mozzarella and tomato dress up these chicken patties. They're wonderful with buttered boiled potatoes or a green salad.

—LISA HUNDLEY ABERDEEN, NORTH CAROLINA

PREP: 30 MIN. • **COOK:** 15 MIN.
MAKES: 4 SERVINGS PLUS ¼ CUP LEFTOVER SPREAD

- 1 tablespoon lemon juice
- ¼ teaspoon Worcestershire sauce
- ½ medium ripe avocado, peeled
- ½ cup mayonnaise
- ¼ cup sour cream
- 4 green onions, coarsely chopped
- ½ teaspoon salt
- ½ teaspoon cayenne pepper

BURGERS
- ¼ cup shredded Parmesan cheese
- 2 tablespoons prepared pesto
- 3 garlic cloves, minced
- ¼ teaspoon salt
- 1 pound ground chicken
- 4 tablespoons olive oil, divided
- ½ pound fresh mozzarella cheese, cut into 4 slices
- 4 slices Italian bread (¾ inch thick)
- 2 cups fresh arugula or baby spinach
- 8 slices tomato
- ¼ teaspoon dried basil
- ¼ teaspoon pepper

1. In a blender, combine the first eight ingredients; cover and process until smooth. Chill until serving. For burgers, in a small bowl, combine the Parmesan cheese, pesto, garlic and salt. Crumble chicken over mixture and mix well. Shape into four patties.

2. In a large skillet over medium heat, cook burgers in 2 tablespoons oil for 5-7 minutes on each side or until a thermometer reads 165° and juices run clear. Top with cheese; cover and cook 1 minute longer.

3. Meanwhile, brush bread with remaining oil; place on a baking sheet. Broil 3-4 in. from the heat for 1-2 minutes on each side or until toasted.

4. Spread each slice of toast with 2 tablespoons avocado spread (refrigerate remaining spread for another use). Top with arugula, a burger and sliced tomato. Sprinkle with basil and pepper.

Beef Barley Soup

This hearty barley soup is a favorite menu item in our house throughout the year. Everyone savors the flavor.

—ELIZABETH KENDALL CAROLINA BEACH, NORTH CAROLINA

PREP: 20 MIN. • **COOK:** 1 HOUR 50 MIN.
MAKES: 9 SERVINGS (2¼ QUARTS)

- 1 pound beef top round steak, cut into ½-inch cubes
- 1 tablespoon canola oil
- 3 cans (14½ ounces each) beef broth
- 2 cups water
- ⅓ cup medium pearl barley
- 1 teaspoon salt
- ⅛ teaspoon pepper
- 1 cup chopped carrots
- ½ cup chopped celery
- ¼ cup chopped onion
- 3 tablespoons minced fresh parsley
- 1 cup frozen peas

1. In a Dutch oven, brown beef in oil; drain. Stir in the broth, water, barley, salt and pepper. Bring to a boil. Reduce heat; cover and simmer for 1 hour.

2. Add the carrots, celery, onion and parsley; cover and simmer for 45 minutes or until meat and vegetables are tender. Stir in peas; heat through.

Chicken Veggie Soup

This satisfying veggie soup hits the spot at lunch or dinner. Add a side salad and some whole grain bread for a filling and nutritious meal.

—**AMY CHEATHAM** SANDUSKY, OHIO

PREP: 25 MIN. • **COOK:** 5 HOURS
MAKES: 7 SERVINGS (2¾ QUARTS)

- 1 large sweet onion, chopped
- 1 cup sliced baby portobello mushrooms
- ½ cup chopped green pepper
- ½ cup chopped sweet red pepper
- 1 tablespoon butter
- 1 tablespoon olive oil
- 5 garlic cloves, minced
- ¾ pound boneless skinless chicken breasts, cut into ½-in. cubes
- 1 can (49½ ounces) chicken broth
- 1 can (28 ounces) crushed tomatoes, undrained
- 2 medium carrots, cut into ¼-inch slices
- ½ cup medium pearl barley
- 1¾ teaspoons Italian seasoning
- 1½ teaspoons pepper
- ½ teaspoon salt

1. In a large skillet, saute the onion, mushrooms and peppers in butter and oil until tender. Add garlic; cook 1 minute longer.

2. Transfer to a 5-qt. slow cooker. Add the remaining ingredients. Cover and cook on low for 5-6 hours or until chicken and barley are tender.

FAST FIX ▶ Asian Turkey Lettuce Wraps

Chopped frozen vegetables make these wraps a snap. Add some Asian chili sauce if you want to spice it up a bit.

—**SUSAN RILEY** ALLEN, TEXAS

PREP/TOTAL TIME: 20 MIN.
MAKES: 5 SERVINGS

- 1¼ pounds extra-lean ground turkey
- 1 package (16 ounces) frozen stir-fry vegetable blend, thawed
- ⅓ cup reduced-sodium teriyaki sauce
- ¼ cup hoisin sauce
- 3 tablespoons reduced-fat creamy peanut butter
- 2 tablespoons minced fresh gingerroot
- 1 tablespoon rice vinegar
- 1 tablespoon sesame oil
- 3 garlic cloves, minced
- 4 green onions, chopped
- 10 Boston lettuce leaves
   Additional hoisin sauce, optional

1. In a large nonstick skillet coated with cooking spray, cook the turkey over medium heat until it is no longer pink.

2. Coarsely chop stir-fry vegetables; add to the pan. Stir in the teriyaki sauce, hoisin sauce, peanut butter, ginger, vinegar and oil. Stir-fry over medium-high heat for 5 minutes. Add garlic; cook 1 minute longer.

3. Remove from the heat; stir in onions. Place a scant ½ cup turkey mixture on each lettuce leaf; fold lettuce over filling. Serve with additional hoisin sauce if desired.

⟨SLOW COOKER⟩ Mexican Chicken Chili

Corn and black beans give this satisfying chili a Mexican flair the whole family will love. Adjust the cayenne if you are looking for a little less zip.

—STEPHANIE RABBITT-SCHAPP
CINCINNATI, OHIO

PREP: 30 MIN. • **COOK:** 5 HOURS
MAKES: 6 SERVINGS

- 1 **pound boneless skinless chicken breasts, cubed**
- 1 **tablespoon canola oil**
- 2 **cans (14½ ounces each) diced tomatoes, undrained**
- 2 **cups frozen corn**
- 1 **can (15 ounces) black beans, rinsed and drained**
- 1 **can (14½ ounces) reduced-sodium chicken broth**
- 1 **can (4 ounces) chopped green chilies**
- 2 **tablespoons chili powder**
- 1 **tablespoon ground cumin**
- ½ **teaspoon salt**
- ¼ **teaspoon cayenne pepper**

In a small skillet, brown chicken in oil. Transfer to a 5-qt. slow cooker. Stir in the remaining ingredients. Cover and cook on low for 5-6 hours or until the chicken is no longer pink.

FAST FIX ▶

Pastrami Deli Wraps

My hubby can't seem to get enough of these pastrami wraps. I sometimes add horseradish for extra flavor.

—NILA GRAHL GURNEE, ILLINOIS

PREP/TOTAL TIME: 20 MIN.
MAKES: 4 SERVINGS

- ¼ **cup reduced-fat spreadable cream cheese**
- ¼ **cup coarsely chopped roasted sweet red pepper**
- 4 **spinach tortillas (8 inches), warmed**
- 4 **lettuce leaves**
- 4 **slices deli pastrami**
- 4 **slices reduced-fat provolone cheese**
- ¼ **cup thinly sliced red onion**
- 1 **small sweet red pepper, julienned**
- ½ **cup chopped cucumber**

Place cream cheese and roasted pepper in a small food processor. Cover and process until blended. Spread over tortillas. Layer with remaining ingredients; roll up. Secure with toothpicks.

PASTRAMI, DEFINED

Pastrami is a deli meat that is made most often from beef brisket. The raw meat is brined and seasoned with herbs and spices. It is then smoked for flavor and steamed until tender.

SLOW COOKER Home-Style Stew

My husband and I both work full time, so quick meals are a must. This stew always tastes great, and is a regular menu item for us.
—**MARIE SHANKS** TERRE HAUTE, INDIANA

PREP: 20 MIN. • **COOK:** 6 HOURS • **MAKES:** 5 SERVINGS

- 2 **packages (16 ounces each) frozen vegetables for stew**
- 1½ **pounds beef stew meat, cut into 1-inch cubes**
- 1 **can (10¾ ounces) condensed cream of mushroom soup, undiluted**
- 1 **can (10¾ ounces) condensed tomato soup, undiluted**
- 1 **envelope reduced-sodium onion soup mix**

1. Place vegetables in a 5-qt. slow cooker. In a large nonstick skillet coated with cooking spray, brown beef on all sides.

2. Transfer to slow cooker. Combine the remaining ingredients; pour over the top.

3. Cover and cook on low for 6-8 hours or until the meat is tender.

Jalapeno Popper Burgers

What do you get when you combine a jalapeno popper and a great burger? This fantastic recipe! It takes the classic components of a popper and encases them in a juicy patty, for a burst of flavor in every delicious bite.
—**JO DAVISON** NAPLES, FLORIDA

PREP: 30 MIN. • **GRILL:** 15 MIN. • **MAKES:** 4 SERVINGS

- 3 **jalapeno peppers, halved lengthwise and seeded**
- 1 **teaspoon olive oil**
- 6 **bacon strips, cooked and crumbled**
- 1 **package (3 ounces) cream cheese, softened**
- 2 **garlic cloves, minced**
- 1 **teaspoon salt**
- 1 **teaspoon lemon-pepper seasoning**
- ½ **teaspoon pepper**
- ¼ **teaspoon paprika**
- 2 **pounds ground beef**
- 4 **slices pepper jack cheese**
- 4 **hamburger buns, split**
- 4 **lettuce leaves**
- 1 **large tomato, sliced**
- ¾ **cup guacamole**

1. Brush jalapenos with oil. Grill, covered, over medium heat for 3-5 minutes or until tender, turning occasionally. When cool enough to handle, finely chop. In a small bowl, combine the bacon, cream cheese and jalapeno until blended.

2. In a large bowl, combine the garlic, salt, lemon-pepper, pepper and paprika. Crumble beef over mixture and mix well. Shape into eight thin patties. Spoon bacon mixture onto center of four patties; top with remaining patties and press edges firmly to seal.

3. Grill burgers, covered, over medium heat or broil 4 in. from heat for 6-7 minutes on each side or until a thermometer reads 160° and juices run clear. Top with pepper jack cheese. Cover and cook 1-2 minutes longer or until cheese is melted.

4. Grill buns, cut side down, over medium heat for 30-60 seconds or until toasted. Serve burgers on buns with lettuce, tomato and guacamole.

NOTE *Wear disposable gloves when cutting hot peppers; the oils can burn skin. Avoid touching your face.*

Hearty Chipotle Chicken Soup

Sweet corn and cool sour cream help tame the smoky hot flavors of chipotle pepper in this well-balanced soup that's perfect for chilly fall nights.

—**SONALI RUDER** NEW YORK, NEW YORK

PREP: 15 MIN. • **COOK:** 30 MIN.
MAKES: 8 SERVINGS (3¼ QUARTS)

- 1 **large onion, chopped**
- 1 **tablespoon canola oil**
- 4 **garlic cloves, minced**
- 4 **cups reduced-sodium chicken broth**
- 2 **cans (15 ounces each) pinto beans, rinsed and drained**
- 2 **cans (14½ ounces each) fire-roasted diced tomatoes, undrained**
- 3 **cups frozen corn**
- 2 **chipotle peppers in adobo sauce, seeded and minced**
- 2 **teaspoons adobo sauce**
- 1 **teaspoon ground cumin**
- ¼ **teaspoon pepper**
- 2 **cups cubed cooked chicken breast**
- ½ **cup fat-free sour cream**
- ¼ **cup minced fresh cilantro**

1. In a Dutch oven, saute onion in oil until tender. Add garlic; cook 1 minute longer. Add the broth, beans, tomatoes, corn, chipotle peppers, adobo sauce, cumin and pepper. Bring to a boil. Reduce heat; simmer, uncovered, for 20 minutes.

2. Stir in chicken; heat through. Garnish with sour cream; sprinkle with cilantro.

Bulgur Chili

This hearty meatless chili is zesty, but also offers a slight hint of sweetness. It doesn't have to simmer for hours like other chili recipes, so it's ideal for drop-in visitors.

—**JERALDINE HALL** RAVENDEN SPRINGS, ARKANSAS

PREP: 10 MIN. + STANDING • **COOK:** 25 MIN. • **MAKES:** 9 SERVINGS

- ¾ **cup bulgur**
- 2 **cups boiling water**
- 1½ **cups finely chopped green peppers**
- 1 **large onion, chopped**
- 2 **teaspoons canola oil**
- 2 **cups reduced-sodium tomato juice**
- 1 **can (16 ounces) kidney beans, rinsed and drained**
- 1 **can (15 ounces) Ranch Style beans (pinto beans in seasoned tomato sauce)**
- 1 **can (14½ ounces) diced tomatoes, undrained**
- 1 **can (8 ounces) tomato sauce**
- 1 **cup water**
- 2 to 3 **tablespoons chili powder**
- 2 **garlic cloves, minced**
- ½ **teaspoon ground cumin**
- ⅛ to ¼ **teaspoon cayenne pepper**
- ¾ **cup shredded reduced-fat cheddar cheese**

1. Place bulgur in a large bowl; stir in boiling water. Cover and let stand for 30 minutes or until most of the liquid is absorbed. Drain and squeeze dry.

2. In a large saucepan, saute green peppers and onion in oil until tender. Stir in the bulgur, tomato juice, beans, tomatoes, tomato sauce, water, chili powder, garlic, cumin and cayenne. Bring to a boil. Reduce heat; cover and simmer for 20-25 minutes or until heated through. Sprinkle with cheese.

SLOW COOKER

Barbecued Beef Sandwiches

Chuck roast makes delicious shredded beef sandwiches after simmering in a rich homemade sauce all day. The meat is tender and juicy, and only takes minutes to prepare, making it a nice meal to enjoy during the busy workweek.

—TATINA SMITH SAN ANGELO, TEXAS

PREP: 20 MIN. • **COOK:** 8¼ HOURS
MAKES: 12 SERVINGS

- 1 **boneless beef chuck roast (3 pounds)**
- 1½ **cups ketchup**
- ¼ **cup packed brown sugar**
- ¼ **cup barbecue sauce**
- 2 **tablespoons Worcestershire sauce**
- 2 **tablespoons Dijon mustard**
- 1 **teaspoon liquid smoke, optional**
- ½ **teaspoon salt**
- ¼ **teaspoon garlic powder**
- ¼ **teaspoon pepper**
- 12 **sandwich buns, split**
   Sliced onions, dill pickles and pickled jalapenos, optional

1. Cut roast in half and place in a 3- or 4-qt. slow cooker. In a small bowl, combine the ketchup, brown sugar, barbecue sauce, Worcestershire sauce, mustard, liquid smoke if desired and seasonings. Pour over beef.
2. Cover and cook on low for 8-10 hours or until meat is tender. Remove meat; cool slightly. Skim fat from cooking liquid.
3. Shred beef with two forks; return to the slow cooker. Cover and cook for 15 minutes or until heated through. Using a slotted spoon, place ½ cup on each bun. Serve with onions, pickles and jalapenos if desired.

Portobello Pockets

This savory recipe is one of my favorites. It's quick, easy and filled with a bounty of veggies. I vary the produce and spices to fit the season. For fuss-free hikes or picnics, bundle them in foil, then take along to toss on a hot grill.

—ELISSA ARMBRUSTER MEDFORD, NEW JERSEY

PREP: 30 MIN. + MARINATING • **COOK:** 10 MIN.
MAKES: 8 SERVINGS

- ¼ **cup water**
- 3 **tablespoons lime juice**
- 2 **tablespoons canola oil**
- 1 **tablespoon Italian seasoning**
- 1 **teaspoon dried minced garlic**
- ½ **teaspoon dried celery flakes**
- ¼ **teaspoon salt**
- ¼ **teaspoon ground cumin**
- ¼ **teaspoon ground nutmeg**
- ¼ **teaspoon pepper**
- ⅛ **teaspoon cayenne pepper**
- 1 **pound sliced baby portobello mushrooms**
- 1 **each medium sweet yellow and red pepper, thinly sliced**
- 1 **medium red onion, thinly sliced**
- 2 **small zucchini, cut into ¼-inch slices**
- 1 **cup (4 ounces) shredded reduced-fat Mexican cheese blend**
- 8 **pita breads (6 inches), cut in half**

1. In a large resealable bag, combine the first 11 ingredients. Add the mushrooms, peppers, onion and zucchini; seal bag and turn to coat. Refrigerate overnight.
2. In a large nonstick skillet coated with cooking spray, cook and stir the vegetable mixture over medium-high heat for 6-8 minutes or until crisp-tender. Stir in cheese; cook 2-3 minutes longer or until cheese is melted. Stuff each pita half with ½ cup vegetable-cheese mixture.

SLOW COOKER Mushroom Salsa Chili

Green, sweet red and yellow peppers give this hearty chili a splash of color. I often fix it for my grandsons. I use mild salsa because they don't like spicy chili, but feel free to use a hotter variety if you want to kick it up a notch.

—RICHARD RUNDELS WAVERLY, OHIO

PREP: 10 MIN. • **COOK:** 8 HOURS • **MAKES:** 8 SERVINGS

- 1 **pound lean ground beef (90% lean)**
- 1 **pound bulk pork sausage**
- 2 **cans (16 ounces each) kidney beans, rinsed and drained**
- 1 **jar (24 ounces) chunky salsa**
- 1 **can (14½ ounces) diced tomatoes, undrained**
- 1 **large onion, chopped**
- 1 **can (8 ounces) tomato sauce**
- 1 **can (4 ounces) mushroom stems and pieces, drained**
- ½ **cup each chopped green, sweet red and yellow peppers**
- ½ **teaspoon dried oregano**
- ¼ **teaspoon garlic powder**
- ⅛ **teaspoon dried thyme**
- ⅛ **teaspoon dried marjoram**
  Shredded cheddar cheese, sour cream and thinly sliced green onions, optional

1. In a large skillet, cook beef and sausage over medium heat until meat is no longer pink; drain. Transfer to a 5-qt. slow cooker.
2. Stir in the beans, salsa, tomatoes, onion, tomato sauce, mushrooms, peppers and seasonings. Cover and cook on low for 8-10 hours or until flavors are blended. Garnish with cheese, sour cream and green onions if desired.

Hearty Chicken Noodle Soup

This satisfying homemade soup with a hint of cayenne is brimming with vegetables, chicken and noodles. The recipe came from my father-in-law, but I made some adjustments to give it my own unique spin.

—NORMA REYNOLDS OVERLAND PARK, KANSAS

PREP: 20 MIN. • **COOK:** 5½ HOURS
MAKES: 12 SERVINGS (3 QUARTS)

- 12 fresh baby carrots, cut into ½-inch pieces
- 4 celery ribs, cut into ½-inch pieces
- ¾ cup finely chopped onion
- 1 tablespoon minced fresh parsley
- ½ teaspoon pepper
- ¼ teaspoon cayenne pepper
- 1½ teaspoons mustard seed
- 2 garlic cloves, peeled and halved
- 1¼ pounds boneless skinless chicken breast halves
- 1¼ pounds boneless skinless chicken thighs
- 4 cans (14½ ounces each) chicken broth
- 1 package (9 ounces) refrigerated linguine

1. In a 5-qt. slow cooker, combine the first six ingredients. Place mustard seed and garlic on a double thickness of cheesecloth; bring up corners of cloth and tie with kitchen string to form a bag. Place in slow cooker. Add chicken and broth. Cover and cook on low for 5-6 hours or until meat is tender.

2. Discard spice bag. Remove chicken; cool slightly. Stir linguine into soup; cover and cook on high for 30 minutes or until tender. Cut chicken into pieces and return to soup; heat through.

Veggie Cheese Soup

My niece makes this in a slow cooker by putting in all the ingredients but the cheese. When the veggies are tender, she adds the cubed cheese and 5 minutes later, a nutritious meal is table-ready.

—JEAN HALL RAPID CITY, SOUTH DAKOTA

PREP: 15 MIN. • **COOK:** 25 MIN. • **MAKES:** 9 SERVINGS

- 1 medium onion, chopped
- 1 celery rib, chopped
- 2 small red potatoes, cut into ½-inch cubes
- 2¾ cups water
- 2 teaspoons reduced-sodium chicken bouillon granules
- 1 tablespoon cornstarch
- ¼ cup cold water
- 1 can (10¾ ounces) reduced-fat reduced-sodium condensed cream of chicken soup, undiluted
- 3 cups frozen California-blend vegetables, thawed
- ½ cup chopped fully cooked lean ham
- 8 ounces reduced-fat process cheese (Velveeta), cubed

1. In a large nonstick saucepan coated with cooking spray, cook onion and celery over medium heat until onion is tender. Stir in the potatoes, water and bouillon. Bring to a boil. Reduce heat; cover and simmer for 10 minutes.

2. Combine cornstarch and cold water until smooth; gradually stir into soup. Return to a boil; cook and stir for 1-2 minutes or until slightly thickened. Stir in condensed soup until blended.

3. Reduce heat; add vegetables and ham. Cook and stir until vegetables are tender. Stir in cheese until melted.

Italian Sausage Kale Soup

My mom dehydrates the last pick of tomatoes from her garden each fall—perfect for quick soups like this one. If I don't have time to prepare dry beans, canned beans work just as well.

—**LORI TERRY** CHICAGO, ILLINOIS

PREP: 15 MIN. • **COOK:** 20 MIN.
MAKES: 8 SERVINGS (2 QUARTS)

- 1½ **pounds Italian turkey sausage links, casings removed**
- 1 **medium onion, chopped**
- 8 **cups chopped fresh kale**
- 2 **garlic cloves, minced**
- ¼ **teaspoon crushed red pepper flakes, optional**
- ½ **cup white wine or chicken stock**
- 1 **carton (26 ounces) chicken stock**
- 1 **can (15 ounces) white kidney or cannellini beans, rinsed and drained**
- 1 **can (14½ ounces) no-salt-added diced tomatoes**
- ½ **cup sun-dried tomatoes (not packed in oil), chopped**
- ¼ **teaspoon pepper**

1. Crumble sausage into a Dutch oven; add onion. Cook and stir over medium heat until meat is no longer pink. Drain, reserving ¼ cup drippings; set sausage aside. Saute kale in reserved drippings until wilted. Add garlic and, if desired, pepper flakes; cook for 1 minute. Add wine; cook 2 minutes longer.
2. Stir in the stock, beans, diced tomatoes, dried tomatoes, pepper and sausage mixture. Bring to a boil. Reduce heat; cover and simmer for 15-20 minutes or until kale is tender.

Paul Bunyan Burgers

This is one of my favorite grilling recipes. I sometimes substitute canned mushrooms and bacon bits when I'm in a time crunch.

—**JO REED** CRAIG, COLORADO

PREP/TOTAL TIME: 30 MIN.
MAKES: 3 SERVINGS

- 6 **bacon strips, diced**
- 1 **cup sliced fresh mushrooms**
- 3 **thin onion slices**
- 1 **egg, lightly beaten**
- 1 **tablespoon Worcestershire sauce**
- ½ **teaspoon seasoned salt**
- ½ **teaspoon salt**
- ½ **teaspoon pepper**
- ½ **teaspoon prepared horseradish**
- 1 **pound ground beef**
- 3 **slices process American cheese**
- 3 **hamburger buns, split**

1. In a large skillet, cook bacon until crisp. Remove with a slotted spoon to paper towels. In the drippings, saute mushrooms and onion until tender. Transfer to a large bowl with a slotted spoon; add bacon.
2. In another bowl, combine the egg, Worcestershire sauce, seasoned salt, salt, pepper and horseradish; sprinkle beef over mixture and mix well. Shape into six ¼-in.-thick patties.
3. Divide bacon mixture among three patties. Top with a cheese slice; fold in corners of cheese. Top with remaining patties; seal edges.
4. Grill burgers, uncovered, over medium-hot heat for 5-6 minutes a side or until a thermometer reads 160° and meat juices run clear. Serve on buns.

3. In an electric skillet, heat ¼ in. of oil to 375°. Cook fillets for 2-3 minutes on each side or until fish flakes easily with a fork. Drain on paper towels.
4. Place fish fillets and coleslaw on bun bottoms; replace bun tops.

Creamy Butternut Squash Soup

I used to live in Australia, where this soup is served often. When I tried it, I knew I had to have the recipe. It's now one of my family's favorites.
—**TIFFANY POPE** DRAPER, UTAH

PREP: 15 MIN. • **COOK:** 20 MIN. • **MAKES:** 2 SERVINGS

　¼　cup chopped onion
　1　tablespoon butter
　3　cups cubed peeled butternut squash
　1　medium potato, peeled and cubed
1½　cups water
1½　teaspoons chicken bouillon granules
　¼　teaspoon salt
　　Dash pepper
　¼　cup evaporated milk

1. In a small saucepan, saute onion in butter until tender. Add squash and potato; cook and stir for 2 minutes. Add the water, bouillon, salt and pepper; bring to a boil. Reduce heat; cover and simmer for 15-20 minutes or until vegetables are tender.
2. Cool slightly. In a blender, cover and process soup until smooth. Return to the pan; stir in evaporated milk and heat through.

FAST FIX ▶ Catfish Po'boys

This tribute to a great Southern staple does fried catfish serious justice. A creative Cajun coleslaw tops perfectly fried fish for a sandwich you won't be able to get enough of.
—**ANN BAKER** TEXARKANA, TEXAS

PREP/TOTAL TIME: 30 MIN. • **MAKES:** 4 SERVINGS

CAJUN COLESLAW
3¾　cups coleslaw mix
　½　cup mayonnaise
　3　tablespoons seafood cocktail sauce
　½　teaspoon Cajun seasoning
　¼　teaspoon seafood seasoning

SANDWICHES
　½　cup cornmeal
　⅓　cup all-purpose flour
　1　teaspoon salt
　1　teaspoon Cajun seasoning
　¼　teaspoon seafood seasoning
　⅔　cup buttermilk
　4　catfish fillets (6 ounces each)
　　Oil for deep-fat frying
　4　hoagie buns, split

1. In a large bowl, toss the coleslaw ingredients; set aside.
2. In a shallow bowl, combine the cornmeal, flour, salt, Cajun seasoning and seafood seasoning. Place buttermilk in another shallow bowl. Dip fish into buttermilk, then coat with cornmeal mixture.

New England Clam Chowder

Living in the Pacific Northwest, I have the pleasure of digging and grinding my own razor clams. I know not everyone has easy access to a local treasure like this, so I recommend canned clams as a good substitute.

—SANDY LARSON PORT ANGELES, WASHINGTON

PREP: 20 MIN. • **COOK:** 35 MIN. • **MAKES:** 5 SERVINGS

- 4 center-cut bacon strips
- 2 celery ribs, chopped
- 1 large onion, chopped
- 1 garlic clove, minced
- 3 small potatoes, peeled and cubed
- 1 cup water
- 1 bottle (8 ounces) clam juice
- 3 teaspoons reduced-sodium chicken bouillon granules
- ¼ teaspoon white pepper
- ¼ teaspoon dried thyme
- ⅓ cup all-purpose flour
- 2 cups fat-free half-and-half, divided
- 2 cans (6½ ounces each) chopped clams, undrained

1. In a Dutch oven, cook bacon over medium heat until crisp. Remove to paper towels to drain; set aside. Saute celery and onion in the drippings until tender. Add garlic; cook 1 minute longer. Stir in the potatoes, water, clam juice, bouillon, pepper and thyme. Bring to a boil. Reduce heat; simmer, uncovered, for 15-20 minutes or until potatoes are tender.

2. In a small bowl, combine flour and 1 cup half-and-half until smooth. Gradually stir into soup. Bring to a boil; cook and stir for 1-2 minutes or until thickened.

3. Stir in clams and remaining half-and-half; heat through (do not boil). Crumble the reserved bacon; sprinkle over each serving.

🍲 SLOW COOKER Shredded Beef au Jus

My mom found this recipe in a farm journal shortly after she got married. The tender beef has become a family favorite, and my dad still requests it after all these years.

—DANIELLE BRANDT RUTHTON, MINNESOTA

PREP: 10 MIN. • **COOK:** 6 HOURS • **MAKES:** 8 SERVINGS

- 1 boneless beef chuck roast (3 pounds)
- 2 cups water
- 2 teaspoons beef bouillon granules
- 1½ teaspoons dried oregano
- 1 teaspoon garlic salt
- 1 teaspoon seasoned salt
- ¼ teaspoon dried rosemary, crushed
- 8 hamburger buns, split

1. Cut roast in half and place in a 4- or 5-qt. slow cooker. Combine the water, bouillon granules and seasonings; pour over the beef.

2. Cover and cook on low for 6-8 hours or until meat is tender. Remove beef; cool slightly. Meanwhile, skim fat from the cooking liquid.

3. Shred meat with two forks; return to the cooking liquid and heat through. Using a slotted spoon, place ½ cup on each bun. Serve with additional cooking liquid on the side.

❝This is a great slow cooker meal! The beef turned out tender and very flavorful. This is one I will be making again.❞

—HEIDI WALBOURN FROM TASTEOFHOME.COM

Pasta Bean Soup

My family loves this soup, especially during our cold New England winters. It's thick and hearty.

—BEVERLY BALLARO
LYNNFIELD, MASSACHUSETTS

PREP: 10 MIN. • **COOK:** 25 MIN. • **MAKES:** 6 SERVINGS

- 1 **large onion, chopped**
- 1 **large carrot, chopped**
- 1 **celery rib, chopped**
- 2 **tablespoons olive oil**
- 3 **garlic cloves, minced**
- 4 **cups vegetable or chicken broth**
- ¾ **cup uncooked small pasta shells**
- 2 **teaspoons sugar**
- 1½ **teaspoons Italian seasoning**
- ¼ **teaspoon crushed red pepper flakes**
- 2 **cans (15 ounces each) white kidney or cannellini beans, rinsed and drained**
- 1 **can (28 ounces) crushed tomatoes**
- 3 **tablespoons grated Parmesan cheese**

1. In a Dutch oven, saute the onion, carrot and celery in oil until crisp-tender. Add garlic; saute 1 minute longer. Add the broth, pasta, sugar, Italian seasoning and pepper flakes.

2. Bring to a boil. Reduce heat; simmer, uncovered, for 15 minutes or until pasta is tender. Add the beans and tomatoes; simmer, uncovered, for 5 minutes. Garnish with Parmesan cheese.

Rustic Italian Tortellini Soup

This soup is quick to fix on a busy night and full of healthy, tasty ingredients. The original recipe called for spicy sausage links, but I've found that turkey sausage or even ground turkey breast is just as good.

—TRACY FASNACHT IRWIN, PENNSYLVANIA

PREP: 20 MIN. • **COOK:** 20 MIN.
MAKES: 6 SERVINGS (2 QUARTS)

- 3 Italian turkey sausage links (4 ounces each), casings removed
- 1 medium onion, chopped
- 6 garlic cloves, minced
- 2 cans (14½ ounces each) reduced-sodium chicken broth
- 1¾ cups water
- 1 can (14½ ounces) diced tomatoes, undrained
- 1 package (9 ounces) refrigerated cheese tortellini
- 1 package (6 ounces) fresh baby spinach, coarsely chopped
- 2¼ teaspoons minced fresh basil or ¾ teaspoon dried basil
- ¼ teaspoon pepper
  Dash crushed red pepper flakes
  Shredded Parmesan cheese, optional

1. Crumble sausage into a Dutch oven; add onion. Cook and stir over medium heat until meat is no longer pink. Add garlic; cook 1 minute longer. Stir in the broth, water and tomatoes. Bring to a boil.
2. Add tortellini; return to a boil. Cook for 7-9 minutes or until tender, stirring occasionally. Reduce heat; add the spinach, basil, pepper and pepper flakes. Cook 2-3 minutes longer or until spinach is wilted. Serve with cheese if desired.

SLOW COOKER

Tex-Mex Chili

Hearty and spicy, this is a hungry man's chili! You can also simmer on the stove—the longer, the better!

—ERIC HAYES ANTIOCH, CALIFORNIA

PREP: 20 MIN. • **COOK:** 6 HOURS
MAKES: 12 SERVINGS (1⅓ CUPS EACH)

- 3 pounds beef stew meat
- 1 tablespoon canola oil
- 3 garlic cloves, minced
- 3 cans (16 ounces each) kidney beans, rinsed and drained
- 3 cans (15 ounces each) tomato sauce
- 1 can (14½ ounces) diced tomatoes, undrained
- 1 cup water
- 1 can (6 ounces) tomato paste
- ¾ cup salsa verde
- 1 envelope chili seasoning
- 2 teaspoons dried minced onion
- 1 teaspoon chili powder
- ½ teaspoon crushed red pepper flakes
- ½ teaspoon ground cumin
- ½ teaspoon cayenne pepper
  Shredded cheddar cheese and minced fresh cilantro

1. In a large skillet, brown beef in oil in batches. Add garlic; cook 1 minute longer. Transfer to a 6-qt. slow cooker.
2. Stir in the beans, tomato sauce, tomatoes, water, tomato paste and salsa verde and seasonings. Cover and cook on low for 6-8 hours or until meat is tender. Garnish each serving with cheese and cilantro.

"I made this for a chili cook-off at our church and won the People's Choice Award. It was amazing!"

—MADCOOKINGMAMA FROM TASTEOFHOME.COM

3. Combine cornstarch and water until smooth; stir into stew. Cover and cook on high for 15 minutes or until thickened. Discard bay leaf.

NOTE *This recipe was tested with McCormick's Montreal Steak Seasoning. Look for it in the spice aisle.*

Stuffed Pepper Soup

One day I was talking to my fellow cooks at the restaurant where I work about our shared love of stuffed peppers, and we decided to stir up similar ingredients for a soup. Customer response to our creation was overwhelming!

—KRISTA MUDDIMAN MEADVILLE, PENNSYLVANIA

PREP: 15 MIN. • **COOK:** 30 MIN.
MAKES: 10 SERVINGS (2½ QUARTS)

- 2 **pounds ground beef**
- 2 **quarts water**
- 1 **can (28 ounces) tomato sauce**
- 1 **can (28 ounces) diced tomatoes, undrained**
- 2 **cups cooked long grain rice**
- 2 **cups chopped green peppers**
- ¼ **cup packed brown sugar**
- 2 **teaspoons salt**
- 2 **teaspoons beef bouillon granules**
- 1 **teaspoon pepper**

In a Dutch oven, cook beef over medium heat until no longer pink; drain. Stir in the remaining ingredients; bring to a boil. Reduce heat; cover and simmer for 30-40 minutes or until peppers are tender.

SLOW COOKER

Apple Cider Beef Stew

I created this slow cooker recipe using convenience products to save time chopping vegetables and browning beef. Apple cider and cinnamon are the unique additions that give a down-home flavor to this oh-so-easy and economical stew.

—MARGARET WILSON SUN CITY, CALIFORNIA

PREP: 20 MIN. • **COOK:** 6¼ HOURS • **MAKES:** 12 SERVINGS

- 4 **cups frozen vegetables for stew (about 24 ounces), thawed**
- 1 **can (8 ounces) sliced water chestnuts, drained**
- 1 **jar (4½ ounces) sliced mushrooms, drained**
- 1 **tablespoon dried minced onion**
- 2 **envelopes brown gravy mix**
- 2 **tablespoons onion soup mix**
- 2 **teaspoons steak seasoning**
- ⅛ **teaspoon ground cinnamon**
- 2 **pounds beef stew meat, cut into 1-inch cubes**
- 1 **can (14½ ounces) beef broth**
- 1¼ **cups apple cider or unsweetened apple juice**
- 1 **can (8 ounces) tomato sauce**
- 1 **bay leaf**
- 3 **tablespoons cornstarch**
- ⅓ **cup cold water**

1. Place the vegetables, water chestnuts, mushrooms and onion in a 5-qt. slow cooker. In a large resealable plastic bag, combine the gravy mix, soup mix, steak seasoning and cinnamon; add beef, a few pieces at a time, and shake to coat. Add to slow cooker.

2. Combine the broth, cider and tomato sauce; pour over beef. Add bay leaf. Cover and cook on low for 6-7 hours or until meat is tender.

FAST FIX ## Italian BLTs

The brilliant method of toasting BLTs in a coating of tangy Italian dressing and crispy bread crumbs takes these sandwiches from satisfying to spectacular!

—**JOYCE MOUL** YORK HAVEN, PENNSYLVANIA

PREP/TOTAL TIME: 20 MIN. • **MAKES:** 2 SERVINGS

- 2 turkey bacon strips, diced
- 4 slices Italian bread (½ inch thick)
- 2 slices reduced-fat provolone cheese
- 2 lettuce leaves
- 1 small tomato, sliced
- 4 teaspoons fat-free Italian salad dressing
- ⅓ cup panko (Japanese) bread crumbs
  Butter-flavored cooking spray
- ½ teaspoon olive oil

1. In a small skillet, cook bacon over medium heat until crisp. Layer two bread slices with cheese, bacon, lettuce and tomato; top with remaining bread.

2. Brush outsides of sandwiches with salad dressing. Place bread crumbs in a shallow bowl. Coat sandwiches with bread crumbs; spray with butter-flavored cooking spray.

3. In a large skillet over medium heat, toast the sandwiches in olive oil for 2-3 minutes on each side or until bread is lightly browned.

Homemade Chicken Broth

This traditional broth is lightly seasoned with herbs and rich with chicken flavor. Besides making wonderful chicken soups, it can be used in casseroles, rice dishes and other recipes that call for chicken broth.

—**TASTE OF HOME TEST KITCHEN**

PREP: 10 MIN. • **COOK:** 2½ HOURS + CHILLING
MAKES: ABOUT 6 CUPS

- 2½ pounds bony chicken pieces
- 2 celery ribs with leaves, cut into chunks
- 2 medium carrots, cut into chunks
- 2 medium onions, quartered
- 2 bay leaves
- ½ teaspoon dried rosemary, crushed
- ½ teaspoon dried thyme
- 8 to 10 whole peppercorns
- 2 quarts cold water

1. Place all ingredients in a soup kettle or Dutch oven. Slowly bring to a boil; reduce heat. Skim foam. Cover and simmer for 2 hours.

2. Set chicken aside until cool enough to handle. Remove meat from bones. Discard bones; save meat for another use. Strain broth, discarding vegetables and seasonings. Refrigerate for 8 hours or overnight. Skim fat from surface.

French Cheeseburger Loaf

Once you prepare this impressive yet simple-to-make sandwich, you'll never look at refrigerated bread dough the same way. It's one of the easiest recipes I have in my files.

—**NANCY DAUGHERTY** CORTLAND, OHIO

PREP: 25 MIN. • **BAKE:** 25 MIN. • **MAKES:** 6 SERVINGS

- ¾ pound lean ground beef (90% lean)
- ½ cup chopped sweet onion
- 1 small green pepper, chopped
- 2 garlic cloves, minced
- 2 tablespoons all-purpose flour
- 2 tablespoons Dijon mustard
- 1 tablespoon ketchup
- 1 tube (11 ounces) refrigerated crusty French loaf
- 4 slices reduced-fat process American cheese product
- 1 egg white, lightly beaten
- 3 tablespoons shredded Parmesan cheese

1. In a large skillet, cook the beef, onion and pepper over medium heat until meat is no longer pink. Add garlic; cook 1 minute longer. Stir in the flour, mustard and ketchup; set aside.

2. Unroll the dough starting at the seam. Pat into a 14x12-in. rectangle. Spoon meat mixture lengthwise down the center of the dough; top with cheese slices. Bring long sides of dough to the center over filling; pinch seams to seal.

3. Place seam side down on a baking sheet coated with cooking spray. Brush with egg white. Sprinkle with Parmesan cheese.

4. With a sharp knife, cut diagonal slits in top of loaf. Bake at 350° for 25-30 minutes or until golden brown. Serve warm.

FAST FIX ▶ Taco Soup

This popular taco soup offers a bright assortment of colors and flavors. Garnish with shredded cheese, sour cream or sliced jalapenos if you like.
—**JENNIFER VILLARREAL** TEXAS CITY, TEXAS

PREP/TOTAL TIME: 30 MIN.
MAKES: 8 SERVINGS (ABOUT 2 QUARTS)

- 1½ pounds ground beef
- 1 envelope taco seasoning
- 2 cans (15¼ ounces each) whole kernel corn, undrained
- 2 cans (15 ounces each) Ranch Style beans (pinto beans in seasoned tomato sauce)
- 2 cans (14½ ounces each) diced tomatoes, undrained
  Tortilla chips and shredded cheddar cheese

In a Dutch oven, cook beef over medium heat until no longer pink; drain. Stir in the taco seasoning, corn, beans and tomatoes. Cover and cook for 15 minutes or until heated through, stirring occasionally. Place tortilla chips in soup bowls; ladle soup over top. Sprinkle with cheese.

FAST FIX ▶
Chunky Chicken Noodle Soup

Marjoram and thyme come through nicely in this old-fashioned soup that tastes just like the one Grandma used to make. You can modify the recipe to include your family's favorite vegetables.
—**COLEEN MARTIN** BROOKFIELD, WISCONSIN

PREP/TOTAL TIME: 25 MIN. • **MAKES:** 6 SERVINGS

- ½ cup finely chopped carrot
- ¼ cup finely chopped celery
- ¼ cup finely chopped onion
- 1 teaspoon butter
- 6 cups chicken broth
- 1½ cups cubed cooked chicken
- 1 teaspoon salt
- ½ teaspoon dried marjoram
- ½ teaspoon dried thyme

- ⅛ teaspoon pepper
- 1¼ cups uncooked medium egg noodles
- 1 tablespoon minced fresh parsley

Saute the carrot, celery and onion in butter in a Dutch oven until tender. Stir in the broth, chicken and seasonings. Bring to a boil. Reduce heat. Add noodles; cook for 10 minutes or until noodles are tender. Sprinkle with parsley.

🍲 SLOW COOKER
Family-Pleasing Turkey Chili

My children really love this recipe, and it's become one of their favorite comfort foods. It's relatively inexpensive, and leftovers are wonderful.
—**SHEILA CHRISTENSEN** SAN MARCOS, CALIFORNIA

PREP: 25 MIN. • **COOK:** 4 HOURS
MAKES: 6 SERVINGS (2¼ QUARTS)

- 1 pound lean ground turkey
- 1 medium green pepper, finely chopped
- 1 small red onion, finely chopped
- 2 garlic cloves, minced
- 1 can (28 ounces) diced tomatoes, undrained
- 1 can (16 ounces) kidney beans, rinsed and drained
- 1 can (15 ounces) black beans, rinsed and drained
- 1 can (14½ ounces) reduced-sodium chicken broth
- 1¾ cups frozen corn, thawed
- 1 can (6 ounces) tomato paste
- 1 tablespoon chili powder
- ½ teaspoon pepper
- ¼ teaspoon ground cumin
- ¼ teaspoon garlic powder
  Optional toppings: reduced-fat sour cream and minced fresh cilantro

1. In a large nonstick skillet, cook the turkey, green pepper and onion over medium heat until meat is no longer pink. Add garlic; cook 1 minute longer. Drain.
2. Transfer to a 4-qt. slow cooker. Stir in the tomatoes, kidney beans, black beans, broth, corn, tomato paste, chili powder, pepper, cumin and garlic powder.
3. Cover and cook on low for 4-5 hours or until heated through. Serve with optional toppings if desired.

CROWD-PLEASING TACO SALAD, PAGE 77

BALSAMIC GREEN BEAN SALAD, 80

FABULOUS FRUIT SALAD, 83

GRANDMA'S POTATO SALAD, 93

SALADS, SIDES & MORE

When it comes to sensational salads and side dishes, this chapter has the pick of the crop! Enjoy mouthwatering medleys of fresh greens, veggies, fruit, pasta, potatoes and more. You and your family will relish every bite when your favorite foods are topped with any of the country-style jams and condiments featured here. See for yourself how these superb sidekicks make the perfect dinner a daily reality!

Grilled Corn with Chive Butter

My family loves grilled corn on the cob, but we got bored with the simple salt and butter topping. So I stirred in some lemon juice and chives to shake things up a bit.

—SUE KIRSCH
EDEN PRAIRIE, MINNESOTA

PREP: 10 MIN. + SOAKING
GRILL: 25 MIN. • **MAKES:** 6 SERVINGS

- 6 **medium ears sweet corn in husks**
- ½ **cup butter, melted**
- 2 **tablespoons minced chives**
- 1 **tablespoon sugar**
- 1½ **teaspoons lemon juice**
  Salt and pepper

1. Soak corn in cold water for 1 hour. In a small bowl, combine the butter, chives, sugar, lemon juice, salt and pepper. Carefully peel back corn husks to within 1 in. of bottom; remove silk. Brush with butter mixture. Rewrap corn in husks and secure with kitchen string.
2. Grill corn, uncovered, over medium heat for 25-30 minutes, turning occasionally.

KERNELS OF CORN FACTS

Fresh corn is at its peak in May through September. Look for ears of corn with bright green, tightly closed husks and golden brown silk. The kernels should be plump, milky and in closely spaced rows all the way to the tip.

FAST FIX ▶ Southwest Chicken Salad

My husband loves chicken salad, and this flavorful recipe is nutritious and tasty. It's also easy, as it calls for convenient rotisserie chicken. Serve it over greens, tucked in a pita or rolled up in a tortilla.

—SARA HOBBS QUINLAN, TEXAS

PREP/TOTAL TIME: 30 MIN.
MAKES: 6 CUPS

- 4 **cups cubed rotisserie chicken**
- 2 **cups frozen corn, thawed**
- 1 **cup chopped roasted sweet red peppers**
- 1 **cup chopped red or sweet onion**
- 1 **cup minced fresh cilantro**

DRESSING
- 3 **tablespoons lime juice**
- 3 **tablespoons olive oil**
- 4 **teaspoons honey**
- 2 **teaspoons ground cumin**
- 1 **teaspoon salt**
- 1 **teaspoon chili powder**
- ½ **teaspoon coarsely ground pepper**

SALADS
  Torn mixed salad greens and sliced almonds

PITAS
  Whole wheat pita pocket halves and lettuce leaves

WRAPS
  Whole wheat tortillas and sliced ripe avocado

In a large bowl, combine the first five ingredients. In a small bowl, whisk the dressing ingredients; pour over chicken mixture and toss to coat. Refrigerate until serving.
SALADS: *Top salad greens with chicken salad; sprinkle with almonds.*
PITAS: *Line pita halves with lettuce leaves; fill with chicken salad.*
WRAPS: *Place chicken salad off-center on tortillas; top with avocado. Roll up.*

FAST FIX ▶ Crowd-Pleasing Taco Salad

This recipe might look complicated, but it can be fixed in just 30 minutes. It always disappears from the potluck table—and I don't have to bring any leftovers home after the shindig!

—ANN CAHOON
BRADENTON, FLORIDA

PREP/TOTAL TIME: 30 MIN.
MAKES: 10 SERVINGS

- 1 **pound ground beef**
- ½ **cup ketchup**
- 1 **teaspoon dried oregano**
- 1 **teaspoon chili powder**
- ½ **teaspoon salt**
- ¼ **teaspoon pepper**
- 1 **medium head iceberg lettuce, torn**
- 2 **medium tomatoes, diced**
- 1 **cup (4 ounces) shredded Mexican cheese blend**
- 1 **can (2¼ ounces) sliced ripe olives, drained**
- ½ **cup mayonnaise**
- ¼ **cup taco sauce**
- 1 **package (10½ ounces) corn chips**

1. In a large saucepan, cook beef over medium heat until no longer pink; drain. Stir in the ketchup, oregano, chili powder, salt and pepper. Bring to a boil. Reduce heat; cover and simmer for 10 minutes.

2. In a large bowl, combine the lettuce, tomatoes, cheese, olives and beef mixture. Combine mayonnaise and taco sauce; pour over salad and toss to coat. Sprinkle with corn chips. Serve taco salad immediately.

FAST FIX ▶ Cherry Brie Tossed Salad

Draped in a light vinaigrette and sprinkled with almonds, this pretty salad is a variation of a recipe that's passed around at school events, church socials and birthday parties. Be adventurous and try new cheeses!

—TONI BORDEN
WELLINGTON, FLORIDA

PREP/TOTAL TIME: 20 MIN.
MAKES: 10 SERVINGS

DRESSING
- 1 **cup cider vinegar**
- ½ **cup sugar**
- ¼ **cup olive oil**
- 1 **teaspoon ground mustard**
- 1½ **teaspoons poppy seeds**

SALAD
- 2 **tablespoons butter**
- ¾ **cup sliced almonds**
- 3 **tablespoons sugar**
- 8 **cups torn romaine**
- 1 **round (8 ounces) Brie or Camembert cheese, rind removed and cubed**
- 1 **package (6 ounces) dried cherries**

1. In a small bowl, whisk the dressing ingredients; set aside.

2. For salad, in a heavy skillet, melt butter over medium heat. Add almonds and cook and stir until nuts are toasted, about 4 minutes. Sprinkle with sugar; cook and stir until sugar is melted, about 3 minutes. Spread on foil to cool; break apart.

3. In a large salad bowl, combine the romaine, cheese and cherries. Whisk dressing; drizzle over salad. Sprinkle with sugared almonds and toss to coat.

NOTE *Swiss cheese can be used in place of the Brie or Camembert.*

Scalloped Potatoes with Ham

This dish is a crowd-pleaser with its smooth sauce, juicy ham and thin potato slices. I always enjoyed it when Mother made it. I added the parsley and the thyme, and now my husband and five children request it.

—WENDY RHOADES YACOLT, WASHINGTON

PREP: 15 MIN. • **BAKE:** 1 HOUR 20 MIN. • **MAKES:** 4 SERVINGS

- 6 tablespoons butter, divided
- ¼ cup all-purpose flour
- 1 teaspoon dried parsley flakes
- 1 teaspoon salt
- ½ teaspoon dried thyme
- ¼ teaspoon pepper
- 3 cups 2% milk
- 6 cups thinly sliced peeled potatoes
- 1½ cups chopped fully cooked ham
- 1 small onion, grated

1. In a large saucepan, melt 4 tablespoons butter. Stir in flour, parsley, salt, thyme and pepper until smooth. Gradually add milk; bring to a boil. Cook and stir for 2 minutes.

2. Combine potatoes, ham and onion; place half in a greased 2½-qt. baking dish. Top with half of the sauce; repeat layers.

3. Cover and bake at 375° for 65-75 minutes or until potatoes are almost tender. Dot with remaining butter. Bake, uncovered, 15-20 minutes longer or until potatoes are tender.

Marvelous Mediterranean Vegetables

With so many barbecues in the summer, I created this simple, tasty dish to complement any entree. I like to prepare it earlier in the day and let it marinate, then I just throw it on the grill.

—CATHY GODBERSON OAKVILLE, ONTARIO

PREP: 25 MIN. + MARINATING • **GRILL:** 10 MIN.
MAKES: 9 SERVINGS

- 3 large portobello mushrooms, sliced
- 1 each medium sweet red, orange and yellow peppers, sliced
- 1 medium zucchini, sliced
- 10 fresh asparagus spears, cut into 2-inch lengths
- 1 small onion, sliced and separated into rings
- ¾ cup grape tomatoes
- ½ cup fresh sugar snap peas
- ½ cup fresh broccoli florets
- ½ cup pitted Greek olives
- 1 bottle (14 ounces) Greek vinaigrette
- ½ cup crumbled feta cheese

1. In a large resealable plastic bag, combine the mushrooms, peppers and zucchini. Add the asparagus, onion, tomatoes, peas, broccoli and olives. Pour vinaigrette into bag; seal bag and turn to coat. Refrigerate for at least 30 minutes.

2. Discard marinade. Transfer vegetables to a grill wok or basket. Grill, uncovered, over medium heat for 8-12 minutes or until tender, stirring frequently. Place on a serving plate; sprinkle with cheese.

NOTE *If you do not have a grill wok or basket, use a disposable foil pan. Poke holes in the bottom of the pan with a meat fork to allow liquid to drain.*

FAST FIX ▸ Emily's Spinach Salad

I've always loved spinach—it's grown in this area of California. I created this recipe after I saw an announcement for a spinach-themed cooking contest. I was delighted when my colorful, tangy salad took the grand prize!

—EMILY FIELDS SANTA ANA, CALIFORNIA

PREP/TOTAL TIME: 15 MIN. • **MAKES:** 6-8 SERVINGS

- ⅔ cup canola oil
- ¼ cup red wine vinegar
- 2 teaspoons lemon juice
- 2 teaspoons soy sauce
- 1 teaspoon sugar
- 1 teaspoon ground mustard
- ½ teaspoon curry powder
- ½ teaspoon salt
- ½ teaspoon seasoned pepper
- ¼ teaspoon garlic powder
- 1 package (10 ounces) fresh spinach, torn
- 5 bacon strips, cooked and crumbled
- 2 hard-cooked eggs, sliced

1. In a small bowl, whisk the first 10 ingredients; set aside. Place the spinach in a large salad bowl.
2. Just before serving, whisk dressing again and drizzle over spinach; toss gently. Garnish with bacon and egg slices.

EASY HOMEMADE BACON BITS

When making bacon bits to sprinkle over a salad, use your kitchen scissors to cut strips of uncooked bacon into small pieces. Fry the pieces in a skillet, stirring often as the bacon cooks. Drain and pat dry on a paper towel. Allow to cool before sprinkling over salad greens.

FAST FIX ▶ Balsamic Green Bean Salad

Serve up traditional green beans in a whole new way! The tangy flavors and crunchy texture of this eye-appealing side dish complement any special meal or holiday spread.

—**MEGAN SPENCER**
FARMINGTON HILLS, MICHIGAN

PREP: 30 MIN. + CHILLING
MAKES: 16 SERVINGS

- 2 **pounds fresh green beans, trimmed and cut into 1½-inch pieces**
- ¼ **cup olive oil**
- 3 **tablespoons lemon juice**
- 3 **tablespoons balsamic vinegar**
- ¼ **teaspoon salt**
- ¼ **teaspoon garlic powder**
- ¼ **teaspoon ground mustard**
- ⅛ **teaspoon pepper**
- 1 **large red onion, chopped**
- 4 **cups cherry tomatoes, halved**
- 1 **cup (4 ounces) crumbled feta cheese**

1. Place beans in a Dutch oven and cover with water. Bring to a boil. Cover and cook for 8-10 minutes or until crisp-tender. Drain and immediately place beans in ice water. Drain and pat dry.
2. In a small bowl, whisk the oil, lemon juice, vinegar, salt, garlic powder, mustard and pepper. Drizzle dressing over beans. Add the onion; toss to coat. Cover and refrigerate for at least 1 hour. Just before serving, stir in the tomatoes and cheese.

FAST FIX ▶ Au Gratin Potato Pancakes

Family and friends say these flavorful potato pancakes are among the best they've ever tasted. They go especially well with barbecued ribs or chicken.

—**CATHY HALL** LYNDHURST, VIRGINIA

PREP/TOTAL TIME: 25 MIN.
MAKES: 8 POTATO PANCAKES

- 2 **cups mashed potatoes (without added milk and butter)**
- 1 **egg, lightly beaten**
- 1 **tablespoon minced chives**
- 1 **teaspoon minced fresh parsley**
- ¾ **teaspoon salt**
- ⅛ **teaspoon dried minced garlic**
- ⅛ **teaspoon pepper**
  Dash dried rosemary, crushed
- ½ **cup shredded sharp cheddar cheese**
- 4 **tablespoons canola oil, divided**

1. In a large bowl, combine the first eight ingredients. Stir in cheese.
2. Heat 2 tablespoons oil in a large nonstick skillet over medium heat. Drop batter by ¼ cupfuls into oil; press lightly to flatten. Cook in batches for 2-3 minutes on each side or until golden brown, using remaining oil as needed. Drain on paper towels.

"Loved this recipe! Sure beats the shredded kind by far. Yum!"

—WYNTERH FROM TASTEOFHOME.COM

FAST FIX ▶ Bacon-Wrapped Asparagus

My husband and I grill dinner almost every night. I serve these bacon-wrapped spears with grilled meat and sliced fresh tomatoes for a complete meal.
—**TRISHA KITTS** DICKINSON, TEXAS

PREP/TOTAL TIME: 30 MIN. • **MAKES:** 2-3 SERVINGS

- 10 fresh asparagus spears, trimmed
- ⅛ teaspoon pepper
- 5 bacon strips, halved lengthwise

1. Place asparagus on a sheet of waxed paper; coat with cooking spray. Sprinkle with pepper; turn to coat. Wrap a bacon piece around each spear; secure ends with toothpicks.
2. Grill, uncovered, over medium heat for 4-6 minutes on each side or until bacon is crisp. Discard toothpicks.

Creamy Red Potato Salad

The color and shape of red spuds work in perfect combination with radishes, green onions and a sharp touch of vinegar in this deliciously different potato salad.
—**BETSY KING** DULUTH, MINNESOTA

PREP: 30 MIN. • **COOK:** 20 MIN.+ CHILLING
MAKES: 12 SERVINGS

- 2½ pounds small red potatoes, cut into ¼-in. slices

VINAIGRETTE
- ⅔ cup canola oil
- ⅓ cup red wine vinegar
- 2 tablespoons Dijon mustard
- ¾ teaspoon salt
- ½ teaspoon dill weed
- ¼ teaspoon garlic salt

- ¼ teaspoon pepper

SALAD
- ⅔ cup mayonnaise
- ⅔ cup sour cream
- 2 cups sliced radishes
- ⅔ cup thinly sliced green onions
- ½ cup minced fresh parsley
- 4 hard-cooked eggs, coarsely chopped

1. Place potatoes in a Dutch oven; cover with water. Bring to a boil. Reduce heat; cover and cook potatoes for 15-18 minutes or until tender. Drain.
2. Transfer potatoes to a large bowl. In a small bowl, whisk the vinaigrette ingredients. Pour over warm potatoes; gently toss to coat. Cool slightly. Cover and refrigerate until chilled.
3. In a small bowl, combine mayonnaise and sour cream; stir in the radishes, onions and parsley. Add to potatoes; mix gently. Top with eggs. Chill until serving.

Poppy Seed Slaw

This colorful side can be put together in minutes for a tasty accompaniment to any backyard barbecue.
—**MARY MCRAE** COLDWATER, MICHIGAN

PREP: 10 MIN. + CHILLING • **MAKES:** 5 SERVINGS

- 1 package (10 ounces) angel hair coleslaw
- ¾ cup dried cranberries
- ¾ cup honey-roasted sliced almonds
- ¾ cup poppy seed salad dressing
- ½ teaspoon salt
- ½ teaspoon pepper

In a large bowl, combine the coleslaw, cranberries and almonds. Combine the salad dressing, salt and pepper; drizzle over salad and toss to coat. Refrigerate for 1 hour before serving.

FAST FIX Orange Rhubarb Spread

This tangy spread is easy to make and tastes especially good on buttered cinnamon toast. The recipe makes enough to have on hand well beyond the growing season.
—**BETTY NYENHUIS** OOSTBURG, WISCONSIN

PREP: 5 MIN. • **COOK:** 20 MIN. + STANDING
MAKES: 5 HALF-PINTS

- 4 **cups diced fresh or frozen rhubarb**
- 2 **cups water**
- 1 **can (6 ounces) frozen orange juice concentrate, thawed**
- 1 **package (1¾ ounces) powdered fruit pectin**
- 4 **cups sugar**

1. In a large saucepan, bring rhubarb and water to a boil. Reduce heat; simmer, uncovered, for 7-8 minutes or until rhubarb is tender. Drain and reserve cooking liquid. Cool rhubarb and liquid to room temperature.
2. Place the rhubarb in a blender; cover and process until pureed. Transfer to a 4-cup measuring cup; add enough reserved cooking liquid to measure 2⅓ cups. Return to the saucepan.
3. Add orange juice concentrate and pectin; bring to a full rolling boil, stirring constantly. Stir in sugar. Return to a full rolling boil; boil and stir for 1 minute. Remove from the heat; skim off foam.
4. Pour into jars or freezer containers; cool to room temperature, about 1 hour. Cover and let stand overnight or until set, but not longer than 24 hours. Refrigerate or freeze. Refrigerate for up to 3 weeks or freeze for up to 12 months.

FAST FIX Tropical Fusion Salad with Spicy Tortilla Ribbons

The fresh taste of this colorful salad makes it a perfect choice for a spring or summer meal. Served with spicy tortilla strips, it's special enough for company.
—**JENNIFER FISHER** AUSTIN, TEXAS

PREP/TOTAL TIME: 30 MIN. • **MAKES:** 4 SERVINGS

- 2 **cups cubed peeled papaya**
- 1 **can (15 ounces) black beans, rinsed and drained**
- 1 **medium ripe avocado, peeled and cubed**
- 1 **cup frozen corn, thawed**
- ½ **cup golden raisins**
- 2 **serrano peppers, seeded and chopped**
- ¼ **cup minced fresh cilantro**
- ¼ **cup orange juice**
- 2 **tablespoons lime juice**
- 1 **tablespoon cider vinegar**
- 2 **garlic cloves, minced**
- 2 **teaspoons ground ancho chili pepper, divided**
- ¼ **teaspoon sugar**
- ¼ **teaspoon salt**
- 2 **corn tortillas (6 inches), cut into ¼-inch strips**

1. In a large bowl, combine the papaya, beans, avocado, corn, raisins, peppers, cilantro, orange juice, lime juice, vinegar, garlic, ½ teaspoon chili pepper, sugar and salt.
2. Place tortilla strips on a baking sheet coated with cooking spray; sprinkle with remaining chili pepper. Bake at 350° for 8-10 minutes or until crisp. Serve with salad.
NOTE *Wear disposable gloves when cutting hot peppers; the oils can burn skin. Avoid touching your face.*

Fabulous Fruit Salad

I first made this fruity creation for a reunion, and now it's always requested for our family gatherings. The sweet and tangy lemonade-pudding coating goes well with any fruit, so feel free to substitute your favorites.
—**RHONDA EADS** JASPER, INDIANA

PREP: 45 MIN. + CHILLING • **MAKES:** 20 SERVINGS (¾ CUP EACH)

- 1 medium honeydew, peeled, seeded and cubed
- 1 medium cantaloupe, peeled, seeded and cubed
- 2 cups cubed seedless watermelon
- 2 medium peaches, peeled and sliced
- 2 medium nectarines, sliced
- 1 cup seedless red grapes
- 1 cup halved fresh strawberries
- 1 can (11 ounces) mandarin oranges, drained
- 2 medium kiwifruit, peeled, halved and sliced
- 2 medium firm bananas, sliced
- 1 large Granny Smith apple, cubed
- 1 can (12 ounces) frozen lemonade concentrate, thawed
- 1 package (3.4 ounces) instant vanilla pudding mix

1. In a large bowl, combine the first nine ingredients. Cover and refrigerate for at least 1 hour.
2. Just before serving, stir in bananas and apple. Combine lemonade concentrate and dry pudding mix; pour over fruit and toss to coat.

FAST FIX ▶ Glazed Orange Carrots

Want your kids to eat more carrots? This tender side dish with a pleasant citrus flavor and a pretty orange glaze will having them asking for seconds.
—**MARILYN HASH** ENUMCLAW, WASHINGTON

PREP/TOTAL TIME: 25 MIN. • **MAKES:** 6 SERVINGS

- 2 pounds fresh carrots, sliced
- 2 tablespoons butter
- ¼ cup thawed orange juice concentrate
- 2 tablespoons brown sugar
- 2 tablespoons minced fresh parsley

1. Place 1 in. of water in a saucepan; add carrots. Bring to a boil. Reduce heat; cover and simmer for 7-9 minutes or until crisp-tender. Drain.
2. Melt butter in a large skillet; stir in orange juice concentrate and brown sugar. Add carrots and parsley; stir to coat. Cook and stir for 1-2 minutes or until glaze is thickened.

FAST FIX ▶ Crunchy Broccoli Salad

I was never a fan of broccoli growing up. But after one bite into this sweet, light salad, I was hooked. Now I can't get enough of this superfood.
—**JESSICA CONREY** CEDAR RAPIDS, IOWA

PREP/TOTAL TIME: 20 MIN. • **MAKES:** 10 SERVINGS

- 8 cups fresh broccoli florets
- 1 bunch green onions, thinly sliced
- ½ cup dried cranberries
- 3 tablespoons canola oil
- 3 tablespoons seasoned rice vinegar
- 2 tablespoons sugar
- ¼ cup sunflower kernels
- 3 bacon strips, cooked and crumbled

In a large bowl, combine the broccoli, onions and cranberries. In a small bowl, whisk the oil, vinegar and sugar; drizzle over broccoli and toss to coat. Chill until serving. Sprinkle with sunflower kernels and bacon.

Summer Corn Salad

This beautiful salad truly captures the summer season. It's chock-full of fresh veggies and basil, and feta cheese gives it a rich, tangy flavor the whole family will love.

—PRISCILLA YEE
CONCORD, CALIFORNIA

PREP: 20 MIN. + STANDING
MAKES: 4 SERVINGS

- 5 teaspoons olive oil, divided
- 1 tablespoon lime juice
- ¼ teaspoon salt
- ¼ teaspoon hot pepper sauce
- 1½ cups fresh or frozen corn, thawed
- 1½ cups cherry tomatoes, halved
- ½ cup finely chopped cucumber
- ¼ cup finely chopped red onion
- 2 tablespoons minced fresh basil or 2 teaspoons dried basil
- ¼ cup crumbled feta cheese

1. In a small bowl, whisk 4 teaspoons oil, lime juice, salt and pepper sauce; set aside.

2. In a large skillet, cook and stir corn in remaining oil over medium-high heat until tender. Transfer to a salad bowl; cool slightly. Add the tomatoes, cucumber, onion and basil. Drizzle with dressing and toss to coat.

3. Let stand for 10 minutes before serving or refrigerate until chilled. Sprinkle salad with cheese just before serving.

Feta Salmon Salad

My son David always ordered the salmon sandwich at a local pub. In trying to replicate it, he came up with this salad. It's the only recipe he's ever made, and our family thinks it's great.

—SUSAN GRIFFITHS
MT. PLEASANT, SOUTH CAROLINA

PREP/TOTAL TIME: 25 MIN.
MAKES: 4 SERVINGS

- ¼ teaspoon salt
- ¼ teaspoon garlic powder
- ¼ teaspoon ground ginger
- ¼ teaspoon dried parsley flakes
- ¼ teaspoon pepper
- 4 salmon fillets (6 ounces each)
- 1 package (5 ounces) spring mix salad greens
- 1 large cucumber, chopped
- 1 large tomato, chopped
- ½ cup crumbled feta cheese
- ¼ cup red wine vinaigrette

1. Combine the seasonings; sprinkle over salmon. Moisten a paper towel with cooking oil; using long-handled tongs, lightly coat the grill rack. Place salmon skin side down on grill rack.

2. Grill, covered, over medium heat or broil 4 in. from the heat for 10-12 minutes or until fish flakes easily with a fork.

3. In a large bowl, combine the salad greens, cucumber, tomato and feta cheese; divide among four plates. Top with salmon; drizzle with vinaigrette.

Golden Potato Surprise

I've had this recipe for as long as I can remember and have tweaked it over the years to perfect it. Now it's a must-have during the holidays.
—**KAREN SHEETS** SHELTON, WASHINGTON

PREP: 30 MIN. • **BAKE:** 30 MIN. • **MAKES:** 4-6 SERVINGS

- 4 **to 5 medium white potatoes, peeled and diced**
- 2 **tablespoons butter**
- 2 **medium red onions, chopped**
- 2 **tablespoons all-purpose flour**
- ½ **teaspoon dried thyme**
- ½ **teaspoon salt**
- ½ **teaspoon pepper**
- 1 **cup half-and-half cream**
- ½ **cup mayonnaise**
- 1 **teaspoon Dijon mustard**
- 4 **bacon strips, cooked and crumbled**

1. Place potatoes in a large saucepan and cover with water. Bring to a boil. Reduce heat; cover and cook for 10-15 minutes or until tender. Drain and set aside.

2. In large saucepan, melt butter. Saute onions until tender; stir in the flour, thyme, salt and pepper until blended. Gradually add cream. Bring to a boil. Cook and stir for 2 minutes or until thickened. Remove from the heat; let cool slightly. Stir in the mayonnaise and mustard. Pour sauce over potatoes; transfer to a 1½-qt. baking dish.

3. Bake, uncovered, at 350° for 30 minutes. Just before serving, sprinkle casserole with crumbled bacon.

Sweet Potato Praline Swirl

Tired of the same old marshmallows on your sweet potatoes? Set this rich, tasty side dish beside the turkey this year and introduce your family to a new favorite.
—**AMANDA DALVINE** ORANGE PARK, FLORIDA

PREP: 25 MIN. • **BAKE:** 30 MIN. • **MAKES:** 6 SERVINGS

- 2 **medium sweet potatoes, peeled and cubed**
- ½ **cup heavy whipping cream**
- 2 **eggs**
- ¼ **cup packed brown sugar**
- 3 **teaspoons vanilla extract**
- 1 **teaspoon ground cinnamon**
- ½ **teaspoon ground ginger**
- ½ **cup chopped pecans**

PRALINE SAUCE
- ⅓ **cup packed brown sugar**
- ¼ **cup sweetened condensed milk**
- 2 **teaspoons butter, melted**
- ½ **teaspoon vanilla extract**

1. Place sweet potatoes in a large saucepan and cover with water. Bring to a boil. Reduce heat; cover and cook for 10-15 minutes or until tender.
2. Drain potatoes and place in a large bowl; mash until smooth. Beat in the cream, eggs, brown sugar, vanilla, cinnamon and ginger; fold in pecans.
3. Transfer to a greased 8-in. square baking dish. Combine sauce ingredients; spoon over potato mixture. Cut through with a knife to swirl the sauce.
4. Bake, uncovered, at 325° for 30-40 minutes or until a thermometer reads 160°.

Spicy Chunky Salsa

Vinegar adds delightful tang to this sweet salsa. I guarantee you'll love the taste. If you prefer for more heat, toss in some of the seeds from the hot peppers.
—**DONNA GOUTERMONT** JUNEAU, ALASKA

PREP: 1½ HOURS • **PROCESS:** 15 MIN./BATCH • **MAKES:** 8 PINTS

- 6 **pounds tomatoes**
- 3 **large green peppers, chopped**
- 3 **large onions, chopped**
- 2 **cups white vinegar**
- 1 **large sweet red pepper, chopped**
- 1 **can (12 ounces) tomato paste**
- 4 **jalapeno peppers, seeded and chopped**
- 2 **serrano peppers, seeded and chopped**
- ½ **cup sugar**
- ½ **cup minced fresh cilantro**
- ½ **cup bottled lemon juice**
- 3 **garlic cloves, minced**
- 4 **teaspoons ground cumin**
- 3 **teaspoons salt**
- 2 **teaspoons dried oregano**
- 1 **teaspoon hot pepper sauce**

1. In a large saucepan, bring 8 cups water to a boil. Using a slotted spoon, place tomatoes, a few at a time, in boiling water for 30-60 seconds. Remove each tomato and immediately plunge in ice water. Drain and pat dry. Peel and finely chop tomatoes to measure 9 cups. In a stock pot, combine the tomatoes and remaining ingredients. Bring to a boil. Reduce heat; simmer, uncovered, for 30 minutes or until slightly thickened.
2. Carefully ladle hot mixture into hot 1-pint jars, leaving ½-in. headspace. Remove air bubbles; wipe rims and adjust lids. Process for 15 minutes in a boiling-water canner.
NOTE *When cutting hot peppers, disposable gloves are recommended. Avoid touching your face. The processing time listed is for altitudes of 1,000 feet or less. For altitudes up to 3,000 feet, add 5 minutes; 6,000 feet, add 10 minutes; 8,000 feet, add 15 minutes; 10,000 feet, add 20 minutes.*

FAST FIX ▶ Grilled Portobellos with Mozzarella Salad

These colorful mushrooms are so filling, they're almost a meal in themselves. They can also be served with a small garden salad or as a hearty side dish.
—**SARAH VASQUES**
MILFORD, NEW HAMPSHIRE

PREP/TOTAL TIME: 30 MIN. • **MAKES:** 4 SERVINGS

- 2 **cups grape tomatoes, halved**
- 3 **ounces fresh mozzarella cheese, cubed**
- 3 **fresh basil leaves, thinly sliced**
- 2 **teaspoons olive oil**
- 2 **garlic cloves, minced**
- ¼ **teaspoon salt**
- ¼ **teaspoon pepper**
- 4 **large portobello mushrooms (4 to 4½ inches), stems removed**
  Cooking spray

1. In a small bowl, combine the first seven ingredients; cover and chill until serving.

2. Spritz mushrooms with cooking spray. Using long-handled tongs, moisten a paper towel with cooking oil and lightly coat the grill rack. Grill mushrooms, covered, over medium heat or broil 4 in. from the heat for 6-8 minutes on each side or until tender. Spoon ½ cup tomato mixture into each mushroom cap.

Three-Cheese Potatoes

My husband and I love these spuds. Oozing with melted cheese and bacon, this easy side dish is great for camping and makes a welcome addition to barbecues.
—**CHERYL HILLE** ASKUM, ILLINOIS

PREP: 15 MIN. • **GRILL:** 35 MIN. • **MAKES:** 4-6 SERVINGS

- 3 **large potatoes, peeled and cut into 1-inch cubes**
- 1 **medium onion, chopped**
- 3 **tablespoons grated Parmesan cheese**
- 1 **tablespoon minced chives**
- ½ **teaspoon seasoned salt**
- ¼ **teaspoon pepper**
- 2 **tablespoons butter**
- ½ **cup crumbled cooked bacon**
- ½ **cup shredded part-skim mozzarella cheese**
- ½ **cup shredded cheddar cheese**

1. In a large bowl, combine the first six ingredients. Transfer to a double thickness of greased heavy-duty foil (about 18 in. square). Dot with butter.

2. Fold foil around potato mixture and seal tightly. Grill, covered, over medium heat for 15-18 minutes on each side or until potatoes are tender.

3. Carefully open foil. Sprinkle the bacon and cheeses over potato mixture. Grill 3-5 minutes longer or until cheese is melted. Open foil carefully to allow steam to escape.

SPEEDY PREP TIME

To speed up the cooking time of Three-Cheese Potatoes, put the diced potatoes and onions in the microwave for a few minutes before grilling.

FAST FIX ▶ Cobb Salad with Chili-Lime Dressing

Spice up dinner tonight with a hearty salad that's got something in it for everyone. I made this salad for a party, and it was a huge hit. Hot sauce gives the dressing a little kick, while cubed avocado cools things off.

—MARY MEEK TOLEDO, OHIO

PREP/TOTAL TIME: 25 MIN. • **MAKES:** 8 SERVINGS

- 1 can (4 ounces) chopped green chilies, undrained
- ⅔ cup sour cream
- ¼ cup fresh cilantro leaves, coarsely chopped
- 2 tablespoons lime juice
- ½ teaspoon pepper
- ¼ to ½ teaspoon hot pepper sauce
- ¼ teaspoon salt
- 1 package (10 ounces) hearts of romaine salad mix
- 1 can (16 ounces) kidney beans, rinsed and drained
- 1 cup (4 ounces) shredded Monterey Jack cheese
- 1 cup chopped tomatoes
- 1 package (7½ ounces) frozen diced cooked chicken breast, thawed
- 1 medium ripe avocado, peeled and cubed
- ½ cup chopped red onion
- ⅓ cup real bacon bits

1. Place the first seven ingredients in a food processor; cover and process until blended. Chill until serving.

2. In a large bowl, layer the salad mix, beans, cheese, tomatoes, chicken, avocado, onion and bacon bits. Drizzle with dressing.

FAST FIX ▸ Candy Bar Apple Salad

This creamy, sweet salad with a crisp apple crunch is a real people-pleaser. The recipe yields a lot, which is good, because it goes fast!
—**CYNDI FYNAARDT** OSKALOOSA, IOWA

PREP/TOTAL TIME: 15 MIN.
MAKES: 12 SERVINGS (¾ CUP EACH)

- 1½ cups cold 2% milk
- 1 package (3.4 ounces) instant vanilla pudding mix
- 1 carton (8 ounces) frozen whipped topping, thawed
- 4 large apples, chopped (about 6 cups)
- 4 Snickers candy bars (2.07 ounces each), cut into ½-inch pieces

In a large bowl, whisk milk and pudding mix for 2 minutes. Let stand for 2 minutes or until soft-set. Fold in whipped topping. Fold in apples and candy bars. Refrigerate until serving.

Festive Broccoli-Cauliflower Salad

I came up with this recipe when unexpected company arrived and I didn't have enough lettuce and tomatoes on hand to make a traditional salad. Everyone enjoyed it so much that it became a regular at our table.
—**AVANELL HEWITT** NORTH RICHLAND HILLS, TEXAS

PREP: 35 MIN. + CHILLING • **MAKES:** 14 SERVINGS (⅔ CUP EACH)

- 1 bunch broccoli, cut into florets
- 3 cups fresh cauliflowerets
- 1 medium green pepper, julienned
- 2 medium carrots, thinly sliced
- ½ cup thinly sliced red onion
- ½ cup small pitted ripe olives, halved
- ½ cup cubed sharp cheddar cheese

DRESSING
- 1 cup mayonnaise
- ½ cup ranch salad dressing
- 1 teaspoon Italian seasoning
- ½ teaspoon garlic powder
- ½ teaspoon dill weed
- ½ cup sunflower kernels

1. In a large bowl, combine the first seven ingredients.
2. In a small bowl, whisk the mayonnaise, salad dressing, Italian seasoning, garlic powder and dill. Pour over salad; toss to coat. Cover and refrigerate for at least 1 hour.
3. Just before serving, sprinkle salad with sunflower kernels.

FAST FIX ▸ Zucchini Parmesan

You'll knock their socks off with this easy-to-prep side that's absolutely delicious. My favorite time to make it is when the zucchini is fresh out of my garden.
—**SANDI GUETTLER** BAY CITY, MICHIGAN

PREP/TOTAL TIME: 25 MIN. • **MAKES:** 6 SERVINGS

- ½ to 1 teaspoon minced garlic
- 1 tablespoon olive oil
- 4 medium zucchini, cut into ¼-inch slices
- 1 can (14½ ounces) Italian diced tomatoes, undrained
- 1 teaspoon seasoned salt
- ¼ teaspoon pepper
- ¼ cup grated Parmesan cheese

1. In a large skillet, saute garlic in oil. Add zucchini; cook and stir for 4-5 minutes or until crisp-tender.
2. Stir in the tomatoes, seasoned salt and pepper. Simmer, uncovered, for 9-10 minutes or until liquid is absorbed and mixture is heated through. Sprinkle with Parmesan cheese. Serve with a slotted spoon.

Greek-Style Squash

My Greek-inspired side dish is a great way to make use of summer squash. You can almost taste the sunshine in this colorful vegetable medley, and the foil packets make for quick and carefree cleanup.
—**BETTY WASHBURN** RENO, NEVADA

PREP: 15 MIN. • **GRILL:** 30 MIN. • **MAKES:** 4 SERVINGS

- 2 **small yellow summer squash, thinly sliced**
- 2 **small zucchini, thinly sliced**
- 1 **medium tomato, seeded and chopped**
- ¼ **cup pitted ripe olives**
- 2 **tablespoons chopped green onion**
- 2 **teaspoons olive oil**
- 1 **teaspoon lemon juice**
- ¾ **teaspoon garlic salt**
- ¼ **teaspoon dried oregano**
- ⅛ **teaspoon pepper**
- 2 **tablespoons grated Parmesan cheese**

1. Place the yellow squash, zucchini, tomato, olives and onion on a double thickness of heavy-duty foil (about 17x18 in.). Combine the oil, lemon juice, garlic salt, oregano and pepper; pour over vegetables. Fold foil around mixture and seal tightly.
2. Grill, covered, over medium heat for 30-35 minutes or until vegetables are tender. Open foil carefully to allow steam to escape. Transfer vegetables to a serving bowl. Sprinkle with cheese.

Creamy Spinach Casserole

Rich and comforting, this savory spinach casserole will be a welcome addition to the table. You will love the short prep time and decadent taste.
—**ANNETTE MARIE YOUNG** WEST LAFAYETTE, INDIANA

PREP: 10 MIN. • **BAKE:** 35 MIN. • **MAKES:** 10 SERVINGS

- 2 **cans (10¾ ounces each) reduced-fat reduced-sodium condensed cream of chicken soup, undiluted**
- 1 **package (8 ounces) reduced-fat cream cheese, cubed**

- ½ **cup fat-free milk**
- ½ **cup grated Parmesan cheese**
- 4 **cups herb seasoned stuffing cubes**
- 2 **packages (10 ounces each) frozen chopped spinach, thawed and squeezed dry**

1. In a large bowl, beat the soup, cream cheese, milk and Parmesan cheese until blended. Stir in stuffing cubes and spinach.
2. Spoon into a 2-qt. baking dish coated with cooking spray. Bake, uncovered, at 350° for 35-40 minutes or until heated through.

Fried Mashed Potato Balls

The key to making this recipe is to use mashed potatoes that are firm from chilling. Serve the balls with sour cream or ranch salad dressing on the side.
—**TASTE OF HOME TEST KITCHEN**

PREP: 25 MIN. + STANDING • **COOK:** 5 MIN./BATCH
MAKES: 6 SERVINGS

- 2 **cups cold mashed potatoes**
- 1 **egg, lightly beaten**
- ¾ **cup shredded cheddar cheese**
- ½ **cup chopped green onions**
- ¼ **cup real bacon bits**
- ½ **cup dry bread crumbs**
  Oil for frying

1. Place mashed potatoes in a large bowl; let stand at room temperature for 30 minutes. Stir in the egg, cheese, onions and bacon bits. Shape into 1-in. balls; roll in bread crumbs. Let stand for 15 minutes.
2. In an electric skillet, heat 1 in. of oil to 375°. Fry potato balls, a few at a time, for 2½ to 3 minutes or until golden brown. Remove with a slotted spoon to paper towels to drain. Serve warm.

FAST FIX ▸ Greek Pasta Salad

My mother-in-law gave me this great recipe, and I have made it many times. I've taken it to church picnics and potlucks and more—always to glowing reviews!
—**LAURA FREEMAN** RUFFIN, NORTH CAROLINA

PREP/TOTAL TIME: 20 MIN. • **MAKES:** 4 SERVINGS

- 1½ cups uncooked penne pasta
- ½ cup cubed cooked turkey or chicken
- 1 can (3.8 ounces) sliced ripe olives, drained
- ¼ cup chopped green pepper
- ¼ cup chopped sweet red pepper
- ¼ cup crumbled feta cheese
- ⅓ cup creamy Caesar salad dressing

1. Cook pasta according to package directions; drain and rinse in cold water. In a serving bowl, combine the pasta, turkey, olives, peppers and feta cheese. Drizzle with dressing and toss to coat. Cover and refrigerate until serving.

NOTE *You may substitute 1½ cups of tricolor spiral pasta for the penne. Proceed as directed.*

FAST FIX ▸ Bacon-Almond Green Beans

I adapted this recipe from one I found in a magazine. The original was time-consuming, so I came up with my own fuss-free version.
—**JACKIE MATTHEWS** YUCCA VALLEY, CALIFORNIA

PREP/TOTAL TIME: 30 MIN. • **MAKES:** 6 SERVINGS

- 1½ pounds fresh green beans, trimmed and cut into 1½-inch pieces
- 3 tablespoons butter
- 3 tablespoons brown sugar
- 2¼ teaspoons soy sauce
- 2¼ teaspoons Worcestershire sauce
- 4 to 5 tablespoons real bacon bits
- 4 to 5 tablespoons sliced almonds, toasted

1. Place beans in a large saucepan and cover with water. Bring to a boil; cook, uncovered, for 8-10 minutes or until crisp-tender.

2. Meanwhile, melt butter in a large skillet over medium heat. Stir in the brown sugar, soy sauce and Worcestershire sauce. Cook for 1 minute or until sugar is dissolved.

3. Drain beans; add to the skillet. Cook and stir for 2 minutes or until heated through. Sprinkle with bacon and almonds; toss to coat. Serve with a slotted spoon.

Colcannon Potatoes

Every Irish family has their own version of this classic dish. My recipe comes from my father's family in Ireland. It's part of my St. Patty's Day menu, along with lamb chops, carrots and traditional Irish soda bread.
—**MARILOU ROBINSON** PORTLAND, OREGON

PREP: 10 MIN. • **COOK:** 35 MIN. • **MAKES:** 12-16 SERVINGS

- 2 pounds cabbage, shredded
- 2 cups water
- 4 pounds potatoes, peeled and quartered
- 2 cups milk
- 1 cup chopped green onions
  Salt and coarsely ground pepper to taste
- ¼ cup butter, melted
  Crumbled cooked bacon and minced fresh parsley

1. In a large saucepan, bring cabbage and water to a boil. Reduce heat; cover and simmer for 10-12 minutes or until tender. Drain, reserving cooking liquid. Keep cabbage warm.

2. Place cooking liquid and potatoes in a large saucepan; add enough additional water to cover the potatoes. Bring to a boil. Reduce heat; cover and cook for 15-17 minutes or until tender. Drain and keep warm.

3. In a small saucepan, bring milk and onions to a boil; remove from the heat. In a large bowl, mash potatoes. Add milk mixture; beat until blended. Beat in the cabbage, salt and pepper. Drizzle with the melted butter, bacon and parsley.

Bacon-Chive Potato Salad

This creamy and colorful potato salad is always requested for all our summer picnics. It's so quick to prepare, goes with almost anything and is really yummy while still warm—but just as delicious when chilled!

—KAREN WHITE
LAWRENCEBURG, TENNESSEE

PREP: 30 MIN. + CHILLING
MAKES: 8 SERVINGS

- 2½ pounds small red potatoes
- ½ cup real bacon bits
- ¼ cup minced chives
- ¾ cup mayonnaise
- ¾ teaspoon ground mustard
- ½ teaspoon salt
- ¼ teaspoon pepper

1. Place potatoes in a large saucepan and cover with water. Bring to a boil. Reduce heat; cover and cook for 15-20 minutes or until tender. Drain and cool. Cut into wedges; place in a serving bowl. Add bacon and chives.
2. In a small bowl, combine the mayonnaise, mustard, salt and pepper. Spoon over salad; toss to coat. Refrigerate for at least 1 hour before serving.

Pina Colada Fruit Salad

Give friends and family a taste of the tropics on warm summer days with this refreshing fruit blend. Add a splash of coconut rum or shredded mint leaves for a little extra flavor punch.

—CAROL FARNSWORTH
GREENWOOD, INDIANA

PREP/TOTAL TIME: 15 MIN.
MAKES: 9 SERVINGS

- 1½ cups green grapes
- 1½ cups seedless red grapes
- 1½ cups fresh blueberries
- 1½ cups halved fresh strawberries
- 1 can (8 ounces) pineapple chunks, drained
- ½ cup fresh raspberries
- 1 can (10 ounces) frozen non-alcoholic pina colada mix, thawed
- ½ cup sugar
- ½ cup pineapple-orange juice
- ⅛ teaspoon almond extract
- ⅛ teaspoon coconut extract

In a serving bowl, combine the first six ingredients. In a small bowl, whisk the pina colada mix, sugar, juice and extracts until sugar is dissolved. Pour over fruit; toss to coat. Chill until serving.

"When I got this recipe and made it for the first time, I knew it was a winner. It was gone within minutes. Love it!"

—SHARON FRANCOIS FROM TASTEOFHOME.COM

Grandma's Potato Salad

Our Fourth of July feast wouldn't be complete without this cool, old-fashioned potato salad. It's Grandma's treasured recipe.

—SUE GRONHOLZ
BEAVER DAM, WISCONSIN

PREP: 45 MIN. + COOLING
COOK: 15 MIN. + CHILLING
MAKES: 24 SERVINGS (¾ CUP EACH)

  6 **pounds medium red potatoes**
     Water

DRESSING

  1 **cup water**
  ½ **cup butter, cubed**
  ¼ **cup white vinegar**
  2 **eggs**
  ½ **cup sugar**
  4½ **teaspoons cornstarch**
  ¾ **cup heavy whipping cream**
  ¾ **cup Miracle Whip**

SALAD

  1 **small onion, finely chopped**
  2 **green onions, sliced**
  1 **teaspoon salt**
  ½ **teaspoon pepper**
  3 **hard-cooked eggs, sliced**
     Paprika

1. Place potatoes in a stockpot and cover with water. Bring to a boil. Reduce heat; cover and cook for 15-20 minutes or until tender. Drain. When cool enough to handle, peel and slice potatoes; cool completely.

2. For dressing, in the top of a double boiler or metal bowl over barely simmering water, heat water, butter and vinegar until butter is melted. In a small bowl, beat eggs; add sugar and cornstarch. Add to butter mixture; cook and stir for 5-7 minutes or until thickened. Transfer to a large bowl; cool completely.

3. In a small bowl, beat cream until stiff peaks form. Stir Miracle Whip into cooled dressing mixture; fold in whipped cream. Stir in onion, green onions, salt and pepper. Add potatoes; toss lightly to combine. Refrigerate, covered, until chilled.

4. To serve, top with hard-cooked eggs; sprinkle with paprika.

Freezer Berry Jam

We live on the farm where my husband was raised. Whenever we find wild blueberries nearby, I make this gorgeous ruby-red jam. It makes a wonderful breakfast spread.

—RITA PISCHKE
WHITEMOUTH, MANITOBA

PREP: 20 MIN. + STANDING
COOK: 10 MIN. + COOLING
MAKES: 3½ PINTS

  4 **cups blueberries**
  2 **cups raspberries**
  5 **cups sugar**
  2 **tablespoons lemon juice**
  ¾ **cup water**
  1 **package (1¾ ounces) powdered fruit pectin**

1. In a large bowl, mash the blueberries. Add raspberries and mash. Stir in sugar and lemon juice. Let stand for 10 minutes. In a small saucepan, bring water and pectin to a boil. Boil for 1 minute, stirring constantly. Add to fruit mixture; stir for 3 minutes or until the sugar is dissolved.

2. Pour mixture into canning jars or freezer containers; cool to room temperature, about 30 minutes. Cover and let stand overnight or until set, but not longer than 24 hours. Refrigerate for up to 3 weeks or freeze for up to 1 year.

STAMP-OF-APPROVAL SPAGHETTI SAUCE, PAGE 100

MAPLE & BLUE CHEESE STEAK, 99

DEEP-DISH SAUSAGE PIZZA, 102

POTATO KIELBASA SKILLET, 111

MAIN DISHES

The choices are almost endless in this chapter of family-pleasing entrees. Whether you want a fancy ham for the holidays, a saucy seafood dish to serve guests or a beefy mainstay for a weeknight delight, your memorable menu starts here. With dishes ranging from skillet suppers and oven-baked wonders to slow cooked sensations, cookout classics, pasta favorites, even meatless options...you're guaranteed to set a winner on the table!

Homemade Pizza

This zesty, palate-pleasing pizza features a crisp, golden crust. Load it up with your family's favorite toppings.
—**MARIANNE EDWARDS** LAKE STEVENS, WASHINGTON

PREP: 25 MIN. + RISING • **BAKE:** 25 MIN.
MAKES: 2 PIZZAS (3 SERVINGS EACH)

- 1 **package (¼ ounce) active dry yeast**
- 1 **teaspoon sugar**
- 1¼ **cups warm water (110° to 115°)**
- ¼ **cup canola oil**
- 1 **teaspoon salt**
- 3½ **cups all-purpose flour**
- ½ **pound ground beef**
- 1 **small onion, chopped**
- 1 **can (15 ounces) tomato sauce**
- 3 **teaspoons dried oregano**
- 1 **teaspoon dried basil**
- 1 **medium green pepper, diced**
- 2 **cups (8 ounces) shredded part-skim mozzarella cheese**

1. In large bowl, dissolve yeast and sugar in water; let stand for 5 minutes. Add oil and salt. Stir in flour, a cup at a time, until a soft dough forms.
2. Turn onto floured surface; knead until smooth and elastic, about 2-3 minutes. Place in a greased bowl, turning once to grease the top. Cover and let rise in a warm place until doubled, about 45 minutes. Meanwhile, cook beef and onion over medium heat until no longer pink; drain.

3. Punch down dough; divide in half. Press each into a greased 12-in. pizza pan. Combine the tomato sauce, oregano and basil; spread over each crust. Top with beef mixture, green pepper and cheese.
4. Bake at 400° for 25-30 minutes or until crust is lightly browned.

FAST FIX ▶

Black Bean Chicken with Rice

With only a few ingredients, I can make this tasty dish in minutes. It's a weeknight go-to, and my family loves it.
—**MOLLY NEWMAN** PORTLAND, OREGON

PREP/TOTAL: 25 MIN. • **MAKES:** 4 SERVINGS

- 3 **teaspoons chili powder**
- 1 **teaspoon ground cumin**
- 1 **teaspoon pepper**
- ¼ **teaspoon salt**
- 4 **boneless skinless chicken breast halves (4 ounces each)**
- 2 **teaspoons canola oil**
- 1 **can (15 ounces) black beans, rinsed and drained**
- 1 **cup frozen corn**
- 1 **cup salsa**
- 2 **cups cooked brown rice**

1. Combine the chili powder, cumin, pepper and salt; rub over chicken. In a large nonstick skillet coated with cooking spray, brown chicken in oil on both sides. Stir in the beans, corn and salsa. Cover and cook over medium heat for 10-15 minutes or until a thermometer reads 165°.
2. Slice chicken; serve with rice and bean mixture.

Steak and Vegetable Kabobs

You can spend the day out of the kitchen by assembling these kabobs in the morning, then letting them marinate all day. Pop them on the grill at dinnertime.

—LORRI CLEVELAND KINGSVILLE, OHIO

PREP: 15 MIN. + MARINATING • **GRILL:** 10 MIN.
MAKES: 10 SERVINGS

- ¼ cup packed brown sugar
- ¼ cup lemon juice
- ¼ cup canola oil
- ¼ cup soy sauce
- 2 garlic cloves, minced
- 3 whole cloves
  Dash dried basil
- 2½ pounds beef top sirloin steak, cut into 1¼ inch pieces
- 24 cherry tomatoes
- 24 large fresh mushrooms
- 1 large green or sweet red pepper, cut into 1½-inch cubes
- 2 small zucchini squash, cut into 1-inch slices
- 1 medium onion, cut into wedges
  Hot cooked rice

1. In a large bowl, combine first seven ingredients; set aside. On metal or soaked wooden skewers, alternately thread the meat and vegetables.

2. Place in a large glass dish. Pour marinade over kabobs; cover and refrigerate for 6 hours or overnight, turning several times. Discard the cloves.

3. Grill over medium-hot heat until the meat reaches desired doneness and vegetables are tender. Serve with rice.

> **GRILLING STEAK**
>
> Trim steaks of fat before cutting into pieces to avoid flare-ups. Leave a thin layer of fat if desired to help maintain juiciness. Pat dry with paper towels before grilling—a dry steak will brown better than a moist one. Grill steak pieces to at least medium-rare, 145°, but don't overcook.

Ham with Apple Raisin Sauce

Since I ran across this recipe several years ago, I've used it often for special dinners. What I really like is the ease of preparation. You don't have a lot of cleanup because everything is done in the roasting bag.

—SANDY OLBERDING SPENCER, IOWA

PREP: 10 MIN. • **BAKE:** 2 HOURS
MAKES: 16 SERVINGS

- 1 tablespoon all-purpose flour
- 1 large oven roasting bag
- 4 medium tart apples, peeled and chopped
- 2 cups apple juice
- 1 cup raisins
- ½ cup packed brown sugar
- 1 teaspoon ground cinnamon
- 1 boneless fully cooked ham (about 6 pounds)

1. Shake flour in oven roasting bag. Place bag in an ungreased 13x9-in. baking pan. Place the apples, apple juice, raisins, brown sugar and cinnamon in bag; mix well. Place ham in bag and close. Cut six ½-in. slits in top of bag.

2. Bake at 350° for 2 to 2¼ hours or until a thermometer reads 140°. Serve with sauce.

FULLY COOKED HAM

A fully cooked ham is a ham that is cooked and smoked and/or cured. It can be eaten without heating but is generally heated to 140° for optimal flavor.

FAST FIX ▶ ## Scallops in Sage Cream

I bought these scallops from a local fisherman and wanted to showcase their fresh flavor. So I used simple seasonings to accent a rich, creamy sauce. The combination was perfect.

—JOAN CHURCHILL
DOVER, NEW HAMPSHIRE

PREP/TOTAL TIME: 20 MIN.
MAKES: 4 SERVINGS

- 1½ pounds sea scallops
- ¼ teaspoon salt
- ⅛ teaspoon pepper
- 3 tablespoons olive oil, divided
- ½ cup chopped shallots
- ¾ cup heavy whipping cream
- 6 fresh sage leaves, thinly sliced
   Hot cooked pasta, optional

1. Sprinkle scallops with salt and pepper. In a large skillet, cook scallops in 2 tablespoons oil for 1½ to 2 minutes on each side or until firm and opaque. Remove scallops and keep warm.

2. In the same skillet, saute shallots in remaining oil until tender. Add cream; bring to a boil. Cook and stir for 30 seconds or until slightly thickened.

3. Return scallops to the pan; heat through. Stir in sage. Serve with pasta if desired.

"This was delicious! The light sauce accents the scallops perfectly."

—CATLOVESBOOKS FROM TASTEOFHOME.COM

Maple & Blue Cheese Steak

This traditional Canadian recipe melts in your mouth. My family loves the tangy blue cheese crumbled on top.

—SUSAN JERROTT
BEDFORD, NOVA SCOTIA

PREP: 20 MIN. + MARINATING
GRILL: 10 MIN. • **MAKES:** 2 SERVINGS

- 6 tablespoons balsamic vinegar
- 6 tablespoons maple syrup, divided
- 2 tablespoons plus 1½ teaspoons Dijon mustard
- 1 tablespoon minced fresh thyme or ¼ teaspoon dried thyme
- ½ pound beef top sirloin steak
- 2 tablespoons chopped pecans
- 1½ teaspoons olive oil
- ⅛ teaspoon salt
- ⅛ teaspoon pepper
- ¼ cup crumbled blue cheese

1. In a small bowl, combine the vinegar, 5 tablespoons maple syrup, mustard and thyme. Pour ⅔ cup marinade into a large resealable plastic bag; add the steak. Seal bag and turn to coat; refrigerate for up to 3 hours. Cover and refrigerate remaining marinade.

2. Meanwhile, in a small skillet, saute pecans in oil until toasted. Stir in remaining maple syrup. Bring to a boil; cook for 1 minute, stirring constantly. Remove from skillet and spread onto waxed paper to cool completely.

3. Drain and discard marinade. Sprinkle steak with salt and pepper. Grill, over medium heat, for 4-6 minutes on each side or until meat reaches desired doneness (for medium-rare, a thermometer should read 145°; medium, 160°; well-done, 170°). Let stand for 5 minutes before slicing.

4. Place reserved marinade in small saucepan. Bring to a boil; cook until liquid is reduced to ¼ cup, about 2 minutes. Divide steak slices between two plates. Drizzle with sauce; sprinkle with blue cheese and pecans.

Cornmeal Oven-Fried Chicken

A coating of cornmeal and Parmesan cheese really perks up fried chicken. It's a crisp and tasty variation from the usual.

—DEB WILLIAMS PEORIA, ARIZONA

PREP: 20 MIN. • **BAKE:** 40 MIN.
MAKES: 6 SERVINGS

- ½ cup dry bread crumbs
- ½ cup cornmeal
- ⅓ cup grated Parmesan cheese
- ¼ cup minced fresh parsley or 4 teaspoons dried parsley flakes
- ¾ teaspoon garlic powder
- ½ teaspoon salt
- ½ teaspoon onion powder
- ½ teaspoon dried thyme
- ½ teaspoon pepper
- ½ cup buttermilk
- 1 broiler/fryer chicken (3 to 4 pounds), cut up and skin removed
- 1 tablespoon butter, melted

1. In a large resealable plastic bag, combine the first nine ingredients. Place the buttermilk in a shallow bowl. Dip chicken in buttermilk, then add to bag, a few pieces at a time, and shake to coat.

2. Place in a 13x9-in. baking pan coated with cooking spray. Bake at 375° for 10 minutes; drizzle with butter. Bake 30-40 minutes longer or until juices run clear.

FAST FIX ▶ Tortellini with Tomato-Cream Sauce

Put frozen food and pantry staples to beautiful use in this warm and satisfying meatless meal.

—BARBRA STANGER WEST JORDAN, UTAH

PREP/TOTAL TIME: 25 MIN. • **MAKES:** 6 SERVINGS

- 1 package (16 ounces) frozen cheese tortellini
- 1 small onion, chopped
- 2 tablespoons olive oil
- 3 garlic cloves, minced
- 1 can (14½ ounces) diced tomatoes, undrained
- 1 package (10 ounces) frozen chopped spinach, thawed and squeezed dry
- 1½ teaspoons dried basil
- 1 teaspoon salt
- ½ teaspoon pepper
- 1½ cups heavy whipping cream
- ½ cup grated Parmesan cheese
  Additional grated Parmesan cheese, optional

1. Cook tortellini according to package directions. Meanwhile, in a large skillet, saute onion in oil until tender. Add garlic; cook 1 minute longer. Add the tomatoes, spinach, basil, salt and pepper. Cook and stir over medium heat until liquid is absorbed, about 3 minutes.

2. Stir in cream and cheese. Bring to a boil. Reduce heat; simmer, uncovered, for 8-10 minutes or until thickened.

3. Drain tortellini; toss with sauce. Sprinkle with additional cheese if desired.

🍲 SLOW COOKER Stamp-of-Approval Spaghetti Sauce

My father is very opinionated—especially about food—and this recipe received his elusive stamp of approval. I have yet to hear a disagreement from anyone who has tried it!

—MELISSA TAYLOR HIGLEY, ARIZONA

PREP: 30 MIN. • **COOK:** 8 HOURS
MAKES: 12 SERVINGS (3 QUARTS)

- 2 pounds ground beef
- ¾ pound bulk Italian sausage
- 4 medium onions, finely chopped
- 8 garlic cloves, minced
- 4 cans (14½ ounces each) diced tomatoes, undrained
- 4 cans (6 ounces each) tomato paste
- ½ cup water
- ¼ cup sugar
- ¼ cup Worcestershire sauce
- 1 tablespoon canola oil
- ¼ cup minced fresh parsley
- 2 tablespoons minced fresh basil or 2 teaspoons dried basil
- 1 tablespoon minced fresh oregano or 1 teaspoon dried oregano
- 4 bay leaves
- 1 teaspoon rubbed sage
- ½ teaspoon salt
- ½ teaspoon dried marjoram
- ½ teaspoon pepper
  Hot cooked spaghetti

1. In a Dutch oven, cook the beef, sausage, onions and garlic over medium heat until the meat is no longer pink; drain.

2. Transfer to a 5-qt. slow cooker. Stir in the tomatoes, tomato paste, water, sugar, Worcestershire sauce, oil and seasonings.

3. Cover and cook on low for 8-10 hours. Discard bay leaves. Serve with spaghetti.

SLOW COOKER

Vegetarian Stuffed Peppers

These filling and flavorful peppers are an updated version of my mom's stuffed peppers, which were a favorite when I was growing up in upstate New York. Whenever I make them, I'm reminded of home.

—**MELISSA MCCABE** LONG BEACH, CALIFORNIA

PREP: 30 MIN. • **COOK:** 3½ HOURS • **MAKES:** 6 SERVINGS

- 6 large sweet peppers
- 2 cups cooked brown rice
- 3 small tomatoes, chopped
- 1 cup frozen corn, thawed
- 1 small sweet onion, chopped
- ⅓ cup canned red beans, rinsed and drained
- ⅓ cup canned black beans, rinsed and drained
- ¾ cup cubed Monterey Jack cheese
- 1 can (4¼ ounces) chopped ripe olives
- 4 fresh basil leaves, thinly sliced
- 3 garlic cloves, minced
- 1 teaspoon salt
- ½ teaspoon pepper
- ¾ cup meatless spaghetti sauce
- ½ cup water
- 4 tablespoons grated Parmesan cheese, divided

1. Cut tops off peppers and remove seeds; set aside. In a large bowl, combine the rice, tomatoes, corn, onion and beans. Stir in the Monterey Jack cheese, olives, basil, garlic, salt and pepper. Spoon into peppers.

2. Combine spaghetti sauce and water; pour half into an oval 5-qt. slow cooker. Add the stuffed peppers. Top with remaining sauce. Sprinkle with 2 tablespoons Parmesan cheese.

3. Cover and cook on low for 3½ to 4 hours or until peppers are tender and filling is heated through. Sprinkle with remaining Parmesan cheese.

BAKED VEGETARIAN STUFFED PEPPERS *Fill peppers as directed. Spoon half of the sauce mixture into an* ungreased 3-qt. baking dish. Add the peppers; top with remaining sauce mixture. Sprinkle with cheese as directed. Cover and bake at 350° for 30-35 minutes or until peppers are tender and filling is heated through.

SLOW COOKER

Slow Cooker Pork Chops

Everyone will enjoy fork-tender pork chops with a light and creamy gravy. I like to serve them with mashed potatoes and coleslaw or a salad. I also like to prepare the recipe with boneless chicken breasts instead of pork, substituting poultry seasoning for the ground mustard.

—**SUE BINGHAM** MADISONVILLE, TENNESSEE

PREP: 15 MIN. • **COOK:** 3 HOURS • **MAKES:** 4 SERVINGS

- ¾ cup all-purpose flour, divided
- ½ teaspoon ground mustard
- ½ teaspoon garlic pepper blend
- ¼ teaspoon seasoned salt
- 4 boneless pork loin chops (4 ounces each)
- 2 tablespoons canola oil
- 1 can (14½ ounces) chicken broth

1. In a large resealable plastic bag, combine ½ cup flour, mustard, garlic pepper and seasoned salt. Add pork chops, one at a time, and shake to coat. In a large skillet, brown chops in oil on both sides.

2. Transfer to a 5-qt. slow cooker. Place remaining flour in a small bowl; whisk in broth until smooth. Pour over chops. Cover and cook on low for 3-4 hours or until meat is tender.

3. Remove pork to a serving plate and keep warm. Whisk cooking liquid until smooth; serve with pork.

Deep-Dish Sausage Pizza

My Grandma made the tastiest snacks for us when we stayed the night at her farm. Her wonderful pizza hot from the oven was covered with cheese and had fragrant herbs in the crust. Now this pizza is a frequent meal for my husband, our two young daughters and me.

—MICHELE MADDEN
WASHINGTON COURT HOUSE, OHIO

PREP: 30 MIN. + RISING • **BAKE:** 30 MIN. + STANDING
MAKES: 8 SLICES

- 1 **package (¼ ounce) active dry yeast**
- ⅔ **cup warm water (110° to 115°)**
- 1¾ to 2 **cups all-purpose flour**
- ¼ **cup vegetable oil**
- 1 **teaspoon each dried oregano, basil and marjoram**
- ½ **teaspoon garlic salt**
- ½ **teaspoon onion salt**

TOPPINGS
- 4 **cups (16 ounces) shredded part-skim mozzarella cheese, divided**
- 2 **medium green peppers, chopped**
- 1 **large onion, chopped**
- ½ **teaspoon each dried oregano, basil and marjoram**
- 1 **tablespoon olive oil**
- 1 **cup grated Parmesan cheese**
- 1 **pound bulk pork sausage, cooked and drained**
- 1 **can (28 ounces) diced tomatoes, well drained**
- 2 **ounces sliced pepperoni**

1. In a large bowl, dissolve yeast in warm water. Add 1 cup flour, oil and seasonings; beat until smooth. Add enough remaining flour to form a soft dough.

2. Turn onto a floured surface; knead until smooth and elastic, about 6-8 minutes. Place in a greased bowl; turn once to greased top. Cover and let rise in a warm place until doubled, about 1 hour.

3. Punch dough down; roll out into a 15-in. circle. Transfer to a well-greased 12-in. heavy ovenproof skillet or round baking pan, letting dough drape over edges. Sprinkle with 1 cup mozzarella.

4. In a skillet, saute the green peppers, onion and seasonings in oil until tender; drain. Layer half of the mixture over crust. Layer with half of the Parmesan, sausage and tomatoes. Sprinkle with 2 cups mozzarella. Repeat layers. Fold crust over to form an edge.

5. Bake for 400° for 20 minutes. Sprinkle with the pepperoni and remaining mozzarella. Bake 10-15 minutes longer or until crust is browned. Let stand for 10 minutes before slicing.

SLOW COOKER
Slow Cooker Chicken Stew

I like to sprinkle this with toasted almonds or cashews and serve it with hot couscous. Flavored with cinnamon and a touch of sweetness from the apricots, this stew tastes like you spent all day in the kitchen!
—**ANGELA BUCHANAN** LONGMONT, COLORADO

PREP: 15 MIN. • **COOK:** 6 HOURS • **MAKES:** 6 SERVINGS

2¼ pounds bone-in chicken thighs, skin removed
1 large onion, chopped
2 medium carrots, sliced
¾ cup unsweetened apple juice
1 garlic clove, minced
1 teaspoon salt
½ teaspoon ground cinnamon
½ teaspoon pepper
1 cup chopped dried apricots
 Hot cooked couscous

1. Place the chicken, onion and carrots in a 3- or 4-qt. slow cooker coated with cooking spray. In a small bowl, combine the apple juice, garlic, salt, cinnamon and pepper; pour over vegetables.
2. Cover and cook on low for 6-8 hours or until the chicken is tender.
3. Remove chicken from slow cooker; shred meat with two forks. Skim fat from cooking juices; stir in apricots. Return shredded chicken to slow cooker; heat though. Serve with couscous.

Moist & Savory Meat Loaf

Stop searching for a go-to meat loaf recipe. This is it! Your family will be delighted with this mixture of beef, pork and sauteed onion, with a sweet-and-tangy sauce baked onto the top. Cheese crackers are the secret ingredient in this one.
—**TASTE OF HOME TEST KITCHEN**

PREP: 20 MIN. • **BAKE:** 1¼ HOURS + STANDING
MAKES: 8 SERVINGS

1 medium onion, chopped
2 teaspoons canola oil
2 eggs, lightly beaten
⅓ cup 2% milk
2 teaspoons Worcestershire sauce
2 teaspoons Dijon mustard
⅔ cup finely crushed cheese crackers
1 teaspoon salt
½ teaspoon pepper
½ teaspoon dried thyme
1½ pounds ground beef
½ pound ground pork
¾ cup ketchup
¼ cup packed brown sugar

1. Saute onion in oil in a small skillet until tender. Cool to room temperature.
2. Combine the eggs, milk, Worcestershire sauce, mustard, crackers, salt, pepper, thyme and onion in a large bowl. Crumble beef and pork over mixture and mix well. Shape into a loaf; place in a greased 11x7-in. baking dish.
3. Bake, uncovered, at 350° for 1 hour. Combine ketchup and brown sugar; spread half of sauce over meat loaf. Bake 15-20 minutes longer or until no pink remains and a thermometer reads 160°. Let stand for 10 minutes before slicing. Serve with remaining sauce.

Savory Grilled T-Bones

Our taste panel flipped for these mouthwatering steaks, marinated and grilled to perfection! They're melt-in-your-mouth delicious and sure to become a warm-weather favorite. Don't let the season go by without trying this recipe.

—ANNA DAVIS HALF WAY, MISSOURI

PREP: 15 MIN. + MARINATING
GRILL: 15 MIN. • **MAKES:** 6 SERVINGS

- ¼ cup chopped onion
- ¼ cup olive oil
- 2 tablespoons lemon juice
- 2 tablespoons soy sauce
- 1 tablespoon sugar
- 1 tablespoon cider vinegar
- 1 tablespoon honey
- 2 teaspoons minced garlic
- 2 teaspoons Worcestershire sauce
- 1 teaspoon salt
- ½ teaspoon pepper
- 6 beef T-bone steaks (1 inch thick and 12 ounces each)

1. In a large resealable plastic bag, combine the first 11 ingredients; add steaks. Seal bag and turn to coat; refrigerate for 2-4 hours.

2. Drain and discard marinade. Grill steaks, covered, over medium heat for 6-10 minutes on each side or until meat reaches desired doneness (for medium-rare, a thermometer should read 145°; medium, 160°; well-done, 170°).

Halibut with Tomato-Basil Sauce

A well-seasoned tomato salsa dresses up these tender, flaky fillets. We're empty-nesters now, but my sons still love this recipe. My husband never complains when I make it either!

—CAROLYN SCHMELING BROOKFIELD, WISCONSIN

PREP: 15 MIN. + MARINATING
GRILL: 10 MIN. • **MAKES:** 2 SERVINGS

- 1 tablespoon lemon juice
- 1½ teaspoons minced fresh rosemary or ½ teaspoon dried rosemary, crushed
- 1½ teaspoons olive oil
- ¼ teaspoon salt
  Dash pepper
- 2 halibut fillets (6 ounces each)
- ¼ cup diced seeded tomato
- 1 tablespoon minced fresh basil or 1 teaspoon dried basil
- 1 tablespoon chopped green onion
- 1½ teaspoons red wine vinegar
- ¼ teaspoon grated orange peel

1. In a large resealable plastic bag, combine the lemon juice, rosemary, oil, salt and pepper; add halibut. Seal bag and turn to coat; refrigerate for up to 1 hour.

2. Drain and discard marinade. Using long-handled tongs, moisten a paper towel with cooking oil and lightly coat the grill rack.

3. Grill halibut, covered, over medium heat or broil 4 in. from the heat for 4-5 minutes on each side or until fish flakes easily with a fork.

4. In a small saucepan, combine the remaining ingredients. Cook over medium heat until heated through. Serve with fish.

Sweet 'n' Smoky Kansas City Ribs

Tender and juicy, these ribs pack a big smoky punch. You won't believe how quickly they go from grill to plate!

—GLORIA WARCZAK CEDARBURG, WISCONSIN

PREP: 35 MIN. + STANDING • **GRILL:** 70 MIN.
MAKES: 5 SERVINGS

- ⅓ cup packed brown sugar
- 2 teaspoons chicken bouillon granules
- 2 teaspoons paprika
- 2 teaspoons chili powder
- 1 teaspoon ground cumin
- ¾ teaspoon garlic powder
- ½ teaspoon each minced fresh basil, rosemary and sage
- ½ teaspoon ground celery seed
- ¼ teaspoon ground coriander
- ⅛ teaspoon fennel seed, crushed
- 2 pork baby back ribs (about 5 pounds)
- 2 cups soaked wood chips (mequite, hickory or alder), optional

SAUCE
- 1 large onion, chopped
- 2 tablespoons olive oil
- 1 tablespoon butter
- 2 tablespoons brown sugar
- 1 tablespoon Worcestershire sauce
- 1 teaspoon each minced fresh basil, marjoram and rosemary, crushed
- 1 teaspoon each minced fresh dill, sage and cilantro
- 1 teaspoon minced chives
- 1 bottle (18 ounces) barbecue sauce

1. In a small bowl, combine the brown sugar, bouillon, seasonings and herbs; rub over ribs. Let stand for 15 minutes.

2. Prepare grill for indirect heat, using a drip pan. Add 1 cup of soaked wood chips if desired. Place ribs in a disposable foil pan. Grill, covered, over indirect medium heat for 30 minutes. Remove ribs from pan and place on grill rack over drip pan. Add remaining wood chips. Grill 30 minutes longer, turning occasionally.

3. Meanwhile, in a small saucepan, saute onion in oil and butter until tender. Stir in the brown sugar, Worcestershire sauce and herbs; cook and stir for 1 minute. Add barbecue sauce. Bring to a boil. Reduce heat; simmer, uncovered, for 5 minutes. Baste ribs with sauce; grill for 10-15 minutes or until meat is tender, turning and basting occasionally.

1. In a large bowl, combine the egg substitute, bread crumbs, onion, pepper and seasoning blend. Crumble turkey over mixture and mix well. Shape into 1-in. balls; place on a rack coated with cooking spray in a shallow baking pan. Bake, uncovered, at 400° for 15 minutes or until no longer pink.

2. Meanwhile, in a 4- or 5-qt. slow cooker, combine the tomato sauce, tomatoes, zucchini, green pepper, onion, tomato paste, bay leaves, garlic and seasonings. Stir in meatballs. Cover and cook on low for 6 hours. Cook spaghetti according to package directions; serve with meatballs and sauce.

Lemon-Pepper Catfish

Nothing beats a late supper of grilled catfish after a hard day's work. It's a fresh family favorite.

—**REGINA ROSENBERRY** GREENCASTLE, PENNSYLVANIA

PREP: 5 MIN. + MARINATING • **GRILL:** 10 MIN.
MAKES: 4 SERVINGS

- 6 tablespoons lemon juice
- ¼ cup butter, melted
- 2 teaspoons Worcestershire sauce
- 4 catfish fillets (about 5 ounces each)
- ½ teaspoon salt
- ½ teaspoon lemon-pepper seasoning

1. In a large resealable plastic bag, combine the lemon juice, butter and Worcestershire sauce. Add the fish; seal bag and turn to coat. Cover and refrigerate for 30 minutes, turning occasionally.

2. Drain and discard marinade. Sprinkle fish with salt and lemon-pepper. Using long-handled tongs, moisten a paper towel with cooking oil and lightly coat the grill rack. Grill, fish, covered, over medium heat or broil 4 in. from the heat for 4-6 minutes on each side or until fish flakes easily with a fork.

SLOW COOKER

Turkey Meatballs and Sauce

My sweetie and I have fought the battle of the bulge forever. This is my less-fattening take on meatballs. They're slow-cooker easy, and so flavorful!

—**JANE MCMILLAN** DANIA BEACH, FLORIDA

PREP: 30 MIN. • **COOK:** 6 HOURS • **MAKES:** 8 SERVINGS

- ¼ cup egg substitute
- ½ cup seasoned bread crumbs
- ⅓ cup chopped onion
- ½ teaspoon pepper
- ¼ teaspoon salt-free seasoning blend
- 1½ pounds lean ground turkey

SAUCE

- 1 can (15 ounces) tomato sauce
- 1 can (14½ ounces) diced tomatoes, undrained
- 1 small zucchini, chopped
- 1 medium green pepper, chopped
- 1 medium onion, chopped
- 1 can (6 ounces) tomato paste
- 2 bay leaves
- 2 garlic cloves, minced
- 1 teaspoon dried oregano
- 1 teaspoon dried basil
- 1 teaspoon dried parsley flakes
- ¼ teaspoon crushed red pepper flakes
- ¼ teaspoon pepper
- 1 package (16 ounces) whole wheat spaghetti

Cinnamon-Apple Pork Chops

When I found this recipe online years ago, it quickly became a favorite. The ingredients are easy to keep on hand, and the one-pan cleanup is a bonus.
—**CHRISTINA PRICE** WHEELING, WEST VIRGINIA

PREP/TOTAL TIME: 25 MIN. • **MAKES:** 4 SERVINGS

- **4 boneless pork loin chops (4 ounces each)**
- **2 tablespoons reduced-fat butter, divided**
- **3 tablespoons brown sugar**
- **1 teaspoon ground cinnamon**
- **½ teaspoon ground nutmeg**
- **¼ teaspoon salt**
- **4 medium tart apples, thinly sliced**
- **2 tablespoons chopped pecans**

1. In a large skillet over medium heat, cook pork chops in 1 tablespoon butter for 4-5 minutes on each side or until a thermometer reads 160°. Meanwhile, in a small bowl, combine the brown sugar, cinnamon, nutmeg and salt.

2. Remove chops and keep warm. Add the apples, pecans, brown sugar mixture and remaining butter to the pan; cook and stir until apples are tender. Serve with chops.

NOTE *This recipe was tested with Land O'Lakes light stick butter.*

Chicken Fajitas

This recipe goes together in a snap and is very popular at my house. If you don't like too much heat, just leave out the red pepper flakes.
—**JULIE STERCHI** JACKSON, MISSOURI

PREP: 20 MIN. + MARINATING • **COOK:** 5 MIN.
MAKES: 6 SERVINGS

- **4 tablespoons canola oil, divided**
- **2 tablespoons lemon juice**
- **1½ teaspoons seasoned salt**
- **1½ teaspoons dried oregano**
- **1½ teaspoons ground cumin**
- **1 teaspoon garlic powder**
- **½ teaspoon chili powder**
- **½ teaspoon paprika**
- **½ teaspoon crushed red pepper flakes, optional**
- **1½ pounds boneless skinless chicken breast, cut into thin strips**
- **½ medium sweet red pepper, julienned**
- **½ medium green pepper, julienned**
- **4 green onions, thinly sliced**
- **½ cup chopped onion**
- **6 flour tortillas (8 inches), warmed**
  Shredded cheddar cheese, taco sauce, salsa, guacamole and sour cream

1. In a large resealable plastic bag, combine 2 tablespoons oil, lemon juice and seasonings; add the chicken. Seal and turn to coat; refrigerate for 1-4 hours.

2. In a large skillet, saute the peppers and onions in remaining oil until crisp-tender. Remove vegetables and keep warm.

3. Discard marinade. In the same skillet, cook chicken over medium-high heat for 5-6 minutes or until no longer pink. Return pepper mixture to pan; heat through.

4. Spoon filling down the center of tortillas; fold in half. Serve with cheese, taco sauce, salsa, guacamole and sour cream.

FAST FIX Tasty Burritos

My cousin is of Mexican heritage, and I've watched her make these crunchy burritos for years. The very first time I made them for my own family, they became an instant favorite meal.

—DEBI LANE
CHATTANOOGA, TENNESSEE

PREP/TOTAL TIME: 30 MIN.
MAKES: 6 SERVINGS

- 1 pound ground beef
- 1 envelope taco seasoning
- 1 can (16 ounces) refried beans
- 6 flour tortillas (12 inches), warmed
- 1 cup (4 ounces) shredded Colby-Monterey Jack cheese
- 4 teaspoons canola oil
  Sour cream and salsa

1. In a large skillet, cook beef over medium heat until no longer pink; drain. Stir in taco seasoning. In a small saucepan, cook refried beans over medium-low heat for 2-3 minutes or until heated through.

2. Spoon about ⅓ cup of beans off-center on each tortilla; top with ¼ cup beef mixture. Sprinkle with cheese. Fold sides and ends of tortilla over filling and roll up.

3. In a large skillet over medium-high heat, brown burritos in oil on all sides. Serve with sour cream and salsa.

Grilled Snapper with Caper Sauce

This recipe uses red snapper fillets, but mahi mahi is also delicious. It's a firm and mild fish that won't fall apart on the grill.

—ALAINA SHOWALTER
CLOVER, SOUTH CAROLINA

PREP: 20 MIN. + MARINATING
GRILL: 10 MIN. • **MAKES:** 4 SERVINGS

- ⅓ cup lime juice
- 1 jalapeno pepper, seeded
- 3 garlic cloves, peeled
- 1¼ teaspoons fresh thyme leaves or ¼ teaspoon dried thyme
- 1 teaspoon salt
- 1 teaspoon pepper
- 4 red snapper fillets (6 ounces each)

SAUCE
- 3 tablespoons lime juice
- 3 tablespoons olive oil
- 2 tablespoons water
- 2 teaspoons red wine vinegar
- ½ cup fresh cilantro leaves
- 1 shallot, peeled
- 1 tablespoon capers, drained
- 1½ teaspoons chopped seeded jalapeno pepper
- 1 garlic clove, peeled and halved
- ¼ teaspoon pepper

1. In a small food processor, combine the first six ingredients; cover and process until blended. Pour into a large resealable plastic bag. Add the red snapper fillets; seal bag and turn to coat. Refrigerate for 30 minutes.

2. Drain and discard marinade. Using long-handled tongs, moisten a paper towel with cooking oil and lightly coat the grill rack. Grill fillets, covered, over medium heat or broil 4 in. from the heat for 3-5 minutes on each side or until fish flakes easily with a fork.

3. Meanwhile, combine sauce ingredients in a small food processor. Cover and process until blended. Serve with fish.

NOTE *Wear disposable gloves when cutting hot peppers; the oils can burn skin. Avoid touching your face.*

Chicken and Red Potatoes

Looking for a classic chicken and potato dish? You'll love this moist and tender slow-cooked sensation with scrumptious gravy. Fix it early in the day, then forget about it until meal time.

—MICHELE TRANTHAM
WAYNESVILLE, NORTH CAROLINA

PREP: 20 MIN. • **COOK:** 3½ HOURS
MAKES: 4 SERVINGS

- 3 **tablespoons all-purpose flour**
- 4 **boneless skinless chicken breast halves (6 ounces each)**
- 2 **tablespoons olive oil**
- 4 **medium red potatoes, cut into wedges**
- 2 **cups fresh baby carrots, halved lengthwise**
- 1 **can (4 ounces) mushroom stems and pieces, drained**
- 4 **canned whole green chilies, cut into ½-inch slices**
- 1 **can (10¾ ounces) condensed cream of onion soup, undiluted**
- ¼ **cup 2% milk**
- ½ **teaspoon chicken seasoning**
- ¼ **teaspoon salt**
- ¼ **teaspoon dried rosemary, crushed**
- ¼ **teaspoon pepper**

1. Place flour in a large resealable plastic bag. Add chicken, one piece at a time; shake to coat. In a large skillet, brown the chicken in oil on both sides.

2. Meanwhile, place the potatoes, carrots, mushrooms and chilies in a greased 5-qt. slow cooker. In a small bowl, combine the remaining ingredients. Pour half of soup mixture over vegetables.

3. Transfer chicken to slow cooker; top with remaining soup mixture. Cover and cook on low for 3½ to 4 hours or until a thermometer reads 170°.

NOTE *This recipe was tested with McCormick's Montreal Chicken Seasoning. Look for it in the spice aisle.*

Spaghetti Squash with Balsamic Vegetables and Toasted Pine Nuts

This light, fresh meal hits the spot. It's low-carb, low-fat, and absolutely delicious! Steaming the squash in the microwave, rather than roasting it, saves a lot of time. The veggies can be prepped and cooked while the squash is cooking, and the meal will be on the table in 30 minutes or less! Chopping all the veggies before beginning the cooking will ensure quick, efficient preparation of this dish.

—DEANNA MCDONALD KALAMAZOO, MICHIGAN

PREP: 20 MIN. • **COOK:** 15 MIN. • **MAKES:** 6 SERVINGS

- 1 medium spaghetti squash (about 4 pounds)
- 1 cup chopped carrots
- 1 small red onion, halved and sliced
- 1 tablespoon olive oil
- 4 garlic cloves, minced
- 1 can (15½ ounces) great northern beans, rinsed and drained
- 1 can (14½ ounces) diced tomatoes, drained
- 1 can (14 ounces) water-packed artichoke hearts, rinsed, drained and halved
- 1 medium zucchini, chopped
- 3 tablespoons balsamic vinegar
- 2 teaspoons minced fresh thyme or ½ teaspoon dried thyme
- ¼ teaspoon salt
- ¼ teaspoon pepper
- ½ cup pine nuts, toasted

1. Cut squash in half lengthwise; discard seeds. Place squash cut side down on a microwave-safe plate. Microwave, uncovered, on high for 15-18 minutes or until tender.

2. Meanwhile, in a large nonstick skillet, saute carrots and onion in oil until tender. Add garlic; cook 1 minute. Stir in beans, tomatoes, artichokes, zucchini, vinegar, thyme, salt and pepper. Cook and stir over medium heat 8-10 minutes or until heated through.

3. When squash is cool enough to handle, use a fork to separate strands. Serve with bean mixture. Sprinkle with nuts.

FAST FIX ▶ Zesty Tacos

Jazz up everyday tacos in a snap! Black-eyed peas and a drizzle of Italian dressing are the surprise ingredients that perk up this recipe.

—SUSIE BONHAM FAIRVIEW, OKLAHOMA

PREP/TOTAL TIME: 30 MIN. • **MAKES:** 8 SERVINGS

- 1 pound ground beef
- 1 cup water
- 1 envelope taco seasoning
- 8 taco shells
- 1 can (15½ ounces) black-eyed peas, rinsed and drained
- 1 cup chopped tomatoes
- 1 cup shredded lettuce
- 1 cup (4 ounces) shredded cheddar cheese
- ½ cup zesty Italian salad dressing

1. In a large skillet, cook beef over medium heat until no longer pink; drain. Stir in water and taco seasoning. Bring to a boil. Reduce heat; simmer, uncovered, for 4-5 minutes or until thickened.

2. Meanwhile, prepare taco shells according to package directions. Stir the peas into skillet; heat through. Spoon ¼ cup beef mixture into each taco shell. Top with tomatoes, lettuce and cheese. Drizzle with salad dressing.

FAST FIX ▸ Mahi Mahi with Nectarine Salsa

A ripe nectarine inspired me to put together a fruity salsa to serve with fish fillets. I received six thumbs up from our three children for this easy, nutritious main dish.

—MICHELLE AUGUSTINE
CINCINNATI, OHIO

PREP/TOTAL TIME: 25 MIN.
MAKES: 2 SERVINGS

- 1   medium nectarine, peeled and chopped
- ¼   cup chopped onion
- 2   tablespoons chopped cucumber
- 1   tablespoon minced fresh cilantro
- 2   teaspoons chopped seeded jalapeno pepper
- 2   teaspoons lime juice
- ¼   teaspoon salt

- ¼   teaspoon pepper
- ¼   teaspoon Louisiana-style hot sauce

FISH FILLETS
- 2   mahi mahi fillets (6 ounces each)
- 1   tablespoon olive oil
     Dash salt

1. For salsa, in a small bowl, combine the first nine ingredients. Cover and refrigerate until serving.
2. Drizzle fillets with oil; sprinkle with salt. Using long-handled tongs, moisten a paper towel with cooking oil and lightly coat the grill rack. Grill fillets, covered, over medium heat or broil 4 in. from the heat for 3-5 minutes on each side or until fish just turns opaque. Serve with salsa.
NOTE *Wear disposable gloves when cutting hot peppers; the oils can burn skin. Avoid touching your face.*

❝This recipe is delicious and so quick to prepare. Since we are watching our calories, it fits right into our diet. It's definitely a keeper!❞

—MARTYLB FROM TASTEOFHOME.COM

FAST FIX ▸ Potato Kielbasa Skillet

Smoky kielbasa steals the show in this home-style, all-in-one meal. Busy cooks love the fact that it's ready to eat in just half an hour.
—TASTE OF HOME TEST KITCHEN

PREP/TOTAL TIME: 30 MIN.
MAKES: 4 SERVINGS

- 1   pound red potatoes, cubed
- 3   tablespoons water
- ¾   pound smoked kielbasa or Polish sausage, cut into ¼-inch slices
- ½   cup chopped onion
- 1   tablespoon olive oil
- 2   tablespoons brown sugar
- 2   tablespoons cider vinegar
- 1   tablespoon Dijon mustard
- ½   teaspoon dried thyme
- ¼   teaspoon pepper
- 4   cups fresh baby spinach
- 5   bacon strips, cooked and crumbled

1. Place potatoes and water in a microwave-safe dish. Cover and microwave on high for 4 minutes or until tender; drain.
2. In a large skillet, saute kielbasa and onion in oil until onion is tender. Add potatoes; saute 3-5 minutes longer or until kielbasa and potatoes are lightly browned.
3. Combine the brown sugar, vinegar, mustard, thyme and pepper; stir into skillet. Bring to a boil. Reduce heat; simmer, uncovered, for 2-3 minutes or until heated through. Add spinach and bacon; cook and stir until spinach is wilted.

Turkey Burritos with Fresh Fruit Salsa

Packed with fruit, veggies, nutrition and flavor, this lighter, whole-grain twist on traditional burritos is sure to be a big hit with your family. Even our pickiest eater loves these with the spicy-sweet fruit salsa. Yum!

—LISA EATON KENNEBUNK, MAINE

PREP: 30 MIN. • **COOK:** 20 MIN. • **MAKES:** 10 SERVINGS

- 1 pint grape tomatoes, quartered
- 1 medium mango, peeled and chopped
- 2 medium kiwifruit, peeled and chopped
- 3 green onions, thinly sliced
- 3 tablespoons finely chopped red onion
- 1 jalapeno pepper, seeded and chopped
- 1 tablespoon lime juice

BURRITOS
- 1 pound lean ground turkey
- ½ teaspoon ground turmeric
- ¼ teaspoon ground cumin
- 1 tablespoon olive oil
- 2 garlic cloves, minced
- ½ cup burgundy wine or reduced-sodium beef broth
- 1 jar (16 ounces) salsa
- 2 cups frozen corn, thawed
- 1 can (15 ounces) black beans, rinsed and drained
- 10 whole wheat tortilla (8 inches), warmed
- 1 cup (4 ounces) shredded reduced-fat cheddar cheese

1. For salsa, combine the first seven ingredients. Chill until serving.

2. In a large nonstick skillet, cook the turkey, turmeric and cumin in oil over medium heat until turkey is no longer pink. Add garlic; cook 1 minute longer. Drain. Stir in wine. Bring to a boil. Reduce heat; simmer, uncovered, for 3-5 minutes or until thickened.

3. Stir in the salsa, corn and black beans. Bring to a boil. Reduce heat; simmer, uncovered, for 10-15 minutes or until thickened. Remove from the heat.

4. Spoon about ½ cup turkey mixture off center on each tortilla. Sprinkle with cheese. Fold sides and ends over filling and roll up. Serve with salsa.

NOTE *Wear disposable gloves when cutting hot peppers; the oils can burn skin. Avoid touching your face.*

66Simply awesome! A must-try for your family.99

—LADYNORTH4EVER FROM TASTEOFHOME.COM

FAST FIX ▶ Barbecued Chicken Pizzas

So fast and so easy with refrigerated pizza crust, this entree will bring raves with its hot-off-the-grill, rustic flavor. It's perfect for a small, spur-of-the-moment party!
—**ALICIA TREVITHICK** TEMECULA, CALIFORNIA

PREP: 25 MIN. • **GRILL:** 10 MIN.
MAKES: 2 PIZZAS (4 PIECES EACH)

- 2 **boneless skinless chicken breast halves (6 ounces each)**
- ¼ **teaspoon salt**
- ¼ **teaspoon pepper**
- 1 **cup barbecue sauce, divided**
- 1 **tube (13.8 ounces) refrigerated pizza crust**
- 2 **teaspoons olive oil**
- 1 **medium red onion, thinly sliced**
- 2 **cups (8 ounces) shredded Gouda cheese**
- ¼ **cup minced fresh cilantro**

1. Sprinkle chicken with salt and pepper. Using long-handled tongs, moisten a paper towel with cooking oil and lightly coat the grill rack. Grill, covered, over medium heat or broil 4 in. from the heat for 5-7 minutes on each side or until a thermometer reads 170°, basting frequently with ½ cup barbecue sauce. Set aside and keep warm.

2. Divide dough in half. On a lightly floured surface, roll each portion into a 12x10-in. rectangle. Lightly brush both sides of dough with oil; place on grill. Cover and grill over medium heat for 1-2 minutes or until the bottom is lightly browned.

3. Remove from grill. Cut the chicken into ½-in. cubes. Spread the grilled side of each pizza with ¼ cup barbecue sauce; layer with chicken, onion, cheese and cilantro. Return to grill. Cover and cook each pizza for 4-5 minutes or until the bottom is lightly browned and cheese is melted.

SLOW COOKER ▶ Mushroom Pot Roast

Wow! The wine-warmed flavors in this recipe are amazing. Packed with wholesome veggies and tender beef, this is one company-special dish all ages will like. Serve with mashed potatoes to enjoy every last drop of the rich, beefy gravy.
—**ANGIE STEWART** TOPEKA, KANSAS

PREP: 25 MIN. • **COOK:** 6 HOURS • **MAKES:** 10 SERVINGS

- 1 **boneless beef chuck roast (3 to 4 pounds)**
- ½ **teaspoon salt**
- ¼ **teaspoon pepper**
- 1 **tablespoon canola oil**
- 1½ **pounds sliced fresh shiitake mushrooms**
- 2½ **cups thinly sliced onions**
- 1½ **cups reduced-sodium beef broth**
- 1½ **cups dry red wine or additional reduced-sodium beef broth**
- 1 **can (8 ounces) tomato sauce**
- ¾ **cup chopped peeled parsnips**
- ¾ **cup chopped celery**
- ¾ **cup chopped carrots**
- 8 **garlic cloves, minced**
- 2 **bay leaves**
- 1½ **teaspoons dried thyme**
- 1 **teaspoon chili powder**
- ¼ **cup cornstarch**
- ¼ **cup water**
  Mashed potatoes

1. Sprinkle roast with salt and pepper. In a Dutch oven, brown roast in oil on all sides. Transfer to a 6-qt. slow cooker. Add the mushrooms, onions, broth, wine, tomato sauce, parsnips, celery, carrots, garlic, bay leaves, thyme and chili powder. Cover and cook on low for 6-8 hours or until meat is tender.

2. Remove meat and vegetables to a serving platter; keep warm. Discard bay leaves. Skim fat from cooking juices; transfer to a small saucepan. Bring liquid to a boil. Combine cornstarch and water until smooth; gradually stir into the pan. Bring to a boil; cook and stir for 2 minutes or until thickened. Serve with mashed potatoes, meat and vegetables.

Caprese Chicken with Bacon

Smoky bacon, fresh basil, ripe tomatoes and gooey mozzarella top these appealing chicken breasts. The aroma as they bake is irresistible!

—**TAMMY HAYDEN** QUINCY, MICHIGAN

PREP: 20 MIN. • **BAKE:** 20 MIN. • **MAKES:** 4 SERVINGS

- 8 bacon strips
- 4 boneless skinless chicken breast halves (6 ounces each)
- 1 tablespoon olive oil
- ½ teaspoon salt
- ¼ teaspoon pepper
- 2 plum tomatoes, sliced
- 6 fresh basil leaves, thinly sliced
- 4 slices part-skim mozzarella cheese

1. Place bacon in an ungreased 15x10x1-in. baking pan. Bake at 400° for 8-10 minutes or until partially cooked but not crisp. Remove to paper towels to drain.

2. Place chicken in an ungreased 13x9-in. baking pan; brush with oil and sprinkle with salt and pepper. Top with tomatoes and basil. Wrap each in two bacon strips, arranging bacon in a crisscross pattern.

3. Bake, uncovered, at 400° for 20-25 minutes or until a meat thermometer reads 170°. Top with cheese; bake 1 minute longer or until melted.

FAST FIX ▶ Simple Shrimp Scampi

This is an extremely easy recipe designed to impress your guests. Serve it to them while you're finishing up the main course and just listen to the raves!

—**LISA BOEHM** DEEPWATER, MISSOURI

PREP/TOTAL TIME: 10 MIN. • **MAKES:** 6 SERVINGS

- ¾ cup butter, cubed
- 2 pounds uncooked medium shrimp, peeled and deveined
- 5 teaspoons lemon-pepper seasoning
- 2 teaspoons garlic powder
  Lemon wedges, optional

In a large skillet over medium heat, melt butter. Add the shrimp, lemon-pepper and garlic powder; cook for 5-8 minutes or until shrimp turn pink. Transfer to individual serving dishes. Serve with the lemon wedges if desired.

FAST FIX ▶ Camping Haystacks

Try this layered dish for a quick but satisfying meal after a day in the great outdoors. We love the easy combination of canned chili, corn chips and taco toppings.

—**GAYLENE ANDERSON** SANDY, UTAH

PREP/TOTAL TIME: 15 MIN. • **MAKES:** 2 SERVINGS

- 1 can (15 ounces) chili with beans
- 2 packages (1½ ounces each) corn chips
- ½ cup shredded cheddar cheese
- 1½ cups chopped lettuce
- 1 small tomato, chopped
- ½ cup salsa
- 2 tablespoons sliced ripe olives
- 2 tablespoons sour cream

In a small saucepan, heat the chili. Divide the corn chips between two plates; top with chili. Layer with cheese, lettuce, tomato, salsa, olives and sour cream. Serve immediately.

Brown Sugar Glazed Salmon

I wasn't a salmon lover until I tried this recipe. Now I'm officially "hooked." I serve this specialty to friends, too.
—**RACHEL GARCIA** FORT KNOX, KENTUCKY

PREP: 15 MIN. • **BAKE:** 20 MIN. • **MAKES:** 8 SERVINGS

- 1 **tablespoon brown sugar**
- 2 **teaspoons butter**
- 1 **teaspoon honey**
- 1 **tablespoon olive oil**
- 1 **tablespoon Dijon mustard**
- 1 **tablespoon reduced-sodium soy sauce**
- ½ to ¾ **teaspoon salt**
- ¼ **teaspoon pepper**
- 1 **salmon fillet (2½ pounds)**

1. In a small saucepan over medium heat, cook and stir the brown sugar, butter and honey until melted. Remove from the heat; whisk in the oil, mustard, soy sauce, salt and pepper. Cool for 5 minutes.

2. Place salmon in a large foil-lined baking pan; spoon brown sugar mixture over salmon. Bake, uncovered, at 350° for 20-25 minutes or until the fish flakes easily with a fork.

FAST FIX ▶ Breaded Pork Chops

I think this recipe came from my maternal grandmother. We had a birthday tradition in our family that we got to choose the entree and Mom would prepare it. These breaded pork chops were my top pick every year.
—**DEBORAH AMRINE** FORT MYERS, FLORIDA

PREP/TOTAL TIME: 20 MIN. • **MAKES:** 6 SERVINGS

- 1 **egg, lightly beaten**
- ½ **cup 2% milk**
- 1½ **cups crushed saltine crackers**
- 6 **boneless pork loin chops (1-inch thick and 4 ounces each)**
- ¼ **cup canola oil**

1. In a shallow bowl, combine egg and milk. Place cracker crumbs in another shallow bowl. Dip each pork chop in egg mixture, then coat with cracker crumbs, patting to make a thick coating.

2. In a large skillet, cook chops in oil for 4-5 minutes on each side or until a thermometer reads 145°. Let meat stand for 5 minutes before serving.

Broccoli-Chicken Cups

I first sampled these when my cousin made them for a bridal shower. All the ladies raved over the fantastic flavor of their individual "casseroles."
—**SHIRLEY GERBER** ROANOKE, ILLINOIS

PREP: 15 MIN. • **BAKE:** 20 MIN. • **MAKES:** 10-12 SERVINGS

- 2 **tubes (10 ounces each) refrigerated biscuits**
- 2 **cups (8 ounces) shredded cheddar cheese, divided**
- 1⅓ **cups crisp rice cereal**
- 1 **cup cubed cooked chicken**
- 1 **can (10¾ ounces) condensed cream of mushroom soup, undiluted**
- 3 **cups frozen chopped broccoli, cooked and drained**

1. Place biscuits in greased muffin cups, pressing dough onto the bottom and up the sides. Add 1 tablespoon cheese and cereal to each cup.

2. In a large bowl, combine the chicken, soup and broccoli; spoon into each muffin cup. Bake at 375° for 20-25 minutes or until bubbly. Sprinkle with remaining cheese.

CAJUN BEEF CASSEROLE, PAGE 118

CREAMY SEAFOOD-STUFFED SHELLS, 120

TURKEY POTPIES, 135

COWBOY CASSEROLE, 137

CASSEROLES & ONE-POT WONDERS

Recipes prepared in just one pot or baking dish are real time-savers for the busy family cook. After all, there's usually little to assemble, and cleanup is a breeze. In this collection of mouthwatering meal-in-one choices, you'll find all the best in bubbly lasagnas, classic potpies, stuffed shells and more. Brimming with meat, potatoes, pasta, rice and veggies, any one of these timeless down-home dishes can become your go-to recipe the next time the kitchen clock is ticking. You'll be saying, "Dinner's ready!" before you know it!

Cajun Beef Casserole

Have little ones who avoid veggies? They won't complain one bit when you bring this cheesy, corn-bread-crusted casserole to the table. For picky eaters, use less Cajun seasoning.
—TASTE OF HOME TEST KITCHEN

PREP: 15 MIN. • **BAKE:** 25 MIN.
MAKES: 6 SERVINGS

- 1 **package (8½ ounces) corn bread/muffin mix**
- 1 **pound ground beef**
- 2 **cans (14½ ounces each) diced tomatoes, drained**
- 2 **cups frozen mixed vegetables, thawed**
- 1 **can (6 ounces) tomato paste**
- 1 **to 2 teaspoons Cajun seasoning**
- 1 **cup (4 ounces) shredded cheddar cheese**
- 2 **green onions, thinly sliced**

1. Prepare corn bread batter according to package directions. Spread into a greased 11x7-in. baking dish.
2. In a large skillet, cook beef over medium heat until meat is no longer pink; drain. Add the tomatoes, vegetables, tomato paste and seasoning. Bring to a boil. Reduce heat; simmer, uncovered, for 5 minutes. Pour over top. Sprinkle with cheese.
3. Bake, uncovered, at 350° for 25-30 minutes or until golden brown. Sprinkle with onions.

Chicken Spaghetti Casserole

This creamy, cheesy casserole is so hearty and homey, second helpings are a must!
—LYNNE GERMAN
CUMMING, GEORGIA

PREP: 25 MIN. • **BAKE:** 25 MIN.
MAKES: 6 SERVINGS

- 8 **ounces uncooked spaghetti, broken into 3-inch pieces**
- 3 **cups cubed cooked chicken**
- 1 **can (10¾ ounces) condensed cream of chicken soup, undiluted**
- 1 **medium onion, chopped**
- 1 **cup 2% milk**
- 1 **cup (4 ounces) shredded sharp cheddar cheese, divided**
- 1 **cup (4 ounces) shredded Swiss cheese, divided**
- 1 **can (4 ounces) mushroom stems and pieces, drained**
- ½ **cup chopped roasted sweet red peppers**
- 3 **tablespoons mayonnaise**
- 1½ **teaspoons steak seasoning**
- ½ **teaspoon dried basil**

1. Cook spaghetti according to package directions. Meanwhile, in a large bowl, combine the chicken, soup, onion, milk, ½ cup cheddar cheese, ½ cup Swiss cheese, mushrooms, peppers, mayonnaise, steak seasoning and basil.
2. Drain spaghetti. Add to chicken mixture; toss to coat. Transfer to a greased 13x9-in. baking dish. Cover and bake at 350° for 20 minutes. Uncover; sprinkle with remaining cheeses. Bake 5-10 minutes longer or until heated through and cheese is melted.
EDITOR'S NOTE: *This recipe was tested with McCormick's Montreal Steak Seasoning. Look for it in the spice aisle.*

Mini Reuben Casseroles

These cute and creamy individual roast beef casseroles boast the flavors of a classic Reuben sandwich.

—TASTE OF HOME TEST KITCHEN

PREP: 20 MIN. • **BAKE:** 20 MIN.
MAKES: 4 SERVINGS

- 1 medium onion, chopped
- 1 medium green pepper, chopped
- 2 teaspoons olive oil
- 2 cups cubed cooked beef roast
- 1 can (14 ounces) sauerkraut, rinsed and well drained
- 1 can (10¾ ounces) condensed cream of chicken soup, undiluted
- 1¼ cups (5 ounces) shredded Swiss cheese, divided
- ⅓ cup 2% milk
- ½ cup Thousand Island salad dressing
- 2 slices rye bread, cubed
- 1 tablespoon butter, melted
- ½ teaspoon onion powder

1. In a large skillet, saute onion and pepper in oil until tender. Stir in the beef roast, sauerkraut, soup, 1 cup cheese, milk and salad dressing; heat through. Transfer to four greased 10-oz. ramekins or custard cups. Place ramekins on a baking sheet.

2. In a small bowl, toss bread cubes with butter and onion powder. Arrange over tops of casseroles. Bake, uncovered, at 350° for 15 minutes. Sprinkle with remaining cheese. Bake 5-10 minutes longer or until cheese is melted.

REUBEN FLAVOR TWIST

To shake up the flavor, feel free to replace the cubed beef roast in Mini Reuben Casseroles with corned beef or beef pastrami.

De-Lightful Tuna Casserole

This mild, homemade tuna casserole will truly satisfy your family's craving for comfort food without all the fat!

—COLLEEN WILLEY
HAMBURG, NEW YORK

PREP: 15 MIN. • **BAKE:** 25 MIN.
MAKES: 5 SERVINGS

- 1 package (7 ounces) elbow macaroni
- 1 can (10¾ ounces) reduced-fat reduced-sodium condensed cream of mushroom soup, undiluted
- 1 cup sliced fresh mushrooms
- 1 cup (4 ounces) shredded reduced-fat cheddar cheese
- 1 cup fat-free milk
- 1 can (6 ounces) light water-packed tuna, drained and flaked
- 2 tablespoons diced pimientos
- 3 teaspoons dried minced onion
- 1 teaspoon ground mustard
- ¼ teaspoon salt
- ⅓ cup crushed cornflakes

1. Cook macaroni according to package directions. Meanwhile, in a large bowl, combine the soup, mushrooms, cheese, milk, tuna, pimientos, onion, mustard and salt. Drain macaroni; add to tuna mixture and mix well.

2. Transfer mixture to a 2-qt. baking dish coated with cooking spray. Sprinkle with cornflakes. Bake, uncovered, at 350° for 25-30 minutes or until bubbly.

Creamy Seafood-Stuffed Shells

Inspired by my love of lasagna, pasta shells and seafood, I created this recipe that's easy to make but special enough to serve company. I serve it with garlic bread and a salad for a complete meal.

—KATIE SLOAN CHARLOTTE, NORTH CAROLINA

PREP: 40 MIN. • **BAKE:** 30 MIN. • **MAKES:** 8 SERVINGS

- 24 uncooked jumbo pasta shells
- 1 tablespoon finely chopped green pepper
- 1 tablespoon chopped red onion
- 1 teaspoon plus ¼ cup butter, divided
- 2 cans (6 ounces each) lump crabmeat, drained
- 1 package (5 ounces) frozen cooked salad shrimp, thawed
- 1 egg, lightly beaten
- ½ cup shredded part-skim mozzarella cheese
- ¼ cup mayonnaise
- 2 tablespoons plus 4 cups 2% milk, divided
- 1½ teaspoons seafood seasoning, divided
- ¼ teaspoon pepper
- ¼ cup all-purpose flour
- ¼ teaspoon coarsely ground pepper
- 1½ cups grated Parmesan cheese

1. Cook pasta according to package directions. Meanwhile, in a small skillet, saute green pepper and onion in 1 teaspoon butter until tender; set aside.

2. In a large bowl, combine the crab, shrimp, egg, mozzarella cheese, mayonnaise, 2 tablespoons milk, 1 teaspoon seafood seasoning, pepper and green pepper mixture.

3. Drain and rinse pasta; stuff each shell with 1 rounded tablespoon of seafood mixture. Place in a greased 13x9-in. baking dish.

4. In a small saucepan, melt remaining butter over medium heat. Whisk in flour and coarsely ground pepper; gradually whisk in remaining milk. Bring to a boil; cook and stir for 2 minutes or until thickened. Stir in Parmesan cheese.

5. Pour over stuffed shells. Sprinkle with remaining seafood seasoning. Bake, uncovered, at 350° for 30-35 minutes or until bubbly.

FAST FIX ▸

Easy Chicken and Dumplings

Perfect for autumn nights, this main course is speedy, comforting and a delicious one-dish meal.
—NANCY TUCK ELK FALLS, KANSAS

PREP/TOTAL TIME: 30 MIN. • **MAKES:** 6 SERVINGS

- 3 celery ribs, chopped
- 1 cup sliced fresh carrots
- 3 cans (14½ ounces each) reduced-sodium chicken broth
- 3 cups cubed cooked chicken breast
- ½ teaspoon poultry seasoning
- ⅛ teaspoon pepper
- 1⅔ cups reduced-fat biscuit/baking mix
- ⅔ cup fat-free milk

1. In a Dutch oven coated with cooking spray, saute celery and carrots for 5 minutes. Stir in the broth, chicken, poultry seasoning and pepper. Bring to a boil; reduce heat to a gentle simmer.

2. For dumplings, combine biscuit mix and milk. Drop by tablespoonfuls onto simmering broth. Cover and simmer for 10-15 minutes or until a toothpick inserted in a dumpling comes out clean (do not lift cover while simmering).

SLOW COOKER

Forgotten Jambalaya

During chilly months, I fix this jambalaya at least once a month. It's so easy—just chop the vegetables, dump everything in the slow cooker and forget it! Even my sons, who are picky about spicy things, like this dish.

—CINDI COSS COPPELL, TEXAS

PREP: 35 MIN. • **COOK:** 4¼ HOURS • **MAKES:** 11 SERVINGS

- 1 can (14½ ounces) diced tomatoes, undrained
- 1 can (14½ ounces) beef or chicken broth
- 1 can (6 ounces) tomato paste
- 3 celery ribs, chopped
- 2 medium green peppers, chopped
- 1 medium onion, chopped
- 5 garlic cloves, minced
- 3 teaspoons dried parsley flakes
- 2 teaspoons dried basil
- 1½ teaspoons dried oregano
- 1¼ teaspoons salt
- ½ teaspoon cayenne pepper
- ½ teaspoon hot pepper sauce
- 1 pound boneless skinless chicken breasts, cut into 1-inch cubes
- 1 pound smoked sausage, halved and cut into ¼-inch slices
- ½ pound uncooked medium shrimp, peeled and deveined
  Hot cooked rice

1. In a 5-qt. slow cooker, combine the tomatoes, broth and tomato paste. Stir in the celery, green peppers, onion, garlic and seasonings. Stir in chicken and sausage.

2. Cover and cook on low for 4-6 hours or until chicken is no longer pink. Stir in shrimp. Cover and cook 15-30 minutes longer or until shrimp turn pink. Serve with rice.

Alfredo Chicken Lasagna

My small-size lasagna makes a great weeknight meal for a twosome, but it's elegant enough for a small dinner party. I've served it often, and everyone comments on its rich flavor. I love the fact that it can be made ahead.

—**BRIDGETTE MONAGHAN** MASONVILLE, IOWA

PREP: 25 MIN. • **BAKE:** 40 MIN. + STANDING
MAKES: 3 SERVINGS

- 6 **ounces boneless skinless chicken breast, cut into bite-size pieces**
- 1 **cup sliced fresh mushrooms**
- 2 **tablespoons chopped onion**
- 1 **tablespoon olive oil**
- 1 **garlic clove, minced**
- 1 **tablespoon all-purpose flour**
- 1 **cup Alfredo sauce**
- ¾ **cup 2% cottage cheese**
- ¼ **cup plus 2 tablespoons shredded Parmesan cheese, divided**
- 1 **egg, lightly beaten**
- ½ **teaspoon Italian seasoning**
- ½ **teaspoon dried parsley flakes**
- 4 **lasagna noodles, cooked and drained**
- 1½ **cups (6 ounces) shredded part-skim mozzarella cheese**

1. In a large skillet, saute the chicken, mushrooms and onion in oil until chicken is no longer pink. Add garlic; cook 1 minute longer. Stir in flour until blended; gradually stir in Alfredo sauce. Bring to a boil. Reduce heat; simmer, uncovered, for 3-5 minutes or until mixture is thickened.

2. In a small bowl, combine the cottage cheese, ¼ cup Parmesan cheese, egg, Italian seasoning and parsley.

3. Spread ½ cup Alfredo mixture in an 8x4-in. loaf pan coated with cooking spray. Layer with two noodles (trimmed to fit pan), half of the cottage cheese mixture, half of the remaining Alfredo mixture and ¾ cup mozzarella cheese. Sprinkle with remaining Parmesan cheese. Repeat layers.

4. Cover and bake at 350° for 30 minutes. Uncover; bake 10 minutes longer or until bubbly. Let stand for 10 minutes before cutting.

🍲 **SLOW COOKER**

Creamy Ham & Potatoes

If you love scalloped potatoes but have a small household, this downsized version with tender chunks of ham is just for you.

—**WENDY ROWLEY** GREEN RIVER, WYOMING

PREP: 20 MIN. • **COOK:** 5 HOURS • **MAKES:** 2 SERVINGS

- 2 **large red potatoes, cubed**
- ⅓ **cup cubed process cheese (Velveeta)**
- ¾ **cup cubed fully cooked ham**
- 1 **tablespoon dried minced onion**
- ⅔ **cup condensed cream of celery soup, undiluted**
- ⅔ **cup 2% milk**
- 1 **tablespoon all-purpose flour**
- ¼ **teaspoon pepper**

1. In a greased 1½-qt. slow cooker, layer the potatoes, cheese, ham and onion.

2. In a small bowl, combine soup and milk; whisk in flour and pepper. Pour over potatoes. Cover and cook on low for 5-6 hours or until potatoes are tender. Stir before serving.

Chili Cheese Dog Casserole

Your hungry clan will dive right into this hearty, comforting dish. With a crispy cheese topping over a warm corn-bread crust, this recipe is definitely a keeper!
—TASTE OF HOME TEST KITCHEN

PREP: 20 MIN. • **BAKE:** 30 MIN. • **MAKES:** 6 SERVINGS

- 1 package (8½ ounces) corn bread/muffin mix
- 1 cup chopped green pepper
- ½ cup chopped onion
- ½ cup chopped celery
- 1 tablespoon olive oil
- 1 package (1 pound) hot dogs, halved lengthwise and cut into bite-size pieces
- 1 can (15 ounces) chili with beans
- 2 tablespoons brown sugar
- ½ teaspoon garlic powder
- ½ teaspoon chili powder
- 1 cup (4 ounces) shredded cheddar cheese, divided

1. Prepare corn bread batter according to package directions. Spread half the batter into a greased 8-in. square baking dish; set aside.

2. In a large skillet, saute the green pepper, onion and celery in oil until crisp-tender. Stir in hot dogs; saute 3-4 minutes longer or until lightly browned. Stir in the chili, brown sugar, garlic powder and chili powder; heat through. Stir in ¾ cup cheese.

3. Spoon over corn bread batter; top with remaining corn bread batter. Sprinkle remaining cheese over the top.

4. Bake, uncovered, at 350° for 28-32 minutes or until a toothpick inserted near the center comes out clean. Let stand for 5 minutes before serving.

Eggplant Zucchini Bolognese

I roast the veggies while the pasta cooks, making this a quick dish. It blends rustic comfort with fresh flavors.
—TRISHA KRUSE EAGLE, IDAHO

PREP: 30 MIN. • **COOK:** 20 MIN.
MAKES: 8 SERVINGS

- 1 package (16 ounces) penne pasta
- 1 small eggplant, peeled and cut into 1-inch pieces
- 1 medium zucchini, cut into ¼-inch slices
- 1 medium yellow summer squash, cut into ¼-inch slices
- 1 cup chopped onion
- 2 tablespoons olive oil
- 2 teaspoons minced garlic
- 1 teaspoon salt
- ½ teaspoon pepper
- 1 pound lean ground beef (90% lean)
- 1 can (28 ounces) tomato puree
- 1 tablespoon Italian seasoning
- 1 tablespoon brown sugar
- 8 teaspoons grated Parmesan cheese

1. Cook pasta according to package directions.

2. In a large bowl, combine the eggplant, zucchini, squash, onion, oil, garlic, salt and pepper. Transfer to two 15x10x1-in. baking pans coated with cooking spray. Bake at 425° for 20-25 minutes or until tender.

3. Meanwhile, in a large skillet, cook beef over medium heat until no longer pink; drain. Stir in the tomato puree, Italian seasoning and brown sugar.

4. Drain pasta; stir in tomato mixture and roasted vegetables. Sprinkle with cheese.

Tastes Like Thanksgiving Casserole

This hearty, rich-tasting dish is sure to be a hit with your family. It's a delicious way to use up Thanksgiving turkey, and you can easily substitute 5½ cups leftover mashed potatoes for the 6 potatoes.

—MARY LOU TIMPSON COLORADO CITY, ARIZONA

PREP: 30 MIN. • **BAKE:** 30 MIN. • **MAKES:** 8 SERVINGS

- 6 **medium potatoes, peeled and cut into chunks**
- 1¼ **cups chopped celery**
- ¾ **cup chopped onion**
- ½ **cup butter, cubed**
- 6 **cups unseasoned stuffing cubes**
- 1 **teaspoon poultry seasoning**
- ¼ **teaspoon rubbed sage**
- 1 **cup chicken broth**
- 4 **cups cubed cooked turkey**
- 2 **cans (10¾ ounces each) condensed cream of chicken soup, undiluted**
- 1 **teaspoon garlic powder**
- ¾ **cup sour cream, divided**
- 4 **ounces cream cheese, softened**
- ½ **teaspoon pepper**
- ¼ **teaspoon salt**
- 1½ **cups (6 ounces) shredded cheddar cheese**

1. Place potatoes in a Dutch oven and cover with water. Bring to a boil. Reduce heat; cover and cook for 10-15 minutes or until tender.

2. Meanwhile, in a large skillet, saute celery and onion in butter until tender. Remove from the heat.

3. In a large bowl, combine the stuffing cubes, poultry seasoning and sage. Stir in broth and celery mixture. Transfer to a greased 13x9-in. baking dish.

4. In another large bowl, combine the turkey, soup, garlic powder and ¼ cup sour cream; spoon over stuffing mixture. Drain potatoes; mash in a large bowl. Beat in the cream cheese, pepper, salt and remaining sour cream; spread over turkey mixture. Sprinkle with cheese.

5. Bake, uncovered, at 350° for 30-35 minutes or until heated through.

FAST FIX ▶ One Skillet Lasagna

Featuring classic flavors and cheesy layers, this skillet lasagna recipe is the best you'll ever taste. Cleanup is a snap because you don't use every pot and pan in the kitchen.
—TASTE OF HOME TEST KITCHEN

PREP/TOTAL TIME: 30 MIN. • **MAKES:** 6 SERVINGS

- ¾ pound ground beef
- 2 garlic cloves, minced
- 1 can (14½ ounces) diced tomatoes with basil, oregano and garlic, undrained
- 2 jars (14 ounces each) spaghetti sauce
- ⅔ cup condensed cream of onion soup, undiluted
- 2 eggs, lightly beaten
- 1¼ cups 1% cottage cheese
- ¾ teaspoon Italian seasoning
- 9 no-cook lasagna noodles
- ½ cup shredded Colby-Monterey Jack cheese
- ½ cup shredded part-skim mozzarella cheese

1. In a large skillet, cook beef and garlic over medium heat until meat is no longer pink; drain. Stir in tomatoes and spaghetti sauce; heat through. Transfer to a large bowl.

2. In a small bowl, combine the soup, eggs, cottage cheese and Italian seasoning.

3. Return 1 cup meat sauce to the skillet; spread evenly. Layer with 1 cup cottage cheese mixture, 1½ cups meat sauce and half of the noodles, breaking to fit. Repeat layers of cottage cheese mixture, meat sauce and noodles. Top with remaining meat sauce. Bring to a boil. Reduce heat; cover and simmer for 15-17 minutes or until noodles are tender.

4. Remove from the heat. Sprinkle with shredded cheeses; cover and let stand for 2 minutes or until cheese is melted.

Texan Ranch Chicken Casserole

I get rave reviews every time I serve this creamy casserole. It's a cinch to make, freezes well and has just a touch of heat. If you want to kick the flavor up a notch, simply toss in some chopped jalapenos.
—KENDRA DOSS COLORADO SPRINGS, COLORADO

PREP: 25 MIN. • **BAKE:** 30 MIN. • **MAKES:** 8 SERVINGS

- 1 large onion, finely chopped
- 2 celery ribs, finely chopped
- 1 medium green pepper, finely chopped
- 1 medium sweet red pepper, finely chopped
- 1 tablespoon canola oil
- 1 garlic clove, minced
- 3 cups cubed cooked chicken breast
- 1 can (10¾ ounces) reduced-fat reduced-sodium condensed cream of celery soup, undiluted
- 1 can (10¾ ounces) reduced-fat reduced-sodium condensed cream of chicken soup, undiluted
- 1 can (10 ounces) diced tomatoes and green chilies, undrained
- 1 tablespoon chili powder
- 12 corn tortillas (6 inches), cut into 1-inch strips
- 2 cups (8 ounces) shredded reduced-fat cheddar cheese, divided

1. In a large nonstick skillet coated with cooking spray, saute the onion, celery and peppers in oil until crisp-tender. Add garlic; cook 1 minute longer. Stir in the chicken, soups, tomatoes and chili powder.

2. Line the bottom of a 3-qt. baking dish with half of the tortilla strips; top with half of the chicken mixture and 1 cup cheese. Repeat layers. Bake, uncovered, at 350° for 30-35 minutes or until bubbly.

Creamy Macaroni and Cheese

This is the ultimate mac and cheese! It's creamy, thick and rich, and it holds the wonderful cheddar flavor. Once you taste it, you will be hooked.

—CINDY HARTLEY
CHESAPEAKE, VIRGINIA

PREP: 20 MIN. • **BAKE:** 35 MIN.
MAKES: 6 SERVINGS

- 2 cups uncooked elbow macaroni
- ½ cup butter, cubed
- ½ cup all-purpose flour
- 1½ cups 2% milk
- 1 cup (8 ounces) sour cream
- 8 ounces process cheese (Velveeta), cubed
- ¼ cup grated Parmesan cheese
- ½ teaspoon salt
- ½ teaspoon ground mustard
- ½ teaspoon pepper
- 2 cups (8 ounces) shredded cheddar cheese

1. Cook macaroni according to package directions. Meanwhile, in a large saucepan, melt butter. Stir in flour until smooth. Gradually add milk. Bring to a boil; cook and stir for 2 minutes or until thickened.

2. Reduce heat; stir in the sour cream, process cheese, Parmesan cheese, salt, mustard and pepper until smooth and cheese is melted.

3. Drain macaroni; toss with cheddar cheese. Transfer to a greased 3-qt. baking dish. Stir in cream sauce.

4. Bake, uncovered, at 350° for 35-40 minutes or until golden brown and bubbly.

Roasted Vegetable Penne Bake

For a twist, toss veggies with seasoning and oil. Poke holes in a disposable foil-lined pan and grill over medium heat, covered, 4-5 minutes per side or until crisp-tender.

—ROBYN CAVALLARO
EASTON, PENNSYLVANIA

PREP: 30 MIN. • **BAKE:** 20 MIN.
MAKES: 6 SERVINGS

- 2 large zucchini, cut into 1-inch pieces
- 1 medium sweet red pepper, cut into 1-inch pieces
- ½ pound medium fresh mushrooms, halved
- 1 small onion, cut into 1-inch pieces
- 2 tablespoons olive oil
- 1½ teaspoons Italian seasoning
- 2 cups uncooked penne pasta
- 1 can (15 ounces) crushed tomatoes, undrained
- 2 ounces provolone cheese, shredded
- ¾ cup frozen peas, thawed
- ¼ cup shredded part-skim mozzarella cheese
- ¼ cup plus 2 tablespoons grated Parmesan cheese, divided
- ½ teaspoon salt
- ½ teaspoon pepper
- 1 tablespoon butter, cubed

1. In a large bowl, combine the zucchini, red pepper, mushrooms, onion, oil and Italian seasoning; toss to coat. Arrange in a single layer in an ungreased 15x10x1-in. baking pan. Bake, uncovered, at 425° for 20-25 minutes or until vegetables are tender.

2. Meanwhile, cook pasta according to package directions; drain. In a large bowl, combine the pasta, roasted vegetables, tomatoes, provolone cheese, peas, mozzarella cheese, ¼ cup Parmesan cheese, salt and pepper.

3. Transfer to a greased 11x7-in. baking dish. Sprinkle with remaining Parmesan cheese; dot with butter. Cover and bake at 350° for 10 minutes. Uncover; bake 10-15 minutes longer or until bubbly.

Italian Spaghetti Bake

In need of a dish to pass at a potluck or want to give one to a neighbor or new parents? My hearty casserole recipe that yields two large casseroles will do the trick. The tasty layers of meat sauce, spaghetti and gooey cheese are sure to appeal to pizza lovers. Don't expect any leftovers!

—JANICE FREDRICKSON ELGIN, TEXAS

PREP: 20 MIN. • **BAKE:** 20 MIN.
MAKES: 2 CASSEROLES
(8 SERVINGS EACH)

- 2 packages (one 16 ounces, one 8 ounces) spaghetti
- 1½ pounds ground beef
- 1 large green pepper, chopped
- 1 medium onion, chopped
- 2 cans (15 ounces each) tomato sauce
- 1 package (8 ounces) sliced pepperoni
- 1 can (8 ounces) mushroom stems and pieces, drained
- 1 can (3.8 ounces) sliced ripe olives, drained
- ½ teaspoon dried basil
- ½ teaspoon dried oregano
- ¼ teaspoon garlic salt
- ¼ teaspoon pepper
- 4 cups (16 ounces) shredded part-skim mozzarella cheese
- ½ cup grated Parmesan cheese

1. Cook spaghetti according to package directions. Meanwhile, in a Dutch oven, cook the beef, green pepper and onion over medium heat until meat is no longer pink; drain. Stir in the tomato sauce, pepperoni, mushrooms, olives and seasonings. Drain spaghetti.

2. Spoon 1 cup meat mixture into each of two greased 13x9-in. baking dishes. Layer with spaghetti and remaining meat mixture. Sprinkle with cheeses.

3. Cover and freeze one casserole for up to 3 months. Bake the remaining casserole, uncovered, at 350° for 20-25 minutes or until heated through.

TO USE FROZEN CASSEROLE *Thaw in the refrigerator overnight. Remove from the refrigerator 30 minutes before baking. Cover and bake at 350° for 40 minutes. Uncover; bake 5-10 minutes longer or until the cheese is melted.*

SLOW COOKER

Slow Cooker Lasagna

Convenient no-cook lasagna noodles take the work out of a traditional favorite adapted for the slow cooker. We like our lasagna with Parmesan bread or garlic cheese toast.

—LISA MICHELETTI
COLLIERVILLE, TENNESSEE

PREP: 25 MIN. • **COOK:** 4 HOURS
MAKES: 6-8 SERVINGS

- 1 pound ground beef
- 1 large onion, chopped
- 2 garlic cloves, minced
- 1 can (29 ounces) tomato sauce
- 1 cup water
- 1 can (6 ounces) tomato paste
- 1 teaspoon salt
- 1 teaspoon dried oregano
- 1 package (8 ounces) no-cook lasagna noodles
- 4 cups (16 ounces) shredded part-skim mozzarella cheese
- 1½ cups (12 ounces) 4% cottage cheese
- ½ cup grated Parmesan cheese

1. In a skillet, cook beef and onion over medium heat until meat is no longer pink. Add garlic; cook 1 minute longer. Drain. Stir in the tomato sauce, water, tomato paste, salt and oregano.

2. Spread a fourth of the meat sauce in an ungreased 5-qt. slow cooker. Arrange a third of the noodles over sauce (break the noodles if necessary). Combine the cheeses; spoon a third of the mixture over noodles. Repeat layers twice. Top with remaining meat sauce.

3. Cover and cook on low for 4-5 hours or until noodles are tender.

Mexican Lasagna

This recipe came from my son's mother-in-law. I've made this fiesta-style lasagna for gatherings of all kinds...and I've never come home with leftovers!

—**ROSE ANN BUHLE** MINOOKA, ILLINOIS

PREP: 20 MIN. • **BAKE:** 65 MIN. + STANDING
MAKES: 12 SERVINGS

- 2 **pounds ground beef**
- 1 **can (16 ounces) refried beans**
- 1 **can (4 ounces) chopped green chilies**
- 1 **envelope taco seasoning**
- 2 **tablespoons hot salsa**
- 12 **ounces uncooked lasagna noodles**
- 4 **cups (16 ounces) shredded Colby-Monterey Jack cheese, divided**
- 1 **jar (16 ounces) mild salsa**
- 2 **cups water**
- 2 **cups (16 ounces) sour cream**
- 1 **can (2¼ ounces) sliced ripe olives, drained**
- 3 **green onions, chopped**
- 1 **medium tomato, chopped, optional**

1. Preheat oven to 350°. In a large skillet, cook beef over medium heat until no longer pink; drain. Stir in beans, chilies, taco seasoning and hot salsa.

2. In a greased 13x9-in. baking dish, layer a third of the noodles and meat mixture. Sprinkle with 1 cup of cheese. Repeat layers twice.

3. Combine mild salsa and water; pour over top. Cover and bake 1 hour or until heated through.

4. Top with sour cream, olives, onions, tomatoes if desired and remaining cheese. Bake, uncovered, 5 minutes. Let stand 10-15 minutes before cutting.

Shrimp & Macaroni Casserole

Mac and cheese goes upscale in this deliciously cheesy variation. The shrimp gives a unique taste twist while spinach adds color to this popular mainstay.

—**MICHAEL COHEN** LOS ANGELES, CALIFORNIA

PREP: 20 MIN. • **BAKE:** 20 MIN. • **MAKES:** 3 SERVINGS

- 1 **cup uncooked elbow macaroni**
- 1 **egg**
- ¼ **cup half-and-half cream**
- 2 **tablespoons butter, melted**
- ½ **cup grated Parmesan cheese**
- ¾ **cup shredded part-skim mozzarella cheese, divided**
- 1 **garlic clove, minced**
- ¼ **teaspoon salt**
- ⅛ **teaspoon pepper**
- ¼ **pound uncooked shrimp, peeled, deveined and chopped**
- ¾ **cup chopped fresh spinach**

1. Cook macaroni according to package directions. Meanwhile, in a small bowl, combine the egg, cream and butter; set aside. Drain macaroni. Add the Parmesan cheese, ½ cup mozzarella cheese, garlic, salt, pepper and reserved egg mixture; toss to coat. Stir in shrimp and spinach.

2. Transfer to a 1-qt. baking dish coated with cooking spray. Sprinkle with remaining mozzarella cheese. Bake, uncovered, at 350° for 20-25 minutes or until shrimp turn pink and cheese is melted.

Black Bean Tortilla Pie

This Southwestern entree makes a great meatless meal. Even my young daughter considers it among her favorites. The corn adds an unexpected touch of sweetness. Serve with a little salsa and a dollop of sour cream.

—WENDY KELLY VOORHEESVILLE, NEW YORK

PREP: 50 MIN. • **BAKE:** 15 MIN. • **MAKES:** 6 SERVINGS

- 1 medium onion, chopped
- 1 medium green pepper, chopped
- 1 teaspoon ground cumin
- ¼ teaspoon pepper
- 1 tablespoon olive oil
- 3 garlic cloves, minced
- 2 cans (15 ounces each) black beans, rinsed and drained
- 1 can (14½ ounces) vegetable broth
- 1 package (10 ounces) frozen corn, thawed
- 4 green onions, thinly sliced
- 4 flour tortillas (8 inches)
- 1 cup (4 ounces) shredded reduced-fat cheddar cheese, divided

1. In a large skillet, saute the onion, green pepper, cumin and pepper in oil until vegetables are tender. Add garlic; cook 1 minute longer. Add beans and broth. Bring to a boil; cook until liquid is reduced to about ⅓ cup. Stir in corn and green onions; remove from the heat.

2. Place one tortilla in a 9-in. springform pan coated with cooking spray. Layer with 1½ cups bean mixture and ¼ cup cheese. Repeat layers twice. Top with remaining tortilla. Place pan on a baking sheet.

3. Bake, uncovered, at 400° for 15-20 minutes or until heated through. Remove sides of pan. Sprinkle with remaining cheese. Cut the pie into wedges.

❝Wonderful recipe! I made this, and my entire family raved about it. The only change I made was to add twice the amount of cheese.❞

—SWAGNER FROM TASTEOFHOME.COM

Chicken 'n' Hash Brown Bake

The first time I served this dish for company was to a family with five children. Both the kids and adults loved it! This is one recipe I often make for potlucks—it goes a long way, and all ages enjoy it.

—RUTH ANDREWSON LEAVENWORTH, WASHINGTON

PREP: 10 MIN. • **BAKE:** 50 MIN. • **MAKES:** 8-10 SERVINGS

- 1 package (32 ounces) frozen cubed hash brown potatoes, thawed
- 1 teaspoon salt
- ¼ teaspoon pepper
- 4 cups diced cooked chicken
- 1 can (4 ounces) mushroom stems and pieces, drained
- 1 cup (8 ounces) sour cream
- 2 cups chicken broth or stock
- 1 can (10¾ ounces) condensed cream of chicken soup, undiluted
- 2 teaspoons chicken bouillon granules
- 2 tablespoons finely chopped onion
- 2 tablespoons finely chopped sweet red pepper
- 1 garlic clove, minced
  Paprika
- ¼ cup sliced almonds

1. Spread potatoes in an ungreased 13x9-in. baking dish. Sprinkle with salt and pepper. Sprinkle chicken and mushrooms over the top. Combine the sour cream, broth, soup, bouillon, onion, red pepper and garlic; pour over mushrooms.

2. Sprinkle casserole with paprika and almonds. Bake, uncovered, at 350° for 50-60 minutes or until heated through.

FAST FIX ▶ # Bacon Cheeseburger Pasta

I try to make foods that are not only kid-friendly, but are also easy to reheat since my husband works long hours and often eats later than our children. If you like, use reduced-fat cheese and ground turkey for a lighter version.

—MELISSA STEVENS ELK RIVER, MINNESOTA

PREP/TOTAL TIME: 30 MIN. • **MAKES:** 4-6 SERVINGS

- 8 ounces uncooked penne pasta
- 1 pound ground beef
- 6 bacon strips, diced
- 1 can (10¾ ounces) condensed tomato soup, undiluted
- ½ cup water
- 1 cup (4 ounces) shredded cheddar cheese
  Barbecue sauce and prepared mustard, optional

1. Cook pasta according to package directions. Meanwhile, in a large skillet, cook beef over medium heat until no longer pink; drain and set aside.

2. In the same skillet, cook bacon until crisp; remove with a slotted spoon to paper towels to drain. Discard drippings. Drain pasta; add to the skillet. Stir in the soup, water, beef and bacon; heat through.

3. Remove from the heat and sprinkle with cheese. Cover and let stand for 2-3 minutes or until the cheese is melted. Serve the pasta with barbecue sauce and mustard if desired.

OVEN-BAKED BACON

Instead of frying bacon, lay strips on a jelly-roll pan and bake at 350° for about 30 minutes. Prepared this way, bacon comes out crisp and flat. Plus, the pan cleans easily, and there's no stove-top spattering.

FAST FIX ▶ Chili Mac

Family and friends love this good-for-you recipe. I use three power foods: tomatoes, black beans and olive oil, plus whole wheat pasta. It's comfort food to feel good about!
—**KRISSY BLACK** MT. VERNON, OHIO

PREP/TOTAL TIME: 30 MIN. • **MAKES:** 6 SERVINGS

- 2 cups uncooked whole wheat elbow macaroni
- 1 pound lean ground turkey
- 1 small onion, chopped
- 2 to 3 jalapeno peppers, seeded and chopped
- 2 teaspoons olive oil
- 2 garlic cloves, minced
- 1 can (15 ounces) black beans, rinsed and drained
- 1 can (14½ ounces) diced tomatoes, undrained
- 1 can (8 ounces) tomato sauce
- 1 to 2 tablespoons hot pepper sauce
- 2 to 3 teaspoons chili powder
- 1 teaspoon ground cumin
- ¼ teaspoon cayenne pepper
- ¼ teaspoon pepper
- ¾ cup shredded reduced-fat cheddar cheese

1. Cook macaroni according to package directions. Meanwhile, in a large nonstick skillet coated with cooking spray, cook the turkey, onion and jalapenos in oil over medium heat until meat is no longer pink. Add garlic; cook 1 minute longer. Drain.

2. Add the beans, tomatoes, tomato sauce, pepper sauce and seasonings. Drain macaroni; stir into turkey mixture. Cook over medium-low heat for 5 minutes or until heated through.

3. Sprinkle with cheese. Remove from the heat; cover and let stand until cheese is melted.

NOTE *Wear disposable gloves when cutting hot peppers; the oils can burn skin. Avoid touching your face.*

Best Shepherd's Pie

I received the recipe for this economical dish from a friend who was a whiz at pinching pennies without sacrificing hearty flavor.
—**VALERIE MERRILL** TOPEKA, KANSAS

PREP: 20 MIN. • **BAKE:** 30 MIN. • **MAKES:** 8-10 SERVINGS

- 2½ pounds potatoes, peeled and cooked
- 1 to 1½ cups (8 to 12 ounces) sour cream
  Salt and pepper to taste
- 2 pounds ground beef
- ½ cup chopped onion
- 1 medium sweet red pepper, chopped
- 1 teaspoon garlic salt
- 1 can (10¾ ounces) condensed cream of mushroom soup, undiluted
- 1 can (16 ounces) whole kernel corn, drained
- ½ cup milk
- 2 tablespoons butter, melted
  Chopped fresh parsley, optional

1. In a large bowl, mash potatoes with sour cream. Add salt and pepper; set aside. In a large skillet, cook beef with onion and red pepper until meat is no longer pink and vegetables are tender; drain. Stir garlic salt into meat mixture. Stir in the soup, corn and milk.

2. Spread meat mixture into a 13x9-in. baking dish. Top with mashed potatoes; drizzle with butter.

3. Bake, uncovered, at 350° for 30-35 minutes or until heated through. For additional browning, place under the broiler for a few minutes. Sprinkle pie with parsley if desired.

SLOW COOKER Coconut Curry Chicken

My husband and I love this yummy dish. It's a breeze to prepare in the slow cooker, and it tastes just like a meal you'd have at your favorite Indian or Thai restaurant.

—ANDI KAUFFMAN
BEAVERCREEK, OREGON

PREP: 20 MIN. • **COOK:** 5 HOURS
MAKES: 4 SERVINGS

- 2 medium potatoes, peeled and cubed
- 1 small onion, chopped
- 4 boneless skinless chicken breast halves (4 ounces each)
- 1 cup light coconut milk
- 4 teaspoons curry powder
- 1 garlic clove, minced
- 1 teaspoon reduced-sodium chicken bouillon granules
- ¼ teaspoon salt
- ¼ teaspoon pepper
- 2 cups hot cooked rice
- ¼ cup thinly sliced green onions
  Raisins, flaked coconut and chopped unsalted peanuts, optional

1. Place potatoes and onion in a 3- or 4-qt. slow cooker. In a large nonstick skillet coated with cooking spray, brown chicken on both sides.

2. Transfer to slow cooker. In a small bowl, combine the coconut milk, curry, garlic, bouillon, salt and pepper; pour over chicken. Cover and cook on low for 5-6 hours or until meat is tender.

3. Serve chicken and sauce with rice; sprinkle with green onions. Garnish with raisins, coconut and peanuts if desired.

Chicken Noodle Casserole

This tasty entree gets even better after it's been refrigerated a day or two, so the leftovers are always superb. We eat it hot in the winter and cold in the summer.

—CHERYL WATTS
NATURAL BRIDGE, VIRGINIA

PREP: 20 MIN. • **BAKE:** 35 MIN.
MAKES: 2 CASSEROLES (8-10 SERVINGS EACH)

- 1 package (16 ounces) egg noodles
- 1 medium sweet red pepper, chopped
- 1 large onion, chopped
- 1 celery rib, chopped
- ¼ cup butter, cubed
- 2 garlic cloves, minced
- 1½ cups sliced fresh mushrooms
- 3 tablespoons all-purpose flour
- 3 cups chicken broth
- 3 cups half-and-half cream
- 2 packages (8 ounces each) cream cheese, cubed
- 12 cups cubed cooked chicken
- 1 to 1½ teaspoons salt

TOPPING
- 1 cup finely crushed cornflakes
- 2 tablespoons butter, melted
- 1 tablespoon canola oil
- 3 tablespoons minced fresh parsley
- ½ teaspoon paprika

1. Cook the noodles according to package directions; drain. In a large skillet, saute the red pepper, onion and celery in butter until tender. Add garlic; cook 1 minute longer. Add mushrooms; cook 2-3 minutes or until tender. Remove the vegetables with a slotted spoon; set aside.

2. Add flour to the skillet; stir until blended. Gradually add broth. Bring to a boil; cook and stir for 2 minutes or until thickened. Reduce heat. Gradually stir in cream. Add the cream cheese; cook and stir until cheese is melted. Remove from the heat.

3. In a large bowl, combine the chicken, salt, noodles, vegetables and cheese sauce. Transfer to two ungreased shallow 3-qt. baking dishes.

4. Combine topping ingredients. Sprinkle over top. Cover and bake casserole at 350° for 20 minutes. Uncover; bake 15-20 minutes longer or until bubbly.

Chicken Potpie

This creamy potpie is great for budget-savvy cooks, as it yields big helpings using ingredients that don't break the bank. Its satisfying taste is worth the extra effort.

—VALERIE BELLEY
ST. LOUIS, MISSOURI

PREP: 70 MIN. + COOLING
BAKE: 25 MIN. • **MAKES:** 7 SERVINGS

- 1 **broiler/fryer chicken (3 to 4 pounds), cut up**
- 4 **cups water**
- 3 **medium carrots, halved widthwise**
- 2 **medium onions, quartered**
- 4 **teaspoons chicken bouillon granules**
- 1 **bay leaf**
- ½ **pound whole fresh mushrooms**
- 2 **celery ribs, cut into 1-inch pieces**
- 3 **tablespoons butter**
- 5 **tablespoons all-purpose flour**
- ½ **cup milk**
- 1 **cup frozen peas**
- 1 **teaspoon dried basil**
- 1 **teaspoon salt**
- ¼ **teaspoon pepper**

BISCUITS
- 1½ **cups all-purpose flour**
- 2 **teaspoons baking powder**
- 2 **teaspoons sugar**
- ¼ **teaspoon salt**
- 5 **tablespoons shortening**
- ½ **cup milk**

1. Place the chicken, water, carrots, onions, bouillon and bay leaf in a Dutch oven; bring to a boil. Reduce heat; cover and simmer for 25 minutes. Add mushrooms and celery; simmer 15 minutes longer or until chicken is tender.

2. Remove chicken; allow to cool. Strain broth, reserving vegetables; skim fat. Set aside 2 cups broth (save remaining broth for another use). Discard bay leaf. Remove meat from bones; discard bones. Chop vegetables and cut chicken into bite-size pieces.

3. In a large saucepan, melt butter. Stir in flour until smooth; gradually add milk and reserved broth. Bring to a boil; cook and stir for 2 minutes or until thickened. Stir in the chicken, cooked vegetables, peas and seasonings. Pour into a greased 2-qt. baking dish; set aside.

4. For biscuits, in a large bowl, combine the flour, baking powder, sugar and salt. Cut in shortening until mixture resembles coarse crumbs. Stir in the milk just until moistened.

5. Turn onto a lightly floured surface; knead 8-10 times. Pat or roll out to ½-in. thickness; cut with a floured 2½-in. biscuit cutter.

6. Place biscuits on top of chicken mixture. Bake, uncovered at 400° for 25 minutes or until biscuits are golden brown.

Enchilada Casser-Ole!

My husband loves this casserole, but it never lasts too long around our house. Packed with black beans, cheese, tomatoes and zesty Southwest flavor, it's an impressive-looking entree that's as simple to make as it is delicious.

—MARSHA WILLS
HOMOSASSA, FLORIDA

PREP: 25 MIN. • **BAKE:** 30 MIN.
MAKES: 8 SERVINGS

- 1 **pound lean ground beef (90% lean)**
- 1 **large onion, chopped**
- 2 **cups salsa**
- 1 **can (15 ounces) black beans, rinsed and drained**
- ¼ **cup reduced-fat Italian salad dressing**
- 2 **tablespoons reduced-sodium taco seasoning**
- ¼ **teaspoon ground cumin**
- 6 **flour tortillas (8 inches)**
- ¾ **cup reduced-fat sour cream**
- 1 **cup (4 ounces) shredded reduced-fat Mexican cheese blend**
- 1 **cup shredded lettuce**
- 1 **medium tomato, chopped**
- ¼ **cup minced fresh cilantro**

1. In a large skillet, cook beef and onion over medium heat until meat is no longer pink; drain. Stir in salsa, beans, dressing, taco seasoning and cumin. Place three tortillas in an 11x7-in. baking dish coated with cooking spray. Layer with half of the meat mixture, sour cream and cheese. Repeat layers.

2. Cover and bake at 400° for 25 minutes. Uncover; bake 5-10 minutes longer or until heated through. Let stand for 5 minutes; top with lettuce, tomato and cilantro.

Cream Cheese and Swiss Lasagna

I like to fix the chunky meat sauce for this dish the day before, so the flavors can blend. It serves 12, unless you have big eaters who will definitely want seconds!
—**BETTY PEARSON** EDGEWATER, MARYLAND

PREP: 40 MIN. + SIMMERING • **BAKE:** 55 MIN. + STANDING
MAKES: 12 SERVINGS

- 1½ pounds lean ground beef (90% lean)
- 1 pound bulk Italian sausage
- 1 medium onion, finely chopped
- 3 garlic cloves, minced
- 2 cans (15 ounces each) tomato sauce
- 1 can (14½ ounces) Italian diced tomatoes, undrained
- 1 can (6 ounces) tomato paste
- 2 teaspoons dried oregano
- 1 teaspoon dried basil
- 1 teaspoon Italian seasoning
- ½ teaspoon sugar
- ½ teaspoon salt
- ¼ teaspoon pepper
- 9 no-cook lasagna noodles
- 12 ounces cream cheese, softened
- 2 cups shredded part-skim mozzarella cheese, divided
- 2 cups shredded Parmesan cheese
- 2 cups shredded Swiss cheese

1. In a Dutch oven over medium heat, cook the beef, sausage and onion until meat is no longer pink. Add garlic; cook 1 minute longer. Drain. Stir in the tomato sauce, tomatoes, tomato paste, oregano, basil, Italian seasoning, sugar, salt and pepper. Bring to a boil. Reduce heat; simmer, uncovered, for 30 minutes.

2. Spread 1 cup sauce in a greased 13x9-in. baking dish. Top with three noodles. Drop a third of the cream cheese by teaspoonfuls over the top. Sprinkle with ½ cup mozzarella and ⅔ cup each of Parmesan cheese and Swiss cheese; spoon a third of the remaining sauce over the top. Repeat with layers of noodles, cheeses and sauce twice (baking dish will be full). Place the dish on a baking sheet.

3. Cover and bake at 350° for 45 minutes. Sprinkle with remaining mozzarella cheese. Bake, uncovered, 10-15 minutes longer or until bubbly and cheese is melted. Let stand for 15 minutes before cutting.

Baked Mostaccioli

I often serve this for dinner parties. It's a homey classic that makes my guests so happy.
—**DONNA EBERT** RICHFIELD, WISCONSIN

PREP: 35 MIN. • **BAKE:** 30 MIN. • **MAKES:** 6 SERVINGS

- 8 ounces uncooked mostaccioli
- ½ pound lean ground turkey
- 1 small onion, chopped
- 1 can (14½ ounces) diced tomatoes, undrained
- 1 can (6 ounces) tomato paste
- ⅓ cup water
- 1 teaspoon dried oregano
- ½ teaspoon salt
- ⅛ teaspoon pepper
- 2 cups (16 ounces) fat-free cottage cheese
- 1 teaspoon dried marjoram
- 1½ cups (6 ounces) shredded part-skim mozzarella cheese
- ¼ cup grated Parmesan cheese

1. Cook mostaccioli according to package directions. Meanwhile, in a large saucepan, cook the turkey and onion over medium heat until meat is no longer pink; drain if necessary.

2. Stir in the tomatoes, tomato paste, water, oregano, salt and pepper. Bring to a boil. Reduce heat; cover and simmer for 15 minutes.

3. In a small bowl, combine cottage cheese and marjoram; set aside. Drain mostaccioli.

4. Spread ½ cup meat sauce into an 11x7-in. baking dish coated with cooking spray. Layer with half of the mostaccioli, meat sauce and mozzarella cheese. Top with cottage cheese mixture. Layer with remaining mostaccioli, meat sauce and mozzarella cheese. Sprinkle with Parmesan cheese (dish will be full).

5. Bake, uncovered, at 350° for 30-40 minutes or until bubbly and heated through.

Turkey Potpies

Some days, comfort-food cravings don't jibe with busy schedules. The solution: whip up a batch of these rich and creamy potpies. Enjoy two tonight and tuck the other two in the freezer for another time. When your busy night hits, you'll have a home-cooked meal on hand that's loaded with comfort and classic taste.

—TASTE OF HOME TEST KITCHEN

PREP: 30 MIN. • **BAKE:** 20 MIN. • **MAKES:** 4 SERVINGS

- 1 small onion, chopped
- 1 medium carrot, chopped
- ½ cup diced peeled potato
- ¼ cup chopped celery
- ¼ cup butter, cubed
- ⅓ cup all-purpose flour
- ½ teaspoon salt
- ½ teaspoon dried parsley flakes
- ¼ teaspoon dried rosemary, crushed
- ¼ teaspoon rubbed sage
- ¼ teaspoon pepper
- 1 cup 2% milk
- 1 cup chicken broth
- 2 cups cubed cooked turkey
- ½ cup frozen peas
- 1 sheet refrigerated pie pastry

1. In a large saucepan, saute the onion, carrot, potato and celery in butter until tender. Add the flour and seasonings until blended; gradually add milk and broth. Bring to a boil; cook and stir for 2 minutes or until thickened. Stir in turkey and peas; divide mixture among four ungreased 5-in. pie plates.

2. Divide pastry into quarters. On a lightly floured surface, roll each quarter into a 6-in. circle; place over filling. Trim, seal and flute edges; cut slits to vent.

3. Cover and freeze two potpies for up to 3 months. Bake the remaining potpies at 375° for 18-22 minutes or until golden brown. Let stand for 10 minutes before serving.

TO USE FROZEN POTPIES *Remove from the freezer 30 minutes before baking. Cover edges of crusts loosely with foil; place on a baking sheet. Bake at 375° for 30 minutes. Remove foil; bake 15-20 minutes longer or until golden brown and filling is bubbly.*

Easy Stuffed Shells

I put this recipe together one day when we had unexpected guests. It was an immediate hit and is now a family favorite. Get the kids involved when putting together this simple, savory dish.

—DOLORES BETCHNER
CUDAHY, WISCONSIN

PREP: 20 MIN. • **BAKE:** 40 MIN.
MAKES: 12 SERVINGS

- 1 package (12 ounces) jumbo pasta shells
- 1 jar (26 ounces) spaghetti sauce
- 36 frozen fully cooked Italian meatballs (½ ounce each), thawed
- 2 cups (8 ounces) shredded part-skim mozzarella cheese

1. Cook pasta according to package directions; drain and rinse in cold water. Place ½ cup sauce in a greased 13x9-in. baking dish. Place a meatball in each shell; transfer to prepared dish. Top with remaining sauce and sprinkle with cheese.
2. Cover and bake at 350° for 35 minutes. Uncover; bake 5-10 minutes longer or until bubbly and cheese is melted.

❝Made this for 'Italian night' with friends. Very easy—and a huge hit!❞
—SAM52687 FROM TASTEOFHOME.COM

FAST FIX ▸

Penne Gorgonzola with Chicken

This rich, creamy pasta dish is a snap to throw together for a weeknight meal, and I serve it to company, too. Feel free to substitute another cheese for the Gorgonzola if you like.

—GEORGE SCHROEDER
PORT MURRAY, NEW JERSEY

PREP/TOTAL TIME: 30 MIN.
MAKES: 8 SERVINGS

- 1 package (16 ounces) penne pasta
- 1 pound boneless skinless chicken breasts, cut into ½-inch pieces
- 1 tablespoon olive oil
- 1 large garlic clove, minced
- ¼ cup white wine
- 1 cup heavy whipping cream
- ¼ cup chicken broth
- 2 cups (8 ounces) crumbled Gorgonzola cheese
- 6 to 8 fresh sage leaves, thinly sliced
  Salt and pepper to taste
  Grated Parmigiano-Reggiano cheese and minced fresh parsley

1. Cook pasta according to package directions. Meanwhile, in a large skillet over medium heat, brown chicken in oil on all sides. Add garlic; cook 1 minute longer. Add wine, stirring to loosen browned bits from pan.
2. Add cream and broth; cook until sauce is slightly thickened and chicken is no longer pink. Stir in the Gorgonzola cheese, sage, salt and pepper; cook just until cheese is melted.
3. Drain pasta; toss with sauce. Sprinkle with Parmigiano-Reggiano cheese and parsley.

Cowboy Casserole

This quick and creamy Tater Tot bake is great comfort food, especially on a cool fall night.

—DONNA DONHAUSER
REMSEN, NEW YORK

PREP: 15 MIN. • **BAKE:** 20 MIN.
MAKES: 2 SERVINGS

- ½ **pound lean ground beef (90% lean)**
- 1 **can (8¾ ounces) whole kernel corn, drained**
- ⅔ **cup condensed cream of chicken soup, undiluted**
- ½ **cup shredded cheddar cheese, divided**
- ⅓ **cup 2% milk**
- 2 **tablespoons sour cream**
- ¾ **teaspoon onion powder**
- ¼ **teaspoon pepper**
- 2 **cups frozen Tater Tots**

1. In a large skillet, cook beef over medium heat until no longer pink. Stir in the corn, soup, ¼ cup cheese, milk, sour cream, onion powder and pepper.
2. Place 1 cup Tater Tots in a greased 3-cup baking dish. Layer with beef mixture and remaining Tater Tots; sprinkle casserole with the remaining cheese. Bake, uncovered, at 375° for 20-25 minutes or until bubbly.

Hamburger Noodle Bake

Cream cheese and cottage cheese nicely balance the saucy ground beef and noodles in this hearty casserole. It's been a favorite for years.

—CHARISSA DUNN
BARTLESVILLE, OKLAHOMA

PREP: 35 MIN. • **BAKE:** 20 MIN.
MAKES: 2 SERVINGS

- 2 **cups uncooked egg noodles**
- ½ **pound lean ground beef (90% lean)**
- 2 **tablespoons finely chopped onion**
- 1 **can (8 ounces) tomato sauce**
- ¼ **teaspoon sugar**
- ⅛ **teaspoon salt**
- ⅛ **teaspoon garlic salt**
  Dash pepper
- ¼ **cup cream-style cottage cheese**
- 2 **ounces cream cheese, softened**
- 1 **tablespoon thinly sliced green onion**
- 1 **tablespoon chopped green pepper**
- 1 **tablespoon sour cream**
- 2 **tablespoons grated Parmesan cheese**

1. Cook noodles according to package directions. Meanwhile, in a large skillet, cook beef and onion until meat is no longer pink; drain. Remove from the heat; stir in the tomato sauce, sugar, salt, garlic salt and pepper.
2. In a small bowl, combine the cottage cheese, cream cheese, green onion, green pepper and sour cream.
3. Drain noodles; place half of noodles in a greased 1-qt. baking dish. Spoon half of beef mixture over the top. Layer with the cottage cheese mixture and the remaining noodles. Top with the remaining beef mixture; sprinkle with the Parmesan cheese.
4. Cover and bake at 350° for 20-25 minutes or until heated through.

CARAMEL APPLE MUFFINS, PAGE 140

GARLIC KNOTS, 146

EASY MOLASSES STICKY BUNS, 146

CHOCOLATE CHIP PUMPKIN BREAD, 149

BREADS, ROLLS & MUFFINS

Nothing draws a family to the kitchen like the aroma of just-baked bread—except of course, the announcement that you're ready to slice into a warm, tasty loaf. Here you'll find just the right baked beauty to accompany your meals, whether you're looking for zippy garlic knots, chewy soft pretzels, tender dinner rolls or deliciously sweet muffins or quick breads. Best of all, most of these fresh-from-the-oven golden goodies go together in a jiffy and have a short baking time.

Jumbo Zucchini Chip Muffins

There's a hint of cinnamon in these moist, delicious treats, and the frosting is just right. For variation, omit the chips and nuts and add 12 ounces of sweetened flaked coconut.
—**SUSANNE SPICKER** NORTH OGDEN, UTAH

PREP: 30 MIN. • **BAKE:** 30 MIN. + COOLING • **MAKES:** 1 DOZEN

- 3 **cups all-purpose flour**
- 1½ **cups sugar**
- 3 **teaspoons ground cinnamon**
- 2 **teaspoons baking powder**
- 1 **teaspoon salt**
- ½ **teaspoon baking soda**
- 3 **eggs, beaten**
- ⅔ **cup canola oil**
- 3 **teaspoons vanilla extract**
- 2 **cups shredded zucchini**
- 1 **package (11½ ounces) milk chocolate chips**
- 1 **cup chopped walnuts**

MASCARPONE FROSTING
- ½ **cup butter, softened**
- 1 **package (3 ounces) cream cheese, softened**
- ⅓ **cup mascarpone cheese**
- ¼ **cup confectioners' sugar**
- ½ **teaspoon vanilla extract**
- ¼ **cup finely chopped walnuts**

1. In a large bowl, combine the first six ingredients. In another bowl, combine the eggs, oil and vanilla. Stir into dry ingredients just until moistened. Fold in zucchini, chips and walnuts.

2. Fill paper-lined jumbo muffin cups three-fourths full. Bake at 350° for 30-35 minutes or until a toothpick inserted near the center comes out clean. Cool for 5 minutes before removing from pans to wire racks to cool completely.

3. In a large bowl, beat the butter, cream cheese and mascarpone cheese until fluffy. Add confectioners' sugar and vanilla; beat until smooth. Pipe a dollop of frosting onto each muffin. Sprinkle with walnuts.

Caramel Apple Muffins

Caramel apple lovers will fall for these dessert-like muffins. They're great served with a hot cup of joe.
—**THERESE PUCKETT** SHREVEPORT, LOUISIANA

PREP: 25 MIN. • **BAKE:** 20 MIN. • **MAKES:** 14 MUFFINS

- 2 **cups all-purpose flour**
- ¾ **cup sugar**
- 2 **teaspoons baking powder**
- 2½ **teaspoons ground cinnamon**
- ½ **teaspoon salt**
- 1 **egg**
- 1 **cup 2% milk**
- ¼ **cup butter, melted**
- 2 **teaspoons vanilla extract**
- ½ **cup chopped peeled tart apple**
- 12 **caramels, chopped**

TOPPING
- ½ **cup packed brown sugar**
- ¼ **cup quick-cooking oats**
- 3 **tablespoons butter, melted**
- 1 **teaspoon ground cinnamon**

1. In a large bowl, combine the flour, sugar, baking powder, cinnamon and salt. In another bowl, whisk the egg, milk, butter and vanilla. Stir into dry ingredients just until moistened. Fold in apple and caramels.

2. Fill paper-lined muffin cups three-fourths full. Combine topping ingredients; sprinkle over batter.

3. Bake at 350° for 20-25 minutes or until a toothpick inserted in cake portion comes out clean. Cool for 5 minutes before removing from pans to wire racks. Serve warm.

Gluten-Free Pizza Crust

Didn't think a gluten-free diet could include pizza? With this inventive crust, gluten-intolerant kids and adults can indulge in their favorite pie.

—SYLVIA GIRMUS TORRINGTON, WYOMING

PREP: 20 MIN. + STANDING • **BAKE:** 20 MIN.
MAKES: 6 SERVINGS

- 1 tablespoon active dry yeast
- ⅔ cup warm water (110° to 115°)
- ½ cup tapioca flour
- 2 tablespoons nonfat dry milk powder
- 2 teaspoons xanthan gum
- 1 teaspoon unflavored gelatin
- 1 teaspoon Italian seasoning
- 1 teaspoon cider vinegar
- 1 teaspoon olive oil
- ½ teaspoon salt
- ½ teaspoon sugar
- 1 to 1⅓ cups brown rice flour
  Pizza toppings of your choice

1. In a small bowl, dissolve yeast in warm water. Add the tapioca flour, milk powder, xanthan gum, gelatin, Italian seasoning, vinegar, oil, salt, sugar and ⅔ cup brown rice flour. Beat until smooth. Stir in enough remaining brown rice flour to form a soft dough (dough will be sticky).

2. On a floured surface, roll dough into a 13-in. circle. Transfer to a 12-in. pizza pan coated with cooking spray; build up edges slightly. Cover and let rest for 10 minutes.

3. Bake at 425° for 10-12 minutes or until golden brown. Add toppings of your choice. Bake 10-15 minutes longer or until crust is golden brown and toppings are lightly browned and heated through.

NOTE *Read all ingredient labels for possible gluten content prior to use. Ingredient formulas can change, and production facilities vary among brands. If you're concerned that your brand may contain gluten, contact the company.*

"We made this tonight for the first time, and the kids loved it! We have only two members of the family that are gluten-free, but everyone said it was the best we had made so far."

—BECKERS68 FROM TASTEOFHOME.COM

Apple Crisp Muffins

Waking up to the smell of apple muffins will start your family's day off right. Cream cheese filling makes them moist and tender, and oats and nuts in the topping add crunch.

—CONNIE BOLL CHILTON, WISCONSIN

PREP: 30 MIN. • **BAKE:** 20 MIN. • **MAKES:** 1 DOZEN

- 2 **cups all-purpose flour**
- ⅓ **cup packed brown sugar**
- 2 **teaspoons baking powder**
- ½ **teaspoon salt**
- ½ **teaspoon ground cinnamon**
- 1 **egg, beaten**
- 1 **cup 2% milk**
- ½ **cup canola oil**
- 2 **cups finely chopped peeled apples**

FILLING
- 1 **package (8 ounces) cream cheese, softened**
- 2 **tablespoons maple syrup**
- 4 **teaspoons grated orange peel**
- ¼ **teaspoon ground nutmeg**

TOPPING
- ¼ **cup all-purpose flour**
- ¼ **cup old-fashioned oats**
- ¼ **cup packed brown sugar**
- ¼ **teaspoon ground cinnamon**
- 3 **tablespoons cold butter**
- ¼ **cup chopped pecans**

1. In a large bowl, combine the flour, sugar, baking powder, salt and cinnamon. In another bowl, combine the egg, milk and oil. Stir into dry ingredients just until moistened. Fold in apples. Fill greased or paper-lined muffin cups three-fourths full.

2. In a small bowl, beat the filling ingredients until smooth. Drop by tablespoonfuls into centers of muffins.

3. For topping, in a small bowl, combine the flour, oats, brown sugar and cinnamon. Cut in butter until crumbly. Stir in pecans. Sprinkle over filling. Bake at 400° for 16-20 minutes or until a toothpick inserted in muffin comes out clean. Cool for 5 minutes before removing from pan to wire rack.

Lemon Meringue Muffins

These muffins taste like lemon meringue pie—my favorite dessert. The fluffy meringue adds a unique twist.
—**NANCY KEARNEY** MASSILLON, OHIO

PREP: 25 MIN. • **BAKE:** 25 MIN. • **MAKES:** 1 DOZEN

- 6 **tablespoons butter, softened**
- 1 **cup sugar, divided**
- 2 **eggs**
- ½ **cup plain yogurt**
- 2 **tablespoons lemon juice**
- 1 **tablespoon grated lemon peel**
- ¼ **teaspoon lemon extract**
- 1⅓ **cups all-purpose flour**
- ½ **teaspoon baking powder**
- ½ **teaspoon baking soda**
- 2 **egg whites**

1. In a large bowl, cream butter and ⅔ cup sugar until light and fluffy. Add eggs, one at a time, beating well after each addition. Beat in the yogurt, lemon juice, peel and extract. Combine the flour, baking powder and baking soda; add to creamed mixture just until moistened.

2. Fill greased or paper-lined muffin cups three-fourths full. Bake at 350° for 18 minutes. Meanwhile, in a small bowl, beat egg whites on medium speed until soft peaks form. Gradually beat in remaining sugar, 1 tablespoon at a time, on high until stiff glossy peaks form and sugar is dissolved.

3. Transfer meringue to a heavy-duty resealable plastic bag; cut a small hole in a corner of bag. Pipe onto muffins. Bake 5-8 minutes longer or until meringue is golden brown and a toothpick inserted into the muffin comes out clean. Cool for 5 minutes before removing from pan to a wire rack. Serve warm. Refrigerate leftovers.

Surprise Monkey Bread

This recipe is traditional Monkey Bread gone wild! I also sometimes make it with garlic and cheese for a savory spin.
—**LOIS RUTHERFORD** ELKTON, FLORIDA

PREP: 25 MIN. • **BAKE:** 40 MIN. • **MAKES:** 1 LOAF (12 SERVINGS)

- 1 **cup packed brown sugar**
- ½ **cup butter, cubed**
- 2 **tubes (12 ounces each) refrigerated flaky buttermilk biscuits**
- ½ **cup sugar**
- 1 **tablespoon ground cinnamon**
- 1 **package (8 ounces) cream cheese, cut into 20 cubes**
- 1½ **cups chopped walnuts**

1. In a small microwave-safe bowl, heat brown sugar and butter on high for 1 minute or until sugar is dissolved; set aside.

2. Flatten each biscuit into a 3-in. circle. Combine sugar and cinnamon; sprinkle ½ teaspoon in the center of each biscuit. Top with a cream cheese cube. Fold dough over filling; pinch edges to seal tightly.

3. Sprinkle ½ cup walnuts into a 10-in. fluted tube pan coated with cooking spray. Layer with half of the biscuits, cinnamon-sugar and butter mixture and ½ cup walnuts. Repeat layers.

4. Bake at 350° for 40-45 minutes or until golden brown. Immediately invert onto a serving platter. Serve warm. Refrigerate leftovers.

Multi-Grain Cinnamon Rolls

This quick and easy recipe is sure to become a family favorite. And the wholesome cinnamon rolls will fill your kitchen with a wonderful, warm aroma.
—**JUDY EDDY** BALDWIN CITY, KANSAS

PREP: 30 MIN. + RISING • **BAKE:** 15 MIN. • **MAKES:** 1 DOZEN

- 1 **package (¼ ounce) active dry yeast**
- ¾ **cup warm water (110° to 115°)**
- ½ **cup quick-cooking oats**
- ½ **cup whole wheat flour**
- ¼ **cup packed brown sugar**
- 2 **tablespoons butter, melted**
- 1 **egg**
- 1 **teaspoon salt**
- 1¾ to 2¼ **cups all-purpose flour**

FILLING
- 3 **tablespoons butter, softened**
- ⅓ **cup sugar**
- 2 **teaspoons ground cinnamon**

GLAZE
- 1 **cup confectioners' sugar**
- 6½ **teaspoons half-and-half cream**
- 4½ **teaspoons butter, softened**

1. In a large bowl, dissolve yeast in warm water. Add the oats, whole wheat flour, brown sugar, butter, egg, salt and 1 cup all-purpose flour. Beat on medium speed until smooth. Stir in enough remaining flour to form a soft dough (dough will be sticky).

2. Turn onto a lightly floured surface; knead until smooth and elastic, about 6-8 minutes. Place in a bowl coated with cooking spray, turning once to coat the top. Cover and let rise in a warm place until doubled, about 1 hour.

3. Punch dough down. Roll into an 18x12-in. rectangle; spread with butter. Combine sugar and cinnamon; sprinkle over dough to within ½ in. of edges.

4. Roll up jelly-roll style, starting with a short side; pinch seams to seal. Cut into 12 slices. Place cut sides down in a 13x9-in. baking pan coated with cooking spray. Cover and let rise until doubled, about 45 minutes.

5. Bake at 375° for 15-20 minutes or until golden brown. For icing, in a small bowl, beat the confectioners' sugar, cream and butter until smooth. Drizzle over warm rolls.

No-Knead Whole Wheat Rolls

Tender and moist, these whole wheat rolls boast a fresh herb flavor. They make a great dinner sidekick.
—**DEBORAH PATRAUCHUK** SICAMOUS, BRITISH COLUMBIA

PREP: 15 MIN. + RISING • **BAKE:** 10 MIN. • **MAKES:** 1 DOZEN

- 1 **package (¼ ounce) active dry yeast**
- 1¼ **cups warm water (110° to 115°)**
- 2 **cups all-purpose flour**
- 1 **cup whole wheat flour**
- 2 **tablespoons butter, softened**
- 1 **tablespoon honey**
- 1 **tablespoon molasses**
- 1 **teaspoon salt**
- 1 **teaspoon Italian seasoning**

1. In a large bowl, dissolve yeast in warm water. Add the remaining ingredients. Beat on medium speed for 3 minutes (dough will be sticky). Do not knead. Cover and let rise in a warm place until doubled, about 30 minutes.

2. Stir dough down. Set aside ¼ cup batter. Fill muffin cups coated with nonstick cooking spray half full. Top each with 1 teaspoon reserved batter. Cover and let rise until doubled, about 8-12 minutes.

3. Bake at 375° for 10-15 minutes or until golden brown. Cool for 1 minute before removing from pan to a wire rack.

Mom's Italian Bread

I think Mom used to bake at least four of these tender loaves at once, and they never lasted long. She served the bread with every Italian meal. I love it toasted, buttered and sprinkled with garlic salt.

—LINDA HARRINGTON WINDHAM, NEW HAMPSHIRE

PREP: 30 MIN. + RISING • **BAKE:** 20 MIN. + COOLING
MAKES: 2 LOAVES (12 SLICES EACH)

- 1 package (¼ ounce) active dry yeast
- 2 cups warm water (110° to 115°)
- 1 teaspoon sugar
- 2 teaspoons salt
- 5½ cups all-purpose flour

1. In a large bowl, dissolve yeast in warm water. Add sugar, salt and 3 cups flour. Beat on medium speed for 3 minutes. Stir in remaining flour to form a soft dough.
2. Turn onto a floured surface; knead until smooth and elastic, about 6-8 minutes. Place in a greased bowl, turning once to grease the top. Cover and let rise in a warm place until doubled, about 1 hour.
3. Punch dough down. Turn onto a floured surface; divide in half. Shape each portion into a loaf. Place each loaf seam side down on a greased baking sheet. Cover and let rise until doubled, about 30 minutes. With a sharp knife, make four shallow slashes across top of each loaf.
4. Bake at 400° for 20-25 minutes or until golden brown. Remove from pans to wire racks to cool.

Everything Bread

I love to make bread from scratch, and this has become one of my tried-and-true favorites to serve with any meal, casual or formal.

—TRACI WYNNE DENVER, PENNSYLVANIA

PREP: 45 MIN. + RISING • **BAKE:** 25 MIN.
MAKES: 1 LOAF (25 SLICES)

- 1 package (¼ ounce) active dry yeast
- ¾ cup warm water (110° to 115°)
- 1 cup warm 2% milk (110° to 115°)
- ¼ cup butter, softened
- 2 tablespoons sugar
- 1 egg yolk
- 1½ teaspoons salt
- 4 to 4½ cups all-purpose flour
- 1 egg white
- 2 teaspoons water
- 1 teaspoon coarse sea salt or kosher salt
- 1 teaspoon dried minced onion
- 1 teaspoon each sesame, caraway and poppy seeds

1. In a large bowl, dissolve yeast in warm water. Add the milk, butter, sugar, egg yolk, salt and 2 cups flour. Beat on medium speed for 3 minutes. Stir in enough remaining flour to form a firm dough.
2. Turn onto a floured surface; knead until smooth and elastic, about 6-8 minutes. Place in a greased bowl, turning once to grease the top. Cover and let rise until doubled, about 1 hour.
3. Punch dough down. Turn onto a lightly floured surface; divide dough into thirds. Shape each into a 20-in. rope. Place ropes on a large greased baking sheet and braid; pinch ends to seal and tuck under. Cover and let rise until doubled, about 45 minutes.
4. Combine egg white and water; brush over dough. Combine the salt, onion and seeds; sprinkle over bread. Bake at 375° for 22-28 minutes or until golden brown. Remove from pan to a wire rack to cool.

FAST FIX ▶ Garlic Knots

Here's a handy bread that can be made in no time flat. Refrigerated biscuits make preparation simple. The Italian flavors complement a variety of meals.

—JANE PASCHKE
UNIVERSITY PARK, FLORIDA

PREP/TOTAL TIME: 30 MIN.
MAKES: 2½ DOZEN

- 1 tube (12 ounces) refrigerated buttermilk biscuits
- ¼ cup canola oil
- 3 tablespoons grated Parmesan cheese
- 1 teaspoon garlic powder
- 1 teaspoon dried oregano
- 1 teaspoon dried parsley flakes

1. Cut each biscuit into thirds. Roll each piece into a 3-in. rope and tie into a knot; tuck ends under. Place 2 in. apart on a greased baking sheet. Bake at 400° for 8-10 minutes or until golden brown.
2. In a large bowl, combine the remaining ingredients; add the warm knots and gently toss to coat.

Bacon Pull-Apart Bread

I made this tender and tasty bread for my husband, and he loved it! Out of bacon? Just substitute bacon bits.

—TERRI CHRISTENSEN
MONTAGUE, MICHIGAN

PREP: 15 MIN. • **BAKE:** 25 MIN.
MAKES: 12 SERVINGS

- 12 bacon strips, diced
- 2 tubes (12 ounces each) refrigerated buttermilk biscuits
- 2 cups (8 ounces) shredded part-skim mozzarella cheese
- 1 tablespoon Italian salad dressing mix
- 2 teaspoons olive oil

1. In a large skillet, cook bacon over medium heat until cooked but not crisp. Using a slotted spoon, remove to paper towels to drain. Separate biscuits; cut each biscuit into quarters.
2. In a large bowl, combine the cheese, dressing mix, oil and bacon. Place half of the biscuit pieces in a greased 10-in. fluted tube pan; sprinkle with half of the cheese mixture. Top with the remaining biscuit pieces and cheese mixture.
3. Bake at 375° for 25-30 minutes or until golden brown. Cool for 5 minutes before inverting onto a serving plate. Serve immediately.

Easy Molasses Sticky Buns

Sleepyheads will leap out of bed when they catch the first whiff of these ooey-gooey caramel rolls baking in the oven. They make a fabulous breakfast for Thanksgiving or Christmas morning. I guarantee these tender treats taste as delicious as they look!

—NANCY FOUST
STONEBORO, PENNSYLVANIA

PREP: 20 MIN. + RISING
BAKE: 25 MIN. • **MAKES:** 1 DOZEN

- 2 loaves (16 ounces each) frozen bread dough, thawed
- ⅓ cup butter, softened
- ½ cup sugar
- 1½ teaspoons ground cinnamon
- **MOLASSES SAUCE**
- 1 cup packed brown sugar
- ½ cup butter, cubed
- ½ cup water
- ¼ cup molasses

1. Roll out each loaf of bread dough into a 10-in. square. Spread with butter to within ½ in. of edges. Combine sugar and cinnamon; sprinkle over butter. Roll up jelly-roll style; pinch seams to seal. Cut each loaf into six slices.
2. For sauce, in a small saucepan, bring the brown sugar, butter, water and molasses to a boil. Pour into a greased 13x9-in. baking dish. Place rolls, cut side down, in molasses sauce.
3. Cover and let rise in a warm place until doubled, about 30 minutes. Bake at 350° for 25-30 minutes or until golden brown. Cool in dish for 5 minutes; invert onto a serving platter. Serve warm.

Chewy Soft Pretzels

These homemade pretzels never last long around our house. My kids love them more than any mall variety. I serve them to company with a variety of dips, such as pizza sauce, ranch dressing, spinach dip or hot mustard.

—ELVIRA MARTENS
ALDERGROVE, BRITISH COLUMBIA

PREP: 1 HOUR + RISING • **BAKE:** 15 MIN.
MAKES: 1 DOZEN

- 1 package (¼ ounce) active dry yeast
- 1½ cups warm water (110° to 115°)
- 1 tablespoon sugar
- 2 teaspoons salt
- 4 to 4¼ cups all-purpose flour
- 8 cups water
- ½ cup baking soda
- 1 egg, lightly beaten
  Kosher salt, sesame seeds, poppy seeds or grated Parmesan cheese

1. In a large bowl, dissolve yeast in warm water. Add the sugar, salt and 2 cups flour; beat until smooth. Stir in enough remaining flour to form a stiff dough.

2. Turn onto a floured surface; knead until smooth and elastic, about 5 minutes. Place in a greased bowl, turning once to grease top. Cover and let rise in a warm place until doubled, about 1 hour.

3. Punch dough down; divide into 12 portions. Roll each into an 18-in. rope; twist into a pretzel shape.

4. In a large saucepan, bring water and baking soda to a boil. Place pretzels into boiling water, one at a time, for 30 seconds. Remove with a slotted spoon; drain on paper towels.

5. Place on greased baking sheets. Brush with egg; sprinkle with desired topping.

6. Bake at 425° for 12-14 minutes or until golden brown. Remove from pans to wire racks. Serve warm.

BOILING SOFT PRETZELS

Boiling the pretzels in water before baking helps create the chewy texture we associate with soft pretzels. Adding baking soda to the water gives the surface of the pretzels a shiny appearance, helps with browning and intensifies the flavor.

Monkey Muffins

These bite-size mini muffins will be a favorite with your family and friends—or anyone who's nuts for bananas, peanut butter and chocolate! It's a nice way to use up a supply of overripe bananas.

—AMIE LONGSTAFF PAINESVILLE TOWNSHIP, OHIO

PREP: 20 MIN. • **BAKE:** 15 MIN./BATCH • **MAKES:** 6 DOZEN

- ½ cup butter, softened
- 1 cup plus 1 tablespoon sugar, divided
- 2 eggs
- 1 cup mashed ripe bananas
- ⅔ cup peanut butter
- 1 tablespoon milk
- 1 teaspoon vanilla extract
- 2 cups all-purpose flour
- 1 teaspoon baking soda
- ½ teaspoon salt
- ¾ cup miniature semisweet chocolate chips

1. In a large bowl, cream butter and 1 cup sugar until light and fluffy. Add eggs, one at a time, beating well after each addition. Beat in the bananas, peanut butter, milk and vanilla. Combine the flour, baking soda and salt; add to creamed mixture just until moistened. Fold in chips.

2. Fill greased or paper-lined miniature muffin cups three-fourths full. Sprinkle with remaining sugar. Bake at 350° for 14-16 minutes or until a toothpick inserted near the center comes out clean. Cool for 5 minutes before removing from pans to wire racks. Serve warm.

NOTE *To freeze, wrap muffins in foil and freeze for up to 3 months.*

TO USE FROZEN MUFFINS *Thaw at room temperature. Warm if desired.*

Lambertville Station Coconut Bread

Hearty bread made with toasted coconut is a long-time specialty at Lambertville Station. Enjoy this sweet treat the next time you crave a distinctive bakery treat.

—LAMBERTVILLE STATION RESTAURANT & INN LAMBERTVILLE, NEW JERSEY

PREP: 10 MIN. • **BAKE:** 40 MIN. + COOLING
MAKES: 1 LOAF (16 SLICES)

- 3 cups all-purpose flour
- 1 cup sugar
- 3 teaspoons baking powder
- ¾ teaspoon salt
- 1 egg
- 1½ cups milk
- ¾ teaspoon vanilla extract
- ¼ teaspoon almond extract
- 1 cup flaked coconut, toasted

1. In a large bowl, combine the flour, sugar, baking powder and salt. Combine the egg, milk and extracts. Stir into dry ingredients just until moistened. Fold in the coconut.

2. Transfer to a greased 9x5-in. loaf pan. Bake at 350° for 40-50 minutes or until a toothpick comes out clean. Cool for 10 minutes before removing from pan to a wire rack.

❝This bread comes out moist and delicious! I have been to the Lambertville Station many times, and I love their coconut bread.❞

—RABBIT391 FROM TASTEOFHOME.COM

Homemade Tortillas

I have to double this recipe for these tender, chewy and simple tortillas because we go through them so quickly. I guarantee you'll never use store-bought again.

—KRISTIN VAN DYKEN WEST RICHLAND, WASHINGTON

PREP/TOTAL TIME: 30 MIN. • **MAKES:** 8 TORTILLAS

- 2 **cups all-purpose flour**
- ½ **teaspoon salt**
- ¾ **cup water**
- 3 **tablespoons olive oil**

1. In a large bowl, combine flour and salt. Stir in water and oil. Turn onto a floured surface; knead 10-12 times, adding a little flour or water if needed to achieve a smooth dough. Let rest for 10 minutes.
2. Divide dough into eight portions. On a lightly floured surface, roll each portion into a 7-in. circle.
3. In a large nonstick skillet coated with cooking spray, cook tortillas over medium heat for 1 minute on each side or until lightly browned. Keep warm.

Party Cheese Bread

You can't go wrong with this cheesy, buttery, finger-licking-good bread! It looks fantastic, and guests flock to it when I set it out on my party spread. It's simple to make and tastes great with pasta dinners, too.

—KAREN GRANT TULARE, CALIFORNIA

PREP: 25 MIN. • **BAKE:** 25 MIN. • **MAKES:** 8 SERVINGS

- ½ **cup butter, melted**
- 2 **tablespoons lemon juice**
- 2 **tablespoons Dijon mustard**
- 1½ **teaspoons garlic powder**
- ½ **teaspoon onion powder**
- ½ **teaspoon celery salt**
- 1 **round loaf sourdough bread (1 pound)**
- 1 **pound Monterey Jack cheese, thinly sliced**

1. In a small bowl, combine the first six ingredients; set aside. Cut bread diagonally into 1-in. slices to within ½ in. of bottom of loaf. Repeat cuts in opposite direction. Arrange cheese slices in cuts. Drizzle butter mixture over bread.
2. Wrap loaf in foil; place on a baking sheet. Bake at 350° for 15 minutes. Uncover; bake 10 minutes longer or until cheese is melted.

Chocolate Chip Pumpkin Bread

A touch of cinnamon accents the chocolate and pumpkin in this tender bread. Because the recipe makes two loaves, I take one to a bake sale and keep one to enjoy at home.

—LORA STANLEY BENNINGTON, KANSAS

PREP: 15 MIN. • **BAKE:** 1 HOUR + COOLING
MAKES: 2 LOAVES (16 SLICES EACH)

- 3 **cups all-purpose flour**
- 2 **teaspoons ground cinnamon**
- 1 **teaspoon salt**
- 1 **teaspoon baking soda**
- 4 **eggs**
- 2 **cups sugar**
- 2 **cups canned pumpkin**
- 1½ **cups canola oil**
- 1½ **cups (6 ounces) semisweet chocolate chips**

1. In a large bowl, combine the flour, cinnamon, salt and baking soda. In another bowl, beat the eggs, sugar, pumpkin and oil. Stir into dry ingredients just until moistened. Fold in chocolate chips.
2. Pour into two greased 8x4-in. loaf pans. Bake at 350° for 60-70 minutes or until a toothpick inserted near the center comes out clean. Cool for 10 minutes before removing from pans to wire racks.

Peanut Butter 'n' Jelly Muffins

Nothing beats the classic peanut butter and jelly combo. These yummy muffins bake up easily, and kids love the fruity surprise inside.
—TASTE OF HOME TEST KITCHEN

PREP: 10 MIN. **BAKE:** 15 MIN. + COOLING
MAKES: 1 DOZEN

- 2 **cups all-purpose flour**
- 2 **teaspoons baking powder**
- ¾ **teaspoon baking soda**
- ¼ **teaspoon salt**
- 2 **eggs**
- ¾ **cup thawed apple juice concentrate**
- ½ **cup reduced-fat chunky peanut butter**
- ¼ **cup fat-free milk**
- 3 **tablespoons butter, melted**
- ⅓ **cup strawberry spreadable fruit**

1. In a large bowl, combine the flour, baking powder, baking soda and salt. Combine the eggs, apple juice concentrate, peanut butter, milk and butter; stir into dry ingredients just until moistened.
2. Coat 12 muffin cups with cooking spray. Spoon half of the batter into cups. Spoon about 1¼ teaspoons spreadable fruit into the center of each; top with remaining batter.
3. Bake at 350° for 15-20 minutes or until a toothpick inserted into muffin comes out clean. Cool for 5 minutes before removing from pan to a wire rack to cool completely.

40-Minute Hamburger Buns

Here on our ranch, I cook for three men who love hamburgers. These fluffy yet hearty buns are just right for their big appetites. I also sometimes serve the buns plain in place of regular dinner rolls.

—JESSIE MCKENNEY
TWODOT, MONTANA

PREP: 20 MIN. + RESTING
BAKE: 10 MIN. • **MAKES:** 1 DOZEN

- 2 **tablespoons active dry yeast**
- 1 **cup plus 2 tablespoons warm water (110° to 115°)**
- ⅓ **cup vegetable oil**
- ¼ **cup sugar**
- 1 **egg**
- 1 **teaspoon salt**
- 3 **to 3½ cups all-purpose flour**

1. In a large bowl, dissolve the yeast in warm water. Add oil and sugar; let stand for 5 minutes. Add the egg, salt and enough flour to form a soft dough.
2. Turn onto a floured surface; knead until smooth and elastic, about 3-5 minutes. Do not let rise. Divide into 12 pieces; shape each into a ball. Place 3 in. apart on greased baking sheets.
3. Cover and let rest for 10 minutes. Bake at 425° for 8-12 minutes or until golden brown. Remove from pans to wire racks to cool.

ACTIVE DRY YEAST VS. QUICK-RISE YEAST

Active dry yeast and quick-rise yeast can be substituted for each other in recipes. However, quick-rise yeast does not need to be dissolved in water before mixing, and it requires only one rise. In place of the first rise, let dough rest, covered, for 10 minutes before shaping. Once shaped, the dough's rise should take about half the time listed in a recipe that calls for active dry yeast.

Lemon-Blueberry Muffins

Bursting with berries and drizzled with a light lemony glaze, these muffins are moist, tender and truly something special. They're great for brunch or to enjoy as an afternoon snack with a cup of tea or coffee.

—KATHY HARDING
RICHMOND, MISSOURI

PREP: 30 MIN. • **BAKE:** 25 MIN.
MAKES: 11 MUFFINS

- ½ cup butter, softened
- 1 cup sugar
- 2 eggs
- ½ cup 2% milk
- 2 tablespoons lemon juice
- 2 teaspoons grated lemon peel
- 2 cups all-purpose flour
- 2 teaspoons baking powder
  Dash salt
- 2 cups fresh or frozen blueberries

GLAZE
- 1½ cups confectioners' sugar
- 2 tablespoons lemon juice
- 1 teaspoon butter, melted
- ¼ teaspoon vanilla extract

1. In a large bowl, cream butter and sugar until light and fluffy. Add eggs, one at a time, beating well after each addition. Beat in the milk, lemon juice and peel. Combine the flour, baking powder and salt; add to creamed mixture just until moistened. Fold in blueberries.

2. Fill paper-lined muffin cups three-fourths full. Bake at 400° for 25-30 minutes or until a toothpick inserted in muffin comes out clean. Cool for 5 minutes before removing from pan to a wire rack.

3. In a small bowl, combine the confectioners' sugar, lemon juice, butter and vanilla; drizzle over warm muffins.

NOTE: *If using frozen blueberries, use without thawing to avoid discoloring the batter.*

Bacon-Apple Cider Biscuits

The sweet and salty flavors of apple and bacon make these special biscuits stand apart from the rest. Be prepared to make more than one batch because they go fast!

—TASTE OF HOME TEST KITCHEN

PREP: 20 MIN. • **BAKE:** 15 MIN.
MAKES: 8 BISCUITS

- 2 cups all-purpose flour
- 2 teaspoons baking powder
- 2 teaspoons brown sugar
- ½ teaspoon salt
- ¼ teaspoon baking soda
- ¼ teaspoon apple pie spice
- 8 tablespoons cold butter, cubed, divided
- 5 bacon strips, cooked and crumbled
- ¾ cup apple cider or juice
- ⅛ teaspoon ground cinnamon

1. In a large bowl, combine the first six ingredients. Cut in 7 tablespoons butter until mixture resembles coarse crumbs. Add bacon. Stir in cider just until combined.

2. Turn onto a lightly floured surface; knead 8-10 times. Roll into a 10x6-in. rectangle. Melt remaining butter; brush over dough. Sprinkle with cinnamon.

3. Cut into eight rectangles. Place 1 in. apart on an ungreased baking sheet. Bake at 450° for 12-15 minutes or until golden brown. Serve warm.

PEANUT BUTTER OATMEAL COOKIES, PAGE 168

DIRT DESSERT, 169

PEACH CRISP, 155

TOFFEE CHIP FUDGE, 166

COOKIES, CANDIES & MORE

Most family cooks agree...there's no easier way to spread a little love than with a yummy sweet treat. Whether you want to bring an old-fashioned fruit cobbler to the table for an after-dinner dessert or simply open up a cookie jar full of bite-size goodies to accompany a cold glass of milk, each of the unforgettable pleasures on the pages that follow will show you just how deliciously fun it is to indulge your sweet tooth. Thanks to these no-fuss ideas, the perfect dessert, classroom treat or after-school snack is always at hand.

FAST FIX ▶ Caramel Apple Dip

My sweet, smooth and fluffy dip is a real crowd-pleaser. Be careful—it's so good that you won't want to stop eating it!
—**TASTE OF HOME TEST KITCHEN**

PREP/TOTAL TIME: 30 MIN. • **MAKES:** 2 CUPS

- 1 package (8 ounces) cream cheese, softened
- ½ cup packed brown sugar
- ¼ cup caramel ice cream topping
- 1 teaspoon vanilla extract
- 1 cup marshmallow creme
- 3 medium tart apples
- 2 tablespoons lemon juice
- 2 tablespoons water

1. In a small bowl, beat the cream cheese, brown sugar, caramel topping and vanilla until smooth; fold in marshmallow creme. Cut apples vertically into thin slices.

2. In a small bowl, combine lemon juice and water; toss apples in lemon juice mixture. Drain.

3. Using Halloween cutters, cut out the center of each slice. Serve apple slices and cutouts with dip.

> ❝This combo is delicious! I've made it several times and have yet to bring any home when I take it somewhere.❞
>
> —**COOKERKATHY** FROM TASTEOFHOME.COM

Big & Buttery Chocolate Chip Cookies

The classic American cookie accidentally got its start when Ruth Wakefield used a Nestle chocolate bar as a substitute for baker's chocolate. The chocolate didn't melt, and the chocolate chip cookie was born. This big, thick and soft version is based on a recipe from the Hungry Bear bakery in California.
—**TASTE OF HOME TEST KITCHEN**

PREP: 35 MIN. + CHILLING • **BAKE:** 10 MIN. • **MAKES:** 2 DOZEN

- 1 cup butter, softened
- 1 cup packed brown sugar
- ¾ cup sugar
- 2 eggs
- 1½ teaspoons vanilla extract
- 2⅔ cups all-purpose flour
- 1¼ teaspoons baking soda
- 1 teaspoon salt
- 1 package (12 ounces) semisweet chocolate chips
- 2 cups coarsely chopped walnuts, toasted

1. In a large bowl, cream the butter, brown sugar and sugar until light and fluffy. Beat in eggs and vanilla. Combine the flour, baking soda and salt; gradually add to creamed mixture and mix well. Stir in chocolate chips and walnuts.

2. Shape quarter cupfuls of dough into balls. Place in an airtight container, separating layers with waxed or parchment paper; cover and refrigerate overnight.

3. To bake, place dough balls 3 in. apart on parchment paper-lined baking sheets. Press a shallow indentation in the center of each with your thumb, reshaping sides to smooth any cracks. Let stand at room temperature for 30 minutes.

4. Preheat oven to 400°. Bake 10-12 minutes or until edges are golden brown. Cool 2 minutes before removing from pans to wire racks; cool.

Peach Crisp

Craving some easy Southern comfort food? My timeless peach cobbler has the perfect balance of sweet and tart. Add a scoop of vanilla ice cream for a dessert that's peachy keen.
—DIANNE ESPOSITE NEW MIDDLETOWN, OHIO

PREP: 20 MIN. • **BAKE:** 40 MIN. • **MAKES:** 6-8 SERVINGS

  1 **cup all-purpose flour**
  ½ **cup packed brown sugar**
  ¼ **teaspoon salt**
  ½ **cup butter, cubed**
FILLING
  2 **cans (15¼ ounces each) sliced peaches**
  1 **cup sugar**
  ¼ **cup cornstarch**
TOPPING
  1½ **cups old-fashioned oats**
  ½ **cup packed brown sugar**
  ¼ **cup all-purpose flour**
  5 **tablespoons butter, cubed**

1. In a large bowl, combine the flour, brown sugar and salt. Cut in butter until crumbly. Pat into a greased 9-in. square baking pan. Bake at 350° for 15 minutes or until lightly browned.
2. Meanwhile, drain the peaches and reserve juice in a small saucepan. Stir in the sugar and cornstarch until smooth. Bring to a boil; cook and stir for 2 minutes or until thickened. Remove from the heat; stir in peaches.
3. Pour into crust. For topping, combine the oats, brown sugar and flour. Cut in the butter until crumbly. Sprinkle over filling. Bake at 350° for 25-30 minutes or until golden brown and bubbly.

Sugared Cherry Jewels

The texture and crunch of the sugar coating make these chewy cookies extra special. The bright cherry center makes them look especially pretty in a holiday gift box or tin.

—JENNIFER BRANUM
O'FALLON, ILLINOIS

PREP: 25 MIN. + CHILLING
BAKE: 15 MIN./BATCH
MAKES: ABOUT 5 DOZEN

1 cup butter, softened
½ cup sugar
⅓ cup light corn syrup
2 egg yolks
½ teaspoon vanilla extract
2½ cups all-purpose flour
Additional sugar
1 jar (10 ounces) maraschino cherries, drained and halved

1. In a large bowl, cream butter and sugar until light and fluffy. Beat in the corn syrup, egg yolks and vanilla. Gradually add the flour and mix well. Cover and refrigerate for 1 hour or until easy to handle.
2. Roll into 1-in. balls; roll each ball in additional sugar. Place 2 in. apart on ungreased baking sheets. Using the end of a wooden spoon handle, make an indentation in the center of each. Press a cherry half in the center of each cookie.
3. Bake at 325° for 14-16 minutes or until lightly browned. Remove to wire racks to cool.

Super Brownies

Loaded with macadamia nuts, these chunky bite-size treats never fail to catch attention on a buffet table. If you prefer, replace the macadamia nuts with pecans.

—BERNICE MUILENBURG
MOLALLA, OREGON

PREP: 20 MIN. • **BAKE:** 55 MIN. + COOLING
MAKES: ABOUT 3½ DOZEN

½ cup butter, cubed
1½ cups sugar
4⅔ cups (28 ounces) semisweet chocolate chips, divided
3 tablespoons hot water
4 eggs
5 teaspoons vanilla extract
1½ cups all-purpose flour
½ teaspoon baking soda
½ teaspoon salt
2 cups coarsely chopped macadamia nuts or pecans, divided

1. In a large saucepan, melt butter with sugar over medium heat. Remove from the heat; stir in 2 cups chocolate chips until melted.
2. Pour into a large bowl; beat in water. Add eggs, one at a time, beating well after each addition. Add vanilla. Combine the flour, baking soda and salt; beat into the chocolate mixture until blended. Stir in 2 cups chocolate chips and 1 cup nuts.
3. Pour into a greased 13x9-in. baking pan. Sprinkle with remaining chips and nuts. Bake at 325° for 55 minutes or until the center is set (do not overbake). Cool on a wire rack.

BROWNIE DESSERT

For a fun and fancy dessert, serve brownies on individual serving plates. Top each with a scoop of chocolate swirl ice cream, add some chocolate sauce and a generous spoonful of whipped cream, then top with a maraschino cherry.

Peach Cobbler

It's the fresh and juicy peaches that make this dessert out of this world. I was raised in Oklahoma, and we used Elberta peaches picked right off our trees whenever we made this outstanding cobbler.

—VIRGINIA CROWELL LYONS, OREGON

PREP: 20 MIN. • **BAKE:** 40 MIN.
MAKES: 8 SERVINGS

- 1 cup all-purpose flour
- ½ cup sugar
- 2 teaspoons baking powder
- ½ teaspoon salt
- ½ cup milk
- 3 cups sliced peeled fresh or frozen peaches

TOPPING
- 2 cups water
- ½ cup sugar
- ½ cup packed brown sugar
- 1 tablespoon butter
- ¼ teaspoon ground nutmeg
  Ground cinnamon, optional
  Half-and-half cream

1. In a large bowl, combine the flour, sugar, baking powder and salt. Stir in the milk just until combined; fold in peaches. Spread into a greased 8-in. square baking dish.

2. In a large saucepan, combine the water, sugars, butter and nutmeg and cinnamon if desired. Bring to boil, stirring until sugars are dissolved. Pour over top.

3. Bake at 400° for 40-50 minutes or until filling is bubbly and a toothpick inserted in topping comes out clean. Serve warm or cold with cream.

Lemon-Berry Shortcake

Here's a quick, easy summertime classic. The shortcake layer is tender and not overly sweet. Add some fresh blueberries to the top for an extra-pretty finish for patriotic celebrations.

—MERYL HERR
GRAND RAPIDS, MICHIGAN

PREP: 30 MIN. • **BAKE:** 20 MIN. + COOLING
MAKES: 8 SERVINGS

- 1⅓ cups all-purpose flour
- ½ cup sugar
- 2 teaspoons baking powder
- ¼ teaspoon salt
- 1 egg
- ⅔ cup buttermilk
- ¼ cup butter, melted
- 1 tablespoon lemon juice
- 1 teaspoon grated lemon peel
- 1 teaspoon vanilla extract
- 1 cup sliced fresh strawberries

TOPPING
- 1½ cups sliced fresh strawberries
- 1 tablespoon lemon juice
- 1 teaspoon sugar
- 2 cups reduced-fat whipped topping

1. In a large bowl, combine the flour, sugar, baking powder and salt. In another bowl, combine the egg, buttermilk, butter, lemon juice, lemon peel and vanilla. Stir into dry ingredients just until moistened. Fold in strawberries. Pour into a greased and floured 9-in. round baking pan.

2. Bake at 350° for 20-25 minutes or until a toothpick inserted near the center comes out clean. Cool for 10 minutes before removing from pan to a wire rack to cool completely.

3. For topping, in a large bowl, combine the strawberries, lemon juice and sugar. Cover and refrigerate until serving. Spread whipped topping over cake. Drain strawberries; arrange over top.

Caramel Cashew Clusters

Several years ago, a co-worker came across candies like these in a store and asked if I could make them. After some trial and error, I came up with a winning recipe.
—**KAREN DANIELS** JEFFERSON CITY, MISSOURI

PREP: 25 MIN. + STANDING • **MAKES:** 2½ DOZEN

- 2 **pounds milk chocolate candy coating, coarsely chopped, divided**
- 1 **cup salted cashew halves**
- 28 **caramels**
- 2 **tablespoons heavy whipping cream**

1. Line baking sheets with waxed paper and butter the paper; set aside.

2. In a microwave, melt 1 pound of candy coating; stir until smooth. Drop by scant tablespoonfuls onto prepared pans. Let stand until partially set, about 3 minutes. Top each with six or seven cashews. Let stand until completely set.

3. In a small heavy saucepan, combine caramels and cream. Cook and stir over low heat until melted; stir until smooth. Spoon over cashews. Reheat caramel over low heat if it thickens. Melt remaining candy coating; spoon over caramel. Let stand until set.

“**These are so easy and delicious! I used my own homemade caramel instead of store-bought, and they turned out wonderful.** ”

—**CARLEY GILES** FROM TASTEOFHOME.COM

Caramel Swirls

Nothing beats a big plate stacked high with cookies when you're craving something sweet. With a crisp outside and chewy caramel filling, these swirls are one of my favorites.
—**JAN SMITH** STAR, TEXAS

PREP: 25 MIN. + CHILLING • **BAKE:** 15 MIN./BATCH
MAKES: 6½ DOZEN

- 1 **cup butter, softened**
- 4 **ounces cream cheese, softened**
- 1 **cup packed brown sugar**
- 1 **egg yolk**
- 1 **teaspoon maple flavoring**
- 2¾ **cups all-purpose flour**

FILLING
- 30 **caramels**
- 2 **packages (3 ounces each) cream cheese, softened**

1. In a large bowl, cream the butter, cream cheese and brown sugar until light and fluffy. Beat in egg yolk and maple flavoring. Gradually add flour and mix well. Refrigerate for 2 hours or until easy to handle.

2. In a microwave-safe bowl, melt caramels; stir until smooth. Stir in cream cheese until blended; set aside. Divide dough in half. Roll each portion between waxed paper to ¼-in. thickness. Spread caramel mixture over dough to within ½ in. of edges.

3. Roll up tightly jelly-roll style, starting with a long side. Wrap rolls in plastic wrap; refrigerate for 4 hours or until firm.

4. Unwrap and cut into ¼-in. slices. Place 1 in. apart on greased baking sheets. Bake at 350° for 12-14 minutes or until golden brown. Remove to wire racks to cool.

Chocolate Peanut Butter Candy

With just three ingredients, these chocolate-swirl treats take just moments to whip up! If you have little ones visiting for the holidays, have them help you with the stirring.
—**HOLLY DEMERS** ABBOTSFORD, BRITISH COLUMBIA

PREP: 10 MIN. + CHILLING • **MAKES:** ABOUT 2½ POUNDS

- 1 pound white candy coating, coarsely chopped
- 1½ cups creamy peanut butter
- 2 cups (12 ounces) semisweet chocolate chips

1. In a large microwave-safe bowl, melt candy coating; stir until smooth. Stir in peanut butter; thinly spread onto a waxed paper-lined baking sheet.
2. In another microwave-safe bowl, melt chocolate chips; stir until smooth. Drizzle over candy coating mixture; cut through mixture with a knife to swirl the chocolate. Chill until firm.
3. Break into pieces. Store in an airtight container in the refrigerator.

Lemon Coconut Squares

The tangy citrus flavor of these no-fuss squares is especially yummy on a hot sticky day. It reminds me of selling lemonade on the sidewalk as a little girl.
—**DONNA BIDDLE** ELMIRA, NEW YORK

PREP: 25 MIN. • **BAKE:** 20 MIN. + COOLING • **MAKES:** 4 DOZEN

- 1½ cups all-purpose flour
- ½ cup confectioners' sugar
- ¾ cup cold butter, cubed
- 4 eggs
- 1½ cups sugar
- ½ cup lemon juice
- 1 teaspoon baking powder
- ¾ cup flaked coconut

1. In a small bowl, combine flour and confectioners' sugar; cut in the butter until crumbly. Press into a lightly greased 13x9-in. baking pan. Bake at 350° for 15 minutes.
2. Meanwhile, in another small bowl, beat the eggs, sugar, lemon juice and baking powder until combined. Pour over crust; sprinkle with coconut.
3. Bake at 350° for 20-25 minutes or until golden brown. Cool on a wire rack. Cut into squares.

FAST FIX ▶ Banana Boats

This recipe, given to me years ago by a good friend, is a favorite with my family when we go camping. It's quick, scrumptious and fun to make.
—**BRENDA LOVELESS** GARLAND, TEXAS

PREP/TOTAL TIME: 20 MIN. • **MAKES:** 4 SERVINGS

- 4 medium unpeeled ripe bananas
- 4 teaspoons miniature chocolate chips
- 4 tablespoons miniature marshmallows

1. Cut banana peel lengthwise about ½ in. deep, leaving ½ in. at both ends. Open peel wider to form a pocket. Fill each with 1 teaspoon chocolate chips and 1 tablespoon marshmallows. Crimp and shape four pieces of heavy-duty foil (about 12 in. square) around bananas, forming boats.
2. Grill, covered, over medium heat for 5-10 minutes or until marshmallows melt and are golden brown.

Pots de Creme

Looking for an easy recipe to make for your sweetheart? Served in pretty, stemmed glasses, this chocolaty custard is sure to set the mood for a special evening.

—CONNIE DREYFOOS CINCINNATI, OHIO

PREP: 15 MIN. + CHILLING • **MAKES:** 5 SERVINGS

  1 **egg**
  2 **tablespoons sugar**
     Dash salt
  ¾ **cup half-and-half cream**
  1 **cup (6 ounces) semisweet chocolate chips**
  1 **teaspoon vanilla extract**
     Whipped cream, optional

1. In a small saucepan, combine the egg, sugar and salt. Whisk in cream. Cook and stir over medium heat until mixture reaches 160° and coats the back of a metal spoon.

2. Remove from the heat; whisk in chocolate chips and vanilla until smooth. Pour into small dessert dishes. Cover and refrigerate for 8 hours or overnight. Garnish with whipped cream if desired.

Stir in water. Bring to a boil; cook and stir for 1-2 minutes or until thickened. Stir in remaining vanilla. Pour mixture over fruit; sprinkle with the remaining crumb mixture.

3. Bake at 350° for 25-30 minutes or until bubbly. Serve with ice cream.

NOTE *If using frozen rhubarb, measure rhubarb while still frozen, then thaw completely. Drain in a colander, but do not press liquid out.*

Pumpkin Chocolate Chip Cookies

I'm one of the cooking project leaders for my daughter's 4-H club. These soft pumpkin cookies studded with chocolate chips were a hit with the kids.
—MARIETTA SLATER JUSTIN, TEXAS

PREP: 10 MIN. • **BAKE:** 15 MIN./BATCH + COOLING
MAKES: 4 DOZEN

- 1 cup butter, softened
- ¾ cup sugar
- ¾ cup packed brown sugar
- 1 egg
- 1 teaspoon vanilla extract
- 2 cups all-purpose flour
- 1 cup quick-cooking oats
- 1 teaspoon baking soda
- 1 teaspoon ground cinnamon
- 1 cup canned pumpkin
- 1½ cups semisweet chocolate chips

1. In a bowl, cream butter and sugars until light and fluffy. Beat in egg and vanilla. Combine the flour, oats, baking soda and cinnamon; stir into creamed mixture alternately with pumpkin. Fold in chocolate chips.

2. Drop by tablespoonfuls onto greased baking sheets. Bake at 350° for 12-13 minutes or until lightly browned. Remove to wire racks to cool.

Berry Delicious Rhubarb Crisp

I sometimes add a tablespoonful of grated orange or lemon zest to the crumb mixture for extra zing. This is a great dessert for warm summer nights.
—SHANNON ARTHUR
PICKERINGTON, OHIO

PREP: 15 MIN. • **BAKE:** 25 MIN. • **MAKES:** 9 SERVINGS

- 1 cup all-purpose flour
- 1 cup packed brown sugar
- ¾ cup old-fashioned oats
- ½ cup butter, melted
- 1½ teaspoons vanilla extract, divided
- 1 teaspoon ground cinnamon
- 1½ cups diced fresh or frozen rhubarb
- 1½ cups sliced fresh strawberries
- 1½ cups fresh blackberries
- ½ cup sugar
- 1 tablespoon cornstarch
- ½ cup water
  Vanilla ice cream

1. In a small bowl, combine the flour, brown sugar, oats, butter, 1 teaspoon vanilla and cinnamon. Set aside 1 cup for topping; press remaining crumb mixture into a greased 8-in. square baking dish. Top with rhubarb, strawberries and blackberries.

2. In a small saucepan, combine sugar and cornstarch.

Chocolate Cream Delight

As a health-conscious cook, I'm grateful for the sugar-free and reduced-fat products available on the market. This dreamy dessert satisfies all my chocolate cravings!

—WANDA BENDA JACKSON, MINNESOTA

PREP: 30 MIN. + CHILLING • **MAKES:** 9 SERVINGS

- 1 cup chocolate wafer crumbs
- 1 tablespoon sugar
- 2 tablespoons butter, melted
- 2 packages (1.3 ounces each) sugar-free cook-and-serve chocolate pudding mix
- 3½ cups fat-free milk
- 3 ounces reduced-fat cream cheese, cubed
- 2 cups reduced-fat whipped topping
- 2 tablespoons chopped pecans

1. In a small bowl, combine the wafer crumbs, sugar and butter; press onto the bottom of an 8-in. square dish coated with cooking spray. Cover and refrigerate.

2. In a large saucepan, combine the pudding mixes and milk until smooth. Bring to a boil, stirring constantly. Remove from the heat; cool slightly.

3. Spread half of the pudding over crust. Stir cream cheese into remaining pudding until smooth; gently spread over pudding layer. Cover and refrigerate for at least 2 hours or until set.

4. Spread whipped topping over dessert. Sprinkle with pecans. Cut into squares.

SHAKE UP THE FLAVOR

Feel free to substitute pistachio, butterscotch, lemon or any pudding flavor of your choice in place of the chocolate in this dessert. You can also use vanilla wafer crumbs instead of chocolate in the crust.

Chocolate Dipped Brownies

My family calls these bars "The World's Chocolatiest Brownies" and is more than happy to gobble up a batch whenever I make them. They're a deliciously jolly part of our holiday cookie collection.

—JACKIE ARCHER CLINTON, IOWA

PREP: 30 MIN. + FREEZING • **BAKE:** 35 MIN. + COOLING
MAKES: 3 DOZEN

- ¾ cup sugar
- ⅓ cup butter, cubed
- 2 tablespoons water
- 4 cups (24 ounces) semisweet chocolate chips, divided
- 1 teaspoon vanilla extract
- 2 eggs
- ¾ cup all-purpose flour
- ½ teaspoon salt
- ¼ teaspoon baking soda
- 2 tablespoons shortening
  Chopped pecans, jimmies and/or nonpareils, optional

1. In a large saucepan, bring the sugar, butter and water to a boil over medium heat. Remove from the heat; stir in 1 cup chocolate chips and vanilla until smooth. Cool for 5 minutes. Beat in eggs. Combine the flour, salt and baking soda; add to chocolate mixture. Stir in 1 cup chocolate chips.

2. Pour into a greased 9-in. square baking pan. Bake at 325° for 35 minutes or until set. Cool completely on a wire rack.

3. Place in the freezer for 30-40 minutes or until firm (do not freeze completely). Cut into bars.

4. In a microwave-safe bowl, melt remaining chips and shortening; stir until smooth. Using a small fork, dip brownies to completely coat; allow excess to drip off. Place on waxed paper-lined baking sheets. Sprinkle with pecans, jimmies and/or nonpareils if desired. Let stand until set. Store in an airtight container in a cool dry place.

Glazed Cinnamon Apples

If you're seeking comfort food on the sweet side, this slow-cooked apple dessert made with cinnamon and nutmeg will warm your heart. It's perfect for cool fall weather.
—MEGAN MAZE OAK CREEK, WISCONSIN

PREP: 20 MIN. • **COOK:** 3 HOURS • **MAKES:** 7 SERVINGS

- 6 large tart apples
- 2 tablespoons lemon juice
- ½ cup packed brown sugar
- ½ cup sugar
- 2 tablespoons all-purpose flour
- 1 teaspoon ground cinnamon
- ¼ teaspoon ground nutmeg
- 6 tablespoons butter, melted
  Vanilla ice cream

1. Peel, core and cut each apple into eight wedges; transfer to a 3-qt. slow cooker. Drizzle with lemon juice. Combine the sugars, flour, cinnamon and nutmeg; sprinkle over apples. Drizzle with butter.
2. Cover and cook on low for 3-4 hours or until apples are tender. Serve in dessert dishes with ice cream.

Peanut Butter Cake Bars

These cakelike bars are packed with peanut butter and chocolate chips, and are perfect for any occasion. Kids and adults alike are in for a treat!
—CHARLOTTE ENNIS LAKE ARTHUR, NEW MEXICO

PREP: 15 MIN. • **BAKE:** 45 MIN. + COOLING • **MAKES:** 2 DOZEN

- ⅔ cup butter, softened
- ⅔ cup peanut butter
- 1 cup sugar
- 1 cup packed brown sugar
- 4 eggs
- 2 teaspoons vanilla extract
- 2 cups all-purpose flour
- 2 teaspoons baking powder
- ½ teaspoon salt
- 1 package (11½ ounces) milk chocolate chips

1. In a large bowl, cream the butter, peanut butter, sugar and brown sugar. Add eggs, one at a time, beating well after each addition. Beat in vanilla. Combine the flour, baking powder and salt; gradually add to creamed mixture. Stir in chocolate chips.
2. Spread into a greased 13x9-in. baking pan. Bake at 350° for 45-50 minutes or until a toothpick inserted near the center comes out clean. Cool on a wire rack. Cut into bars.

Almond Toffee

Crisp and delicious, this toffee is sandwiched between two layers of heavenly chocolate. It's brimming with toasted almond flavor.
—SUE GRONHOLZ
BEAVER DAM, WISCONSIN

PREP: 50 MIN. + STANDING • **MAKES:** ABOUT 1½ POUNDS

- 1 tablespoon plus 2 cups butter, divided
- 2 cups sugar
- 1 cup slivered almonds
- ¼ cup water
- 1 teaspoon salt
- 1 teaspoon vanilla extract
- 1 package (11½ ounces) milk chocolate chips, divided
- ½ cup finely chopped almonds

1. Grease a 15x10x1-in. pan with 1 tablespoon butter; set aside. In a large heavy saucepan, melt the remaining butter. Add the sugar, slivered almonds, water and salt; cook and stir over medium heat until a candy thermometer reads 295° (approaching hard-crack stage). Remove from the heat; stir in vanilla.
2. Quickly pour into prepared pan. Let stand at room temperature until cool, about 1 hour.
3. In a microwave, melt 1 cup chocolate chips; spread over toffee. Refrigerate for 45 minutes or until set. Invert onto an ungreased large baking sheet. Melt remaining chips; spread over toffee. Sprinkle with chopped almonds. Let stand for 1 hour. Break into bite-size pieces. Store in an airtight container.

NOTE *We recommend that you test your candy thermometer before each use by bringing water to a boil; the thermometer should read 212°. Adjust your recipe temperature up or down based on your test.*

Hot Caramel Apples

Who ever thinks of making dessert in a slow cooker? This old-time favorite goes together quickly, and it's such a treat to come home to the comforting aroma of cinnamony baked apples.

—**PAT SPARKS** ST. CHARLES, MISSOURI

PREP: 15 MIN. • **COOK:** 4 HOURS
MAKES: 4 SERVINGS

- 4 **large tart apples, cored**
- ½ **cup apple juice**
- ½ **cup packed brown sugar**
- 12 **red-hot candies**
- ¼ **cup butter**
- 8 **caramels**
- ¼ **teaspoon ground cinnamon**
  Whipped cream, optional

1. Peel about ¾ in. off the top of each apple; place in a 3-qt. slow cooker. Pour juice over apples. Fill the center of each apple with 2 tablespoons of sugar, three red-hots, 1 tablespoon butter and two caramels. Sprinkle with cinnamon.
2. Cover and cook on low for 4-6 hours or until the apples are tender. Serve immediately with whipped cream if desired.

Oat Apple Crisp

A yellow cake mix sets this easy, tasty crisp apart from others. Serve it a la mode for an extra-special treat.

—**RUBY HODGE**
RICHLAND CENTER, WISCONSIN

PREP: 25 MIN. • **BAKE:** 45 MIN.
MAKES: 8 SERVINGS

- 7 **cups thinly sliced peeled tart apples (about 7 medium)**
- 1 **cup sugar**
- 1 **tablespoon all-purpose flour**
- 1 **teaspoon ground cinnamon**
  Dash salt
- ¼ **cup water**
- 1 **package (9 ounces) yellow cake mix**
- ¾ **cup quick-cooking oats**
- ⅓ **cup butter, softened**
- ¼ **cup packed brown sugar**
- ¼ **teaspoon baking powder**
- ¼ **teaspoon baking soda**
  Vanilla ice cream

1. Place apples in a greased 2½ qt. shallow baking dish. In a small bowl, combine the sugar, flour, cinnamon and salt; sprinkle over apples. Drizzle with water. In a large bowl, combine the cake mix, oats, butter, brown sugar, baking powder and baking soda. Sprinkle over apples.
2. Bake, uncovered, at 350° for 45-50 minutes or until apples are tender and topping is golden brown. Serve warm with ice cream.

FAST FIX ▸ No-Bake Peanut Butter Treats

This quick and tasty dessert is perfect for a road trip. The treats won't stick to your hands, so you'll crave more than one. Keep them on hand in the refrigerator for an easy snack.

—SONIA ROHDA WAVERLY, NEBRASKA

PREP/TOTAL TIME: 10 MIN.
MAKES: 15 TREATS

- ⅓ cup chunky peanut butter
- ¼ cup honey
- ½ teaspoon vanilla extract
- ⅓ cup nonfat dry milk powder
- ⅓ cup quick-cooking oats
- 2 tablespoons graham cracker crumbs

In a small bowl, combine the peanut butter, honey and vanilla. Stir in the milk powder, oats and graham cracker crumbs. Shape into 1-in. balls. Cover and refrigerate until serving.

Warm Chocolate Melting Cups

These cakes have become a favorite of our guests. They're always so surprised that these little desserts are so light and less sinful than they look.

—KISSA VAUGHN TROY, TEXAS

PREP: 20 MIN. • **BAKE:** 20 MIN.
MAKES: 10 SERVINGS

- 1¼ cups sugar, divided
- ½ cup baking cocoa
- 2 tablespoons all-purpose flour
- ⅛ teaspoon salt
- ¾ cup water
- ¾ cup plus 1 tablespoon semisweet chocolate chips
- 1 tablespoon brewed coffee
- 1 teaspoon vanilla extract
- 2 eggs
- 1 egg white
- 10 fresh strawberry halves, optional

1. In a small saucepan, combine ¾ cup sugar, cocoa, flour and salt. Gradually stir in water. Bring to a boil; cook and stir for 2 minutes or until thickened. Remove from the heat; stir in the chocolate chips, coffee and vanilla until smooth. Transfer to a large bowl.

2. In another bowl, beat the eggs and egg white until slightly thickened. Gradually add the remaining sugar, beating until thick and lemon-colored. Fold into the chocolate mixture.

3. Transfer mixture to ten 4-oz. ramekins coated with cooking spray. Place ramekins in a baking pan; add 1 in. of boiling water to pan. Bake, uncovered, at 350° for 20-25 minutes or just until the centers are set. Garnish with strawberry halves if desired. Serve cups immediately.

Peanut Butter Granola Mini Bars

Kids will flip over this deliciously oaty sweet snack! With honey, peanut butter, brown sugar and two types of chips, what's not to love? And at less than 100 calories, you can afford to have seconds.

—VIVIAN LEVINE SUMMERFIELD, FLORIDA

PREP: 20 MIN.
BAKE: 15 MIN. + COOLING
MAKES: 3 DOZEN

- ½ cup reduced-fat creamy peanut butter
- ⅓ cup honey
- 1 egg
- 2 tablespoons canola oil
- 1 teaspoon vanilla extract
- 3½ cups old-fashioned oats
- ½ cup packed brown sugar
- ¾ teaspoon salt
- ⅓ cup peanut butter chips
- ⅓ cup miniature semisweet chocolate chips

1. In a large bowl, beat the peanut butter, honey, egg, oil and vanilla until blended. Combine the oats, brown sugar and salt; add to the peanut butter mixture and mix well. Stir in chips. (Batter will be sticky.)

2. Press into a 13x9-in. baking dish coated with cooking spray. Bake at 350° for 12-15 minutes or until set and edges are lightly browned. Cool on a wire rack. Cut into bars.

Toffee Chip Fudge

My grandchildren savor the job of taste-testing my baking experiments. I combined two recipes to come up with this yummy fudge dotted with crisp toffee bits. The kids gave it a "thumbs-up" before requesting a batch to take home.
—**MAXINE SMITH** OWANKA, SOUTH DAKOTA

PREP: 15 MIN. + CHILLING • **COOK:** 10 MIN. • **MAKES:** 2 POUNDS

- 1½ teaspoons plus ¼ cup butter, divided
- 1½ cups sugar
- 1 can (5 ounces) evaporated milk
- ¼ teaspoon salt
- 1½ cups semisweet chocolate chips
- 2 cups miniature marshmallows
- ½ cup milk chocolate English toffee bits plus 2 tablespoons milk chocolate English toffee bits, divided
- 1 teaspoon vanilla extract

1. Line a 9-in. square pan with foil. Grease the foil with 1½ teaspoons butter; set aside.

2. In a large heavy saucepan, combine the sugar, milk, salt and remaining butter. Cook and stir over medium heat until sugar is dissolved. Bring to a rapid boil; boil for 5 minutes, stirring constantly.

3. Remove from the heat; stir in chocolate chips and marshmallows until melted. Fold in ½ cup toffee bits and vanilla. Pour into a prepared pan. Sprinkle with remaining toffee bits. Chill until firm. Remove from pan and cut into 1-in. squares. Store in the refrigerator.

> **FOILED FUDGE**
>
> When making fudge, you can simply butter or grease the pan with nonstick cooking spray to prevent the candy from sticking. But many recipes suggest first lining the pan with foil. The foil allows the fudge to be lifted out of the pan in one piece. Cutting the fudge outside of the pan prevents the pan from being scratched and also allows for more evenly cut pieces.

Sensational Tiramisu

This light version of the popular Italian dessert is moist and creamy, and cuts so well into pretty layered squares. You'll love the blend of coffee, Kahlua and cream cheese flavors.
—**MARY WALTERS** WESTERVILLE, OHIO

PREP: 25 MIN. • **COOK:** 10 MIN. + CHILLING
MAKES: 12 SERVINGS

- 1 package (8 ounces) reduced-fat cream cheese
- ⅔ cup confectioners' sugar, divided
- 1½ cups reduced-fat whipped topping, divided
- ½ cup plus 1 tablespoon sugar
- 3 egg whites
- ¼ cup water
- 2 packages (3 ounces each) ladyfingers, split
- ½ cup boiling water
- 2 tablespoons coffee liqueur
- 1 tablespoon instant coffee granules
- ½ teaspoon baking cocoa

1. In a small bowl, beat cream cheese and confectioners' sugar until smooth. Fold in 1 cup whipped topping; set aside.

2. Combine ½ cup sugar, egg whites and water in a small heavy saucepan over low heat. With a hand mixer, beat on low speed for 1 minute. Continue beating on low over low heat until mixture reaches 160°, about 8-10 minutes. Pour into a large bowl. Beat on high until stiff peaks form, about 7 minutes. Fold into cream cheese mixture.

3. Arrange half of ladyfingers in an ungreased 11-in. x 7-in. dish. Combine the boiling water, coffee liqueur, coffee granules and remaining sugar; brush half of mixture over ladyfingers. Top with half of cream cheese mixture. Repeat layers. Spread remaining whipped topping over the top; sprinkle with cocoa. Refrigerate for 2 hours before serving.

Peanut Butter Brownie Trifle

Too full for dessert? Once you set your eyes on this elaborate creation, you'll think again. It feeds a crowd and features the classic pairing of chocolate and peanut butter.

—NANCY FOUST STONEBORO, PENNSYLVANIA

PREP: 1 HOUR + CHILLING
MAKES: 20 SERVINGS (1 CUP EACH)

- 1 **fudge brownie mix (13-inch x 9-inch pan size)**
- 1 **package (10 ounces) peanut butter chips**
- 2 **packages (13 ounces each) miniature peanut butter cups**
- 4 **cups cold 2% milk**
- 2 **packages (5.1 ounces each) instant vanilla pudding mix**
- 1 **cup creamy peanut butter**
- 4 **teaspoons vanilla extract**
- 3 **cartons (8 ounces each) frozen whipped topping, thawed**

1. Prepare brownie batter according to package directions; stir in peanut butter chips. Bake in a greased 13x9-in. baking pan at 350° for 20-25 minutes or until a toothpick inserted near the center comes out with moist crumbs (do not overbake). Cool on a wire rack; cut into ¾-in. pieces.

2. Cut peanut butter cups in half; set aside ⅓ cup for garnish. In a large bowl, whisk milk and pudding mixes for 2 minutes (mixture will be thick). Add peanut butter and vanilla; mix well. Fold in 1½ cartons whipped topping.

3. Place a third of the brownies in a 5-qt. glass bowl; top with a third of the remaining peanut butter cups. Spoon a third of the pudding mixture over the top. Repeat layers twice. Cover with remaining whipped topping; garnish with reserved peanut butter cups. Refrigerate until chilled.

Gooey Butterscotch Bars

These bars definitely live up to their name. With caramels, butterscotch chips and pudding, they're finger-lickin' good! Sugar cookie mix speeds up prep time.

—**CAROL BREWER** FAIRBORN, OHIO

PREP: 20 MIN. • **BAKE:** 20 MIN. + COOLING
MAKES: ABOUT 3 DOZEN

- 1 package (17½ ounces) sugar cookie mix
- 1 package (3.4 ounces) instant butterscotch pudding mix
- ½ cup butter, softened
- 1 egg
- 14 ounces caramels
- ½ cup evaporated milk
- 2 cups mixed nuts
- 1 teaspoon vanilla extract
- 1 cup butterscotch chips

1. In a large bowl, combine the sugar cookie mix, pudding mix, butter and egg. Press into an ungreased 13x9-in. baking pan. Bake at 350° for 20-25 minutes or until set.

2. In a large saucepan, combine caramels and milk. Cook and stir over medium-low heat until melted. Remove from the heat. Stir in nuts and vanilla. Pour over crust. Sprinkle with butterscotch chips.

3. Cool completely. Cut into bars. Store bars in an airtight container.

FAST FIX

Peanut Butter Oatmeal Cookies

These delightful cookies taste great with a glass of cold milk. With their peanutty flavor, the scrumptious treats really hit the spot.

—**MARILYN BLANKSCHIEN** CLINTONVILLE, WISCONSIN

PREP/TOTAL TIME: 20 MIN. • **MAKES:** 2 DOZEN

- ½ cup chunky peanut butter
- ½ cup packed brown sugar
- 1 egg
- 1¼ cups quick-cooking oats
- ½ teaspoon baking soda

1. In a small bowl, cream peanut butter and brown sugar until fluffy. Beat in egg. Add oats and baking soda to creamed mixture; mix well.

2. Drop by tablespoonfuls 2 in. apart onto greased baking sheets; flatten slightly. Bake at 350° for 6-8 minutes. Remove to wire racks to cool. Store in an airtight container.

Fudgy Brownies

Rich brownies are topped with a peanut butter pudding frosting, making this a recipe the whole family will love. These are perfect for a potluck, bake sale or yummy after-dinner treat to turn a weeknight into a special occasion.

—**AMY CROOK** SYRACUSE, UTAH

PREP: 20 MIN. • **BAKE:** 25 MIN. + CHILLING • **MAKES:** 2½ DOZEN

- 1 package fudge brownie mix (13x9-inch pan size)
- 1½ cups confectioners' sugar
- ½ cup butter, softened
- 2 to 3 tablespoons peanut butter
- 2 tablespoons cold 2% milk
- 4½ teaspoons instant vanilla pudding mix
- 1 can (16 ounces) chocolate fudge frosting

1. Prepare and bake brownies according to package directions. Cool on a wire rack.
2. Meanwhile, in a small bowl, beat the confectioners' sugar, butter, peanut butter, milk and pudding mix until smooth. Spread over brownies. Refrigerate for 30 minutes or until firm. Frost with chocolate fudge frosting just before cutting.

FAST FIX Chocolate Chip Dip

Think dunking cookies into milk is fun? Just wait until you dip a graham cracker stick into my indulgent cream cheese-based sensation. You can also serve it alongside apple wedges or fresh strawberries for a fruity twist.
—**HEATHER KOENIG** PRAIRIE DU CHIEN, WISCONSIN

PREP/TOTAL TIME: 15 MIN. • **MAKES:** 2 CUPS

- 1 package (8 ounces) cream cheese, softened
- ½ cup butter, softened
- ¾ cup confectioners' sugar
- 2 tablespoons brown sugar
- 1 teaspoon vanilla extract
- 1 cup (6 ounces) miniature semisweet chocolate chips
  Graham cracker sticks

In a small bowl, beat cream cheese and butter until light and fluffy. Add the sugars and vanilla; beat until smooth. Stir in chocolate chips. Serve with graham cracker sticks.

Dirt Dessert

I loved this yummy dessert that was a specialty of my mom's when I was growing up. If you're entertaining kids, add some gummy worms on top for extra silliness.
—**KRISTI LINTON** BAY CITY, MICHIGAN

PREP: 30 MIN. + CHILLING • **MAKES:** 20 SERVINGS

- 1 package (8 ounces) cream cheese, softened
- ¼ cup butter, softened
- 1 cup confectioners' sugar
- 3½ cups cold 2% milk
- 2 packages (3.4 ounces each) instant vanilla pudding mix
- 1 carton (12 ounces) frozen whipped topping, thawed
- 1 package (15½ ounces) Oreo cookies
  Shaved white chocolate, optional

1. In a large bowl, beat the cream cheese, butter and confectioners' sugar until smooth. In a large bowl, whisk milk and pudding mixes for 2 minutes; let stand for 2 minutes or until soft-set. Gradually stir into cream cheese mixture. Fold in whipped topping.
2. Spread 1⅓ cups of crushed cookies into an ungreased 13x9-in. dish. Layer with half of the pudding mixture and half of the remaining cookies. Repeat layers. Refrigerate for at least 1 hour before serving. Serve with shaved white chocolate if desired.

Microwave Marshmallow Fudge

Calling for only five ingredients from your pantry and fridge, this decadent delight is made to be shared!

—SUE ROSS CASA GRANDE, ARIZONA

PREP: 15 MIN. + CHILLING
MAKES: ABOUT 2 POUNDS

- 1 **teaspoon butter**
- 1 **can (16 ounces) chocolate frosting**
- 2 **cups (12 ounces) semisweet chocolate chips**
- ½ **cup chopped walnuts**
- ½ **cup miniature marshmallows**

1. Line a 9-in. square pan with foil and grease the foil with butter; set aside. In a microwave, melt frosting and chocolate chips; stir until smooth. Stir in walnuts; cool for 10 minutes. Stir in marshmallows. Transfer to prepared pan. Cover and refrigerate until firm.

2. Using foil, lift fudge out of pan. Discard foil; cut into 1-in. squares. Store in an airtight container in the refrigerator.

STICKY MARSHMALLOWS

To easily separate sticky marshmallows, place a spoonful of powdered sugar in the bag and shake it well. A few stubborn marshmallows might still need to be separated by hand, but this generally works great.

Peanut Butter Custard Blast

Ooey, gooey, great! That's how folks describe my chocolate-peanut butter dessert. I appreciate the make-ahead convenience.

—MARILEE EVENSON
WISCONSIN RAPIDS, WISCONSIN

PREP: 30 MIN. • **COOK:** 25 MIN. + CHILLING
MAKES: 15 SERVINGS

- 2 **cups cream-filled chocolate sandwich cookie crumbs**
- 2 **tablespoons sugar**
- ⅓ **cup butter, melted**

FILLING
- 1½ **cups sugar**
- ⅓ **cup cornstarch**
- 2 **tablespoons all-purpose flour**
- ½ **teaspoon salt**
- 6 **cups 2% milk**
- 6 **egg yolks, beaten**
- 1 **cup creamy peanut butter**

TOPPING
- 2 **cups heavy whipping cream**
- 1 **tablespoon confectioners' sugar**
- 6 **peanut butter cups, chopped**
- ½ **cup chopped salted peanuts**
- 2 **tablespoons chocolate syrup**

1. In a small bowl, combine cookie crumbs and sugar; stir in butter. Press onto the bottom of a greased 13x9-in. baking dish. Bake at 375° for 8 minutes or until set. Cool on a wire rack.

2. For filling, in a large saucepan, combine the sugar, cornstarch, flour and salt. Stir in milk until smooth. Cook and stir over medium-high heat until thickened and bubbly. Reduce heat; cook and stir 2 minutes longer. Remove from the heat. Stir a small amount of hot mixture into egg yolks; return all to pan, stirring constantly. Bring to a gentle boil; cook and stir 2 minutes longer.

3. Remove from the heat. Stir 1 cup into peanut butter until smooth. Gently stir peanut butter mixture into the pan. Pour over crust. Cool to room temperature. Cover and refrigerate for at least 2 hours.

4. In a large bowl, beat cream until it begins to thicken. Add confectioners' sugar; beat until stiff peaks form. Spread over peanut butter mixture. Sprinkle with peanut butter cups and peanuts. Drizzle with chocolate syrup.

TO MAKE AHEAD *After peanut butter custard is pour over the crust, refrigerate overnight. Before serving, top with the sweetened whipped cream, peanuts, peanut butter candy and chocolate drizzle.*

Rum Balls

Rum flavor comes through nicely in these traditional holiday cookies. Try rolling half in confectioners' sugar and the other half in crushed vanilla wafers for added visual appeal on your dessert platter.

—AUDREY LARSON BLOOMINGTON, MINNESOTA

PREP: 40 MIN. • **MAKES:** 3½ DOZEN

> 2½ cups crushed vanilla wafers (about 75 wafers)
> 1 cup ground pecans
> 1 cup confectioners' sugar
> 2 tablespoons plus 2 teaspoons baking cocoa
> ¼ cup rum
> 3 tablespoons honey
> 2 tablespoons water
>   Additional confectioners' sugar and/or crushed vanilla wafers

1. In a large bowl, combine the wafer crumbs, pecans, confectioners' sugar and cocoa. Combine the rum, honey and water; stir into crumb mixture.

2. Shape into 1-in. balls. Roll in additional confectioners' sugar and/or wafer crumbs. Store in an airtight container.

Raspberry Swirl Frozen Dessert

Rich, creamy and delicious describe this raspberry treat. It's so luscious it's worth the time it takes to make it.

—KAREN SUDERMAN SUGAR LAND, TEXAS

PREP: 45 MIN. • **COOK:** 20 MIN. + FREEZING • **MAKES:** 12 SERVINGS

> ⅔ cup graham cracker crumbs
> 2 tablespoons butter, melted
> 5 teaspoons sugar

FILLING

> 3 eggs, separated
> ¼ cup plus 1 tablespoon water, divided
> 1 cup sugar, divided
> ⅛ teaspoon salt
> ⅛ teaspoon cream of tartar
> 1 package (8 ounces) reduced-fat cream cheese
> 1½ cups reduced-fat whipped topping
> 1 package (10 ounces) frozen sweetened raspberries, thawed

1. In a small bowl, combine the cracker crumbs, butter and sugar. Press into an 11x7-in. dish coated with cooking spray. Cover and refrigerate crust for at least 15 minutes.

2. Meanwhile, for filling, in a small heavy saucepan, combine the egg yolks, ¼ cup water, ½ cup sugar and salt. Cook and stir over low heat until mixture reaches 160° or is thick enough to coat the back of a metal spoon. Cool quickly by placing pan in a bowl of ice water; stir for 2 minutes. Set aside.

3. In a small heavy saucepan over low heat, combine the egg whites, cream of tartar and remaining water and sugar. With a portable mixer, beat on low speed until mixture reaches 160°. Transfer to a small bowl; beat on high until soft peaks form.

4. In a large bowl, beat cream cheese until smooth. Gradually beat in egg yolk mixture. Fold in whipped topping, then egg white mixture. Drain raspberries, reserving 3 tablespoons juice. In a small bowl, crush half of berries with 1 tablespoon juice. Set remaining berries and juice aside.

5. Spread one third of the cream cheese mixture over the crust; spoon half of the crushed berry mixture over the top. Repeat layers. Cut through with a knife to swirl raspberries.

6. Top with remaining cream cheese mixture. Sprinkle with reserved berries and drizzle with remaining juice. Cover and freeze for 5 hours or until firm. Remove from the freezer 15 minutes before cutting.

Over-the-Top Blueberry Bread Pudding

Delicious warm or at room temperature, this dessert is out of this world. It's a favorite for family celebrations. For a change, top it with fresh mint and sweetened whipped cream.
—MARILYN HAYNES SYLACAUGA, ALABAMA

PREP: 15 MIN. + STANDING • **BAKE:** 50 MIN.
MAKES: 12 SERVINGS

- 3 **eggs**
- 4 **cups heavy whipping cream**
- 2 **cups sugar**
- 3 **teaspoons vanilla extract**
- 2 **cups fresh or frozen blueberries**
- 1 **package (10 to 12 ounces) white baking chips**
- 1 **loaf (1 pound) French bread, cut into 1-inch cubes**

SAUCE

- 1 **package (10 to 12 ounces) white baking chips**
- 1 **cup heavy whipping cream**

1. In a large bowl, combine the eggs, cream, sugar and vanilla. Stir in blueberries and baking chips. Stir in bread cubes; let stand for 15 minutes or until bread is softened.
2. Transfer to a greased 13x9-in. baking dish. Bake, uncovered, at 350° for 50-60 minutes or until a knife inserted near the center comes out clean. Let stand for 5 minutes before serving.
3. For sauce, place the baking chips in a small bowl. In a small saucepan, bring the cream just to a boil. Pour over baking chips; whisk until smooth. Serve with bread pudding.

FAST FIX ▶ Lemon Drop Cookies

After we'd visited at her house, my sister sent a care package for the trip home. These delightful cookies were tucked inside. Crushed lemon drop candies and grated lemon peel lend refreshingly zesty taste.
—PAT ZIMMERMAN MIDLAND, TEXAS

PREP/TOTAL TIME: 25 MIN. • **MAKES:** ABOUT 3½ DOZEN

- ½ **cup butter, softened**
- ¾ **cup sugar**
- 1 **egg**
- 1 **tablespoon half-and-half cream**
- 1 **teaspoon grated lemon peel**
- 1½ **cups all-purpose flour**
- ½ **cup finely crushed lemon drops**
- 1 **teaspoon baking powder**
- ¼ **teaspoon salt**

1. In a large bowl, cream butter and sugar until light and fluffy. Beat in the egg, cream and peel. Combine the flour, lemon drops, baking powder and salt; gradually add to the creamed mixture and mix well.
2. Drop by rounded teaspoonfuls 3 in. apart onto greased baking sheets. Bake at 350° for 8-10 minutes or until edges are lightly browned. Cool for 2 minutes before removing to wire racks.

Peanut Butter-Chocolate Ice Cream Torte

What's not to love about peanut butter, chocolate, ice cream and Oreo cookies? This indulgent frozen dessert is a cinch to put together. It's great to have on hand for unexpected guests during the warm weather months.
—**DANA SOUTHWICK** MANTON, CALIFORNIA

PREP: 30 MIN. + FREEZING • **MAKES:** 12 SERVINGS

- 24 **Oreo cookies**
- ⅓ **cup butter, melted**

FILLING
- 1 **quart chocolate ice cream, softened**
- 1½ **cups creamy peanut butter**
- 1 **quart peanut butter ice cream with peanut butter cup pieces, softened**

TOPPING
- 2 **cups (12 ounces) semisweet chocolate chips**
- 1 **cup heavy whipping cream**
- 1½ **cups coarsely chopped miniature peanut butter cups**

1. Place cookies in a food processor. Cover and pulse until fine crumbs form. Transfer to a large bowl and stir in butter. Press onto the bottom and 1 in. up the sides of a greased 10-in. springform pan; cover and freeze for at least 15 minutes.
2. Spread chocolate ice cream into crust; cover and freeze until firm. Spread peanut butter over chocolate layer and top with peanut butter ice cream. Cover and freeze until firm.
3. Place chocolate chips in a large bowl. In a small saucepan, bring cream just to a boil. Pour over chocolate; whisk until smooth. Cool to room temperature, stirring occasionally. Spread over top of dessert. Immediately sprinkle with peanut butter cups. Cover and freeze for 1 hour before serving.

Giant Molasses Cookies

My cookie-loving clan can't get enough of these chewy delights. Send some as holiday gifts to long-distance loved ones or include in care packages to troops overseas.
—**KRISTINE CHAYES** SMITHTOWN, NEW YORK

PREP: 30 MIN. • **BAKE:** 15 MIN./BATCH • **MAKES:** 2 DOZEN

- 1½ **cups butter, softened**
- 2 **cups sugar**
- 2 **eggs**
- ½ **cup molasses**
- 4½ **cups all-purpose flour**
- 4 **teaspoons ground ginger**
- 2 **teaspoons baking soda**
- 1½ **teaspoons ground cinnamon**
- 1 **teaspoon ground cloves**
- ¼ **teaspoon salt**
- ¼ **cup chopped pecans**
- ¾ **cup coarse sugar**

1. Preheat oven to 350°. In a large bowl, cream butter and sugar until light and fluffy. Beat in eggs and molasses. Combine the flour, ginger, baking soda, cinnamon, cloves and salt; gradually add to creamed mixture and mix well. Fold in pecans.
2. Shape into 2-in. balls and roll in coarse sugar. Place 2½ in. apart on ungreased baking sheets. Bake 13-15 minutes or until tops are cracked. Remove to wire racks to cool.

STRAWBERRY CAKE, PAGE 187

ZUCCHINI CUPKCAKES, 176

TOFFEE POKE CAKE, 185

FIVE-FRUIT PIE, 180

CAKES & PIES

A slice of freshly frosted cake or a just-baked pie stirs up warm feelings of comfort, hope and joy, whether you're celebrating a birthday, graduation or retirement—or just treating the ones you love. If you want to bake up some of that goodness, you've come to the right place. Not only is this chapter chock-full of oven-fresh cakes and pies, you'll also find tangy, fruit-filled tarts, luscious cheesecakes, dreamy frosting recipes, and everyone's favorite petite treat—cupcakes. Bakers, start your ovens. This is your time to shine!

Zucchini Cupcakes

I asked my grandmother for this recipe after trying her irresistible spice cupcakes at her home. I love the creamy caramel frosting. They're so scrumptious, you actually forget you're getting a big dose of veggies, too!
—**VIRGINIA LAPIERRE** GREENSBORO BEND, VERMONT

PREP: 20 MIN. • **BAKE:** 20 MIN. + COOLING
MAKES: 1½ TO 2 DOZEN

- 3 **eggs**
- 1⅓ **cups sugar**
- ½ **cup canola oil**
- ½ **cup orange juice**
- 1 **teaspoon almond extract**
- 2½ **cups all-purpose flour**
- 2 **teaspoons ground cinnamon**
- 2 **teaspoons baking powder**
- 1 **teaspoon baking soda**
- 1 **teaspoon salt**
- ½ **teaspoon ground cloves**
- 1½ **cups shredded zucchini**

CARAMEL FROSTING
- 1 **cup packed brown sugar**
- ½ **cup butter, cubed**
- ¼ **cup 2% milk**
- 1 **teaspoon vanilla extract**
- 1½ **to 2 cups confectioners' sugar**

1. In a large bowl, beat the eggs, sugar, oil, orange juice and extract. Combine dry ingredients; gradually add to egg mixture and mix well. Stir in zucchini.

2. Fill paper-lined muffin cups two-thirds full. Bake at 350° for 20-25 minutes or until toothpick inserted near the center comes out clean. Cool for 10 minutes before removing to a wire rack.

3. For frosting, combine the brown sugar, butter and milk in a saucepan. Bring to a boil over medium heat;

cook and stir for 2 minutes or until thickened. Remove from the heat; stir in vanilla. Cool to lukewarm.

4. Gradually beat in confectioners' sugar until frosting reaches spreading consistency. Frost cupcakes.

Grasshopper Pie

This deliciously minty pie is a longtime Christmas classic in our family. We love it so much, I now make it throughout the year. It's perfect for St. Patty's Day!
—**MELISSA SOKASITS** WARRENVILLE, ILLINOIS

PREP: 15 MIN. + CHILLING • **MAKES:** 8 SERVINGS

- 1½ **cups cold milk**
- 1 **package (3.9 ounces) instant chocolate pudding mix**
- 2¾ **cups whipped topping, divided**
- 1 **package (4.67 ounces) mint Andes candies, chopped, divided**
- 1 **chocolate crumb crust (9 inches)**
- ¼ **teaspoon mint extract**
- 2 **drops green food coloring, optional**

1. In a small bowl, whisk milk and pudding mix for 2 minutes. Let stand for 2 minutes or until soft-set. Fold in ¾ cup whipped topping. Fold in ¾ cup candies. Spoon into crust.

2. In another bowl, combine extract and remaining whipped topping; add food coloring if desired. Spread over pudding layer; sprinkle with remaining candies. Cover and refrigerate for 4 hours or until set.

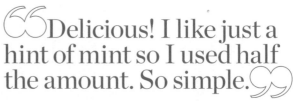

❝Delicious! I like just a hint of mint so I used half the amount. So simple.❞

—**CHERRYLADY** FROM TASTEOFHOME.COM

Cinnamon Apple Cheesecake

An attractive topping of cinnamon-spiced apples slices and a homemade oat-walnut crust make this creamy dessert a definite showstopper.
—EMILY YOUNG TROPHY CLUB, TEXAS

PREP: 40 MIN. • **BAKE:** 40 MIN. + CHILLING
MAKES: 12 SERVINGS

- ½ **cup butter, softened**
- ¼ **cup packed brown sugar**
- 1 **cup all-purpose flour**
- ¼ **cup quick-cooking oats**
- ¼ **cup finely chopped walnuts**
- ½ **teaspoon ground cinnamon**

FILLING
- 2 **packages (8 ounces each) cream cheese, softened**
- 1 **can (14 ounces) sweetened condensed milk**
- ½ **cup thawed apple juice concentrate**
- 3 **eggs, lightly beaten**

TOPPING
- 2 **medium tart apples, peeled and sliced**
- 1 **tablespoon butter**
- 1 **teaspoon cornstarch**
- ¼ **teaspoon ground cinnamon**
- ¼ **cup thawed apple juice concentrate**

1. In a small bowl, cream butter and brown sugar until light and fluffy. Gradually add flour, oats, walnuts and cinnamon until well blended. Press onto the bottom and 1½ in. up the sides of a greased 9-in. springform pan. Place on a baking sheet. Bake at 325° for 10 minutes or until set. Cool on a wire rack.

2. In a large bowl, beat cream cheese until fluffy. Beat in milk and apple juice concentrate until smooth. Add eggs; beat on low speed just until combined (batter will be thin). Pour into crust. Return pan to baking sheet.

3. Bake at 325° for 40-45 minutes or until center is almost set. Cool cheesecake on a wire rack for 10 minutes. Carefully run a knife around edge of the pan to loosen; cool 1 hour longer. Refrigerate overnight.

4. In a large skillet, cook and stir apples in butter over medium heat until crisp-tender, about 5 minutes. Cool to room temperature. Arrange over cheesecake.

5. In a small saucepan, combine the cornstarch, cinnamon and juice concentrate until smooth. Bring to a boil. Reduce heat; cook and stir for 1 minute or until thickened. Immediately brush the topping over apples. Refrigerate for 1 hour or until chilled. Refrigerate leftovers.

Turtle Praline Tart

This rich, gooey dessert is my own homemade creation. I love to serve it to guests and bring it to potlucks, but I'm thankful it's easy enough to make for an everyday pick-me-up, too!

—KATHLEEN SPECHT
CLINTON, MONTANA

PREP: 35 MIN. + CHILLING
MAKES: 16 SERVINGS

- 1 sheet refrigerated pie pastry
- 36 caramels
- 1 cup heavy whipping cream, divided
- 3½ cups pecan halves
- ½ cup semisweet chocolate chips, melted

1. Unroll pastry on a lightly floured surface. Transfer to an 11-in. fluted tart pan with removable bottom; trim edges.

2. Line unpricked pastry shell with a double thickness of heavy-duty foil. Bake at 450° for 8 minutes. Remove foil; bake 5-6 minutes longer or until light golden brown. Cool on a wire rack.

3. In a large saucepan, combine the caramels and ½ cup cream. Cook and stir over medium-low heat until the caramels are melted. Stir in pecans. Spread the filling evenly into the crust. Drizzle with the melted chocolate.

4. Refrigerate for 30 minutes or until set. Whip remaining cream; serve with tart.

Carrot-Spice Cake with Caramel Frosting

This cake starts with an easy boxed mix, but it's loaded with extras to give it that "from-scratch" flavor. It's so moist and delicious—everyone asks for the recipe!

—NORA FITZGERALD
SEVIERVILLE, TENNESSEE

PREP: 45 MIN. • **BAKE:** 25 MIN. + COOLING
MAKES: 12 SERVINGS

- 1 package spice cake mix (regular size)
- 1 package (3.4 ounces) instant vanilla pudding mix
- 4 eggs
- ¾ cup water
- ½ cup sour cream
- ¼ cup canola oil
- 1 cup shredded carrots
- 1 can (8 ounces) unsweetened crushed pineapple, drained
- ½ cup flaked coconut
- ½ cup chopped pecans
- ¼ cup raisins

FROSTING
- 1 cup butter, softened
- 1 package (8 ounces) cream cheese, softened
- 6 cups confectioners' sugar
- ½ cup caramel ice cream topping
- 1 to 2 tablespoons 2% milk

1. In a large bowl, combine the cake mix, pudding mix, eggs, water, sour cream and oil; beat on low speed for 30 seconds. Beat on medium for 2 minutes. Fold in the carrots, pineapple, coconut, pecans and raisins just until blended. Pour into two greased and floured 9-in. round baking pans.

2. Bake at 350° for 25-30 minutes or until a toothpick inserted near the center comes out clean. Cool for 10 minutes before removing from pans to wire racks to cool completely.

3. For frosting, in a large bowl, beat butter and cream cheese until fluffy. Add the confectioners' sugar, ice cream topping and enough milk to achieve desired consistency. Spread frosting between layers and over the top and sides of cake. Store in the refrigerator.

Banana Cupcakes

Go bananas when baking—especially when you have a bunch to use up. Ripe bananas are the secret to these down-home cupcakes. They look, smell and taste the best!

—JANE DEARING
NORTH LIBERTY, INDIANA

PREP: 25 MIN. • **BAKE:** 20 MIN. + COOLING
MAKES: 1½ DOZEN

- ½ cup shortening
- 1½ cups sugar
- 2 eggs
- 1 cup mashed ripe bananas (about 2 medium)
- 1 teaspoon vanilla extract
- 2 cups all-purpose flour
- ¾ teaspoon baking soda
- ½ teaspoon baking powder
- ½ teaspoon salt
- ½ cup buttermilk

LEMON BUTTER FROSTING

- 2 cups confectioners' sugar
- ⅓ cup butter, softened
- 3 tablespoons mashed ripe banana
- 1 tablespoon lemon juice

1. In a large bowl, cream shortening and sugar until light and fluffy. Add eggs, one at a time, beating well after each addition. Beat in bananas and vanilla. Combine the flour, baking soda, baking powder and salt; add dry ingredients to creamed mixture alternately with buttermilk, beating well after each addition.
2. Fill paper-lined muffin cups two-thirds full. Bake at 375° for 18-22 minutes or until a toothpick inserted near the center comes out clean. Cool for 10 minutes before removing from pan to a wire rack to cool completely.
3. In a small bowl, combine the frosting ingredients; beat until light and fluffy. Frost cupcakes.

CHERRY BANANA CUPCAKES *Fold ⅓ cup each chopped maraschino cherries and walnuts into the batter. In the frosting, substitute milk for lemon juice.*

FROST CUPCAKES IN A FLASH

To quickly frost cupcakes, place frosting in a bowl. The frosting should be a soft, spreadable consistency. If it's too stiff, add milk a teaspoon at a time until it reaches desired consistency. Dip top of cupcake into the frosting, twist slightly and lift up.

Southern Sweet Potato Pie

This recipe is popular in the South. It's a particular favorite at our house because we always have plenty of sweet potatoes in our garden. Try it with a dollop of whipped cream.

—BONNIE HOLCOMB
FULTON, MISSISSIPPI

PREP: 15 MIN. • **BAKE:** 55 MIN. + CHILLING
MAKES: 8 SERVINGS

- 3 tablespoons all-purpose flour
- 1⅔ cups sugar
- ¼ teaspoon ground nutmeg
   Pinch salt
- 1 cup mashed sweet potatoes
- 2 eggs
- ¼ cup light corn syrup
- ½ cup butter, softened
- ¾ cup evaporated milk
- 1 unbaked pastry shell (9 inches)

1. In a small bowl, combine the flour, sugar, nutmeg and salt. In a large bowl, beat the potatoes, eggs, corn syrup, butter and sugar mixture. Gradually stir in milk. Pour into pastry shell.
2. Bake at 350° for 55-60 minutes. Cool on a wire rack for 1 hour. Refrigerate for at least 3 hours before serving. Refrigerate any leftovers.

Caramel-Pecan Cheesecake Pie

This rich, nutty pie is one I'm proud to serve any time of year, although it's especially good around Halloween and Thanksgiving. It's impressive, but a snap to make.
—**REBECCA RUFF** MCGREGOR, IOWA

PREP: 15 MIN. • **BAKE:** 35 MIN. + CHILLING
MAKES: 6-8 SERVINGS

- 1   **sheet refrigerated pie pastry**
- 1   **package (8 ounces) cream cheese, softened**
- ½   **cup sugar**
- 4   **eggs**
- 1   **teaspoon vanilla extract**
- 1¼ **cups chopped pecans**
- 1   **jar (12¼ ounces) fat-free caramel ice cream topping**
      Additional fat-free caramel ice cream topping, optional

1. Line a 9-in. deep-dish pie plate with pastry. Trim and flute edges. In a small bowl, beat the cream cheese, sugar, 1 egg and vanilla until smooth. Spread into pastry shell; sprinkle with pecans.

2. In a small bowl, whisk remaining eggs; gradually whisk in caramel topping until blended. Pour slowly over pecans.

3. Bake at 375° for 35-40 minutes or until lightly browned (loosely cover edges with foil after 20 minutes if pie browns too quickly). Cool on a wire rack for 1 hour. Refrigerate for 4 hours or overnight before slicing. If desired, garnish with additional caramel ice cream topping.

NOTE *This recipe was tested with Smucker's ice cream topping.*

Five-Fruit Pie

My fruity sensation gets compliments galore. I give it to new neighbors or anyone who needs a pie pan full of sweet sunshine. They all love it!
—**JEAN ROSS** OIL CITY, PENNSYLVANIA

PREP: 40 MIN. • **BAKE:** 45 MIN. + COOLING • **MAKES:** 8 SERVINGS

- 1½ **cups sugar**
- 3   **tablespoons cornstarch**
- 2   **tablespoons quick-cooking tapioca**
- 1   **cup chopped peeled tart apples**
- 1   **cup chopped fresh or frozen rhubarb**
- 1   **cup each fresh or frozen raspberries, blueberries and sliced strawberries**

CRUST
- 2   **cups all-purpose flour**
- ½   **teaspoon salt**
- ½   **cup shortening**
- 1   **egg**
- ¼   **cup cold water**
- 2   **teaspoons white vinegar**
- 2   **tablespoons half-and-half cream**
- 2   **tablespoons coarse sugar**

1. In a large bowl, combine the sugar, cornstarch, tapioca and fruit; let stand for 15 minutes. In another bowl, combine flour and salt; cut in shortening until mixture resembles coarse crumbs. Combine the egg, water and vinegar; stir into flour mixture just until moistened.

2. Divide dough in half so that one portion is slightly larger than the other. On a lightly floured surface, roll out larger portion to fit a 9-in. pie plate. Transfer pastry to pie plate; trim pastry to ½ in. beyond edge of plate. Spoon fruit mixture into crust.

3. Roll out remaining pastry to fit top of pie; make a lattice crust. Trim, seal and flute edges. Brush with cream; sprinkle with coarse sugar.

4. Bake at 375° for 45-55 minutes or until crust is golden brown and filling is bubbly. Cool completely on a wire rack.

NOTE *If using frozen fruit, measure fruit while still frozen, then thaw completely. Drain in a colander, but do not press liquid out.*

Hummingbird Cupcakes

Turn the traditional hummingbird cake—flavored with pineapple, bananas and walnuts—into a bite-sized treat with these moist cupcakes.

—JESSIE OLESON SEATTLE, WASHINGTON

PREP: 40 MIN. • **BAKE:** 20 MIN. + COOLING
MAKES: ABOUT 2 DOZEN

- 1 cup butter, softened
- 2 cups sugar
- 3 eggs
- 2 teaspoons vanilla extract
- 2 cups mashed ripe bananas
- ½ cup drained canned crushed pineapple
- 3 cups all-purpose flour
- 1 teaspoon baking soda
- 1 teaspoon ground cinnamon
- ½ teaspoon salt
- 1 cup flaked coconut
- 1 cup chopped walnuts

CREAM CHEESE FROSTING
- 1 package (8 ounces) cream cheese, softened
- ½ cup butter, softened
- 3¾ cups confectioners' sugar
- 1 teaspoon vanilla extract

1. In a large bowl, cream butter and sugar until light and fluffy. Add eggs, one at a time, beating well after each addition. Beat in vanilla. In a small bowl, combine bananas and pineapple.

2. Combine the flour, baking soda, cinnamon and salt; add to the creamed mixture alternately with banana mixture, beating well after each addition. Fold in coconut and walnuts.

3. Fill paper-lined muffin cups two-thirds full. Bake at 350° for 20-25 minutes or until a toothpick inserted near the center comes out clean. Cool cupcakes for 10 minutes before removing from pans to wire racks to cool completely.

4. In a small bowl, beat cream cheese and butter until fluffy. Add confectioners' sugar and vanilla; beat until smooth. Frost cupcakes.

Chocolate Banana Cream Cake

My inspiration for this cake came from my desire to create a dessert combining my father's love for cake, my mother's love for chocolate and my love for bananas. It's divine!

—SUSIE PATTISON DUBLIN, OHIO

PREP: 30 MIN. • **BAKE:** 20 MIN. + COOLING
MAKES: 12 SERVINGS

- ½ cup butter, softened
- 1¼ cups sugar
- 2 eggs, separated
- 1½ cups mashed ripe bananas (about 3 medium)
- ¼ cup sour cream
- 2 teaspoons vanilla extract
- 1½ cups all-purpose flour
- 1 teaspoon baking soda
- ¼ teaspoon salt

FILLING/FROSTING
- 1½ cups cold 2% milk
- 1 package (3.4 ounces) instant banana cream pudding mix
- 1 can (16 ounces) chocolate frosting
- 2 medium firm bananas, sliced
- 3 tablespoons lemon juice

1. In a large bowl, cream butter and sugar until light and fluffy. Beat in egg yolks. Beat in the bananas, sour cream and vanilla. Combine the flour, baking soda and salt; add to the creamed mixture and mix well.

2. In a small bowl, beat egg whites until stiff peaks form. Fold into batter. Transfer to two greased and floured 9-in. round baking pans. Bake at 350° for 20-25 minutes or until a toothpick inserted near the center comes out clean. Cool for 10 minutes before removing from pans to wire racks to cool completely.

3. For filling, in a small bowl, whisk milk and pudding mix for 2 minutes. Let stand for 2 minutes or until soft-set. Cover and refrigerate until chilled.

4. In a small bowl, beat frosting until light and fluffy. Place bananas in a small bowl; toss with lemon juice.

5. Place one cake layer on a serving plate; spread with 3 tablespoons frosting. Stir pudding; spread half over the frosting. Top with half of the bananas and the remaining cake layer. Repeat frosting, filling and banana layers. Frost sides and decorate top edge of cake with remaining frosting. Store in the refrigerator.

Zucchini Chocolate Cake

This moist, chocolaty cake is a great way to use up a bounty of zucchini. Serve it alone or with fresh berries.

—WEDA MOSELLIE
PHILLIPSBURG, NEW JERSEY

PREP: 25 MIN.
BAKE: 45 MIN. + COOLING
MAKES: 15 SERVINGS

- ½ cup butter, softened
- 1¾ cups sugar
- ½ cup canola oil
- 2 eggs
- 1 teaspoon vanilla extract
- 1 cup 2% milk
- ½ cup buttermilk
- 2½ cups all-purpose flour
- ¼ cup baking cocoa
- 1 teaspoon baking soda
- ½ teaspoon baking powder
- ½ teaspoon salt
- 2 cups shredded zucchini
- ½ cup semisweet chocolate chips
  Confectioners' sugar

1. In a large bowl, beat the butter, sugar and oil until smooth. Add eggs, one at a time, beating well after each addition. Beat in vanilla. Combine milk and buttermilk. Combine the flour, cocoa, baking soda, baking powder and salt; add to batter alternately with milk mixture, beating well after each addition. Fold in zucchini.
2. Transfer to a greased 13x9-in. baking pan. Sprinkle batter with chocolate chips. Bake at 325° for 45-50 minutes or until a toothpick inserted near the center comes out clean. Cool on a wire rack. Dust with confectioners' sugar.

Chocolate Almond Cheesecake

This cheesecake is easy to make but it's definitely not easy to wait till the next day to eat it! It's a spectacular make-ahead treat for a party.

—DARLENE BRENDEN
SALEM, OREGON

PREP: 25 MIN. + CHILLING
BAKE: 50 MIN. + CHILLING
MAKES: 12-16 SERVINGS

CRUST
- 1 package (9 ounces) chocolate wafer cookies, crushed (about 2 cups)
- ¼ cup sugar
- ¼ teaspoon ground cinnamon
- ¼ cup butter, melted

FILLING
- 2 packages (8 ounces each) cream cheese, softened
- 1 cup sugar
- 1 cup (8 ounces) sour cream
- 8 ounces semisweet chocolate, melted and cooled
- ½ teaspoon almond extract
- 2 eggs, lightly beaten

TOPPING
- 1 cup (8 ounces) sour cream
- ¼ teaspoon baking cocoa
- 2 tablespoons sugar
- ½ teaspoon almond extract

1. In a small bowl, combine crust ingredients; reserve 2 tablespoons for garnish. Press remaining crumbs evenly onto the bottom and 2 in. up the sides of a 9-in. springform pan. Chill.
2. For filling, in a large bowl, beat cream cheese and sugar until smooth. Beat in the sour cream, chocolate and extract. Add eggs; beat on low speed just until combined. Pour into crust.
3. Place pan on a baking sheet. Bake at 350° for 40 minutes (filling will not be set). Remove from oven and let stand for 5 minutes.
4. Meanwhile, combine topping ingredients. Gently spread over filling. Sprinkle with reserved crumbs. Bake 10 minutes longer.
5. Cool on a wire rack for 10 minutes. Carefully run a knife around edge of pan to loosen; cool 1 hour longer. Refrigerate overnight.

Marvelous Cannoli Cake

A luscious, chocolate-studded cannoli filling separates the tender vanilla layers of this heavenly cake, which starts with a handy packaged mix. It's best served well chilled.

—ANTOINETTE OWENS
RIDGEFIELD, CONNECTICUT

PREP: 30 MIN. + CHILLING
BAKE: 25 MIN. + COOLING
MAKES: 12 SERVINGS

- 1 package French vanilla cake mix (regular size)

FILLING
- 1 carton (16 ounces) ricotta cheese
- ½ cup confectioners' sugar
- 2 teaspoons ground cinnamon
- 1 teaspoon almond extract
- 1 teaspoon rum extract
- 1 teaspoon vanilla extract
- 2 ounces semisweet chocolate, finely chopped

FROSTING
- 2 cartons (8 ounces each) mascarpone cheese
- ¾ cup confectioners' sugar, sifted
- ¼ cup whole milk
- 2 teaspoons almond extract
- 1 teaspoon vanilla extract
- 1 cup sliced almonds
- 2 tablespoons miniature semisweet chocolate chips

1. Prepare and bake cake mix according to the package directions, using two greased and floured 9-in. round baking pans. Cool for 10 minutes before removing from pans to wire racks to cool completely.

2. In a large bowl, combine the ricotta cheese, confectioners' sugar, cinnamon and extracts; stir in chocolate. In another bowl, beat the mascarpone cheese, confectioners' sugar, milk and extracts on medium speed until creamy (do not overmix).

3. Place one cake layer on a serving plate; spread with 1 cup filling. Top with second cake layer. Spread remaining filling over the top of cake to within 1 in. of edges. Frost sides and top edge of cake with 2 cups frosting.

4. Press almonds into sides of cake. Sprinkle chocolate chips over top. Refrigerate until serving.

Ultimate Chocolate Cake

Semisweet chocolate chips add rich flavor to this moist cake that's lower in fat than its traditional counterpart. It makes an excellent dessert or snack.

—KAY MCMICKEN
CHARLOTTE, NORTH CAROLINA

PREP: 15 MIN. • **BAKE:** 45 MIN. + COOLING
MAKES: 12 SERVINGS

- 1 package devil's food cake mix (regular size)
- 1 package (1.4 ounces) sugar-free instant chocolate pudding mix
- 1 cup (8 ounces) fat-free sour cream
- ½ cup unsweetened applesauce
- ½ cup water
- 2 eggs
- ½ cup egg substitute
- ½ cup semisweet chocolate chips
- 1½ teaspoons confectioners' sugar

1. In a bowl, combine the first seven ingredients; mix well. Stir in chocolate chips. Coat a 10-in. fluted tube pan with cooking spray and dust with flour; add batter.

2. Bake at 350° for 45-50 minutes or until a toothpick inserted near the center comes out clean. Cool for 10 minutes before removing from the pan to a wire rack to cool completely. Lightly dust cake with confectioners' sugar.

Vermont Maple-Pecan Cake

This nutty maple cake has become a hands-down favorite. Chopped pecans add delicious flavor, and the rich cream cheese frosting is accented with a teaspoon of real maple syrup.

—TERESA CARDIN MANSFIELD, MISSOURI

PREP: 40 MIN. • **BAKE:** 20 MIN. + COOLING
MAKES: 6 SERVINGS

- ¾ cup plus 1 tablespoon all-purpose flour
- ¼ cup sugar
- ¼ cup packed brown sugar
- ½ teaspoon baking soda
- ¼ teaspoon salt
- ½ cup buttermilk
- ¼ cup butter, melted
- 3 tablespoons maple syrup
- ¼ teaspoon vanilla extract
- ⅓ cup finely chopped pecans, toasted

GLAZED PECANS
- 3 tablespoons light corn syrup
- ⅓ cup pecan halves

FROSTING
- 1 package (3 ounces) cream cheese, softened
- 3 tablespoons butter, softened
- 1 tablespoon plus 1 teaspoon maple syrup
- 1½ cups confectioners' sugar

1. In a large bowl, combine the flour, sugars, baking soda and salt. Combine the buttermilk, butter, syrup and vanilla; stir into dry ingredients just until combined. Fold in chopped pecans.

2. Pour into two 6-in. round baking pans coated with cooking spray. Bake at 350° for 20-25 minutes or until a toothpick inserted near the center comes out clean. Cool for 10 minutes before removing from pans to wire racks to cool completely.

3. In a small saucepan, bring corn syrup to a boil. Cook and stir for 1 minute or until slightly thickened. Remove from the heat; stir in pecan halves until coated. Place in a single layer on a foil-lined baking sheet. Bake at 425° for 2-3 minutes or until golden brown. Cool.

4. For frosting, in a small bowl, beat the cream cheese, butter and syrup until smooth. Beat in confectioners' sugar. Place one cake layer on a serving plate; spread with ½ cup frosting. Top with second layer; frost top and sides of cake. Garnish with glazed pecans. Store in the refrigerator.

NOTE *This recipe does not use eggs.*

Makeover Peanut Butter Cup Cheesecake

No one will ever guess this decadent cheesecake is light. The firm texture and yummy peanut butter cups make it over-the-top indulgent!

—SHARON ANDERSON
LYONS, ILLINOIS

PREP: 30 MIN. • **BAKE:** 50 MIN. + CHILLING
MAKES: 16 SERVINGS

- ¾ cup graham cracker crumbs
- 2 tablespoons sugar
- 2 tablespoons butter, melted
- ¾ cup creamy peanut butter

FILLING

- 2 packages (8 ounces each) fat-free cream cheese
- 1 package (8 ounces) reduced-fat cream cheese
- 1 cup (8 ounces) reduced-fat sour cream
- ¾ cup sugar
- 2 eggs, lightly beaten
- 1½ teaspoons vanilla extract
- ¾ cup hot fudge ice cream topping, divided
- 6 peanut butter cups, cut into small wedges

1. In a small bowl, combine the cracker crumbs, sugar and butter. Press onto the bottom of a 9-in. springform pan coated with cooking spray.

2. Place pan on a baking sheet. Bake at 350° for 10 minutes. Cool on a wire rack. In a microwave-safe bowl, heat peanut butter on high for 30 seconds or until softened. Spread over the crust to within 1 in. of edges.

3. In a large bowl, beat the cream cheese, sour cream and sugar until smooth. Add eggs; beat on low speed just until combined. Stir in vanilla. Pour 1 cup into a bowl; set aside. Pour remaining filling over peanut butter layer.

4. In a microwave-safe bowl, heat ¼ cup fudge topping on high for 30 seconds or until thin; fold into reserved cream cheese mixture. Carefully pour over filling; cut through with a knife to swirl.

5. Return pan to baking sheet. Bake for 50-60 minutes or until center is almost set. Cool on a wire rack for 10 minutes. Carefully run a knife around edge of pan to loosen; cool 1 hour longer.

6. Microwave the remaining fudge topping on high for 30 seconds or until warmed; spread topping over cheesecake. Garnish with chopped peanut butter cups. Refrigerate cheesecake overnight.

Toffee Poke Cake

This simple recipe is a favorite among family and friends. The oozing caramel tastes wonderful with the smooth chocolate cake.

—JEANETTE HOFFMAN
OSHKOSH, WISCONSIN

PREP: 25 MIN. • **BAKE:** 25 MIN. + CHILLING
MAKES: 15 SERVINGS

- 1 package chocolate cake mix (regular size)
- 1 jar (17 ounces) butterscotch-caramel ice cream topping
- 1 carton (12 ounces) frozen whipped topping, thawed
- 3 Heath candy bars (1.4 ounces each), chopped

1. Prepare and bake cake according to package directions, using a greased 13x9-in. baking pan. Cool on a wire rack.

2. Using the handle of a wooden spoon, poke holes in cake. Pour ¾ cup caramel topping into holes. Spoon remaining caramel over cake. Top with whipped topping. Sprinkle with candy. Refrigerate for at least 2 hours before serving.

> ❝This is so delicious it should be declared sinful! I've made this numerous times for picnics, and it's always a huge hit.❞
>
> **—MKONK** FROM TASTEOFHOME.COM

Easy Vanilla Buttercream Frosting

This basic buttery frosting has unmatchable homemade taste. With a few simple variations, you can come up with different colors and flavors.
—**DIANA WILSON** DENVER, COLORADO

PREP/TOTAL TIME: 10 MIN. • **MAKES:** ABOUT 3 CUPS

- ½ cup butter, softened
- 4½ cups confectioners' sugar
- 1½ teaspoons vanilla extract
- 5 to 6 tablespoons 2% milk

In a large bowl, cream butter until light and fluffy. Beat in the confectioners' sugar, vanilla and enough milk to achieve desired consistency.

ALMOND BUTTERCREAM FROSTING *Substitute ½ to ¾ teaspoon almond extract for the vanilla.*

CHOCOLATE BUTTERCREAM FROSTING *Reduce confectioners' sugar to 4 cups and add ½ cup baking cocoa; increase milk to 6-7 tablespoons.*

LEMON BUTTERCREAM FROSTING *Substitute 5-6 tablespoons lemon juice for the milk; add 1 teaspoon grated lemon peel.*

ORANGE BUTTERCREAM FROSTING *Substitute 5-6 tablespoons orange juice for the milk; add 1 teaspoon grated orange peel.*

PEANUT BUTTER FROSTING *Substitute peanut butter for the butter; increase milk to 6-8 tablespoons.*

PEPPERMINT BUTTERCREAM FROSTING *Substitute ½ to ¾ teaspoon peppermint extract for the vanilla.*

Magnolia Dream Cheesecake

Your guests will be amazed when they learn this gorgeous Italian-style dessert is your own homemade creation, not store-bought! It's flavored with a delightful combination of hazelnut and peach.
—**CHARLENE CHAMBERS** ORMOND BEACH, FLORIDA

PREP: 50 MIN. • **BAKE:** 1½ HOURS + CHILLING
MAKES: 16 SERVINGS

- 1 cup hazelnuts, toasted
- 12 whole graham crackers
- ¼ cup sugar
- 6 tablespoons unsalted butter, melted

FILLING
- 1½ pounds ricotta cheese
- 2 packages (8 ounces each) cream cheese, softened
- 2 cups (16 ounces) sour cream
- 1½ cups sugar
- 6 tablespoons all-purpose flour
- 4 tablespoons hazelnut liqueur, divided
- 6 eggs, lightly beaten
- 3 medium peaches, sliced

1. Place a greased 10-in. springform pan on a double thickness of heavy-duty foil (about 18 in. square). Securely wrap foil around pan.
2. Place hazelnuts in a food processor; cover and pulse until coarsely chopped. Set aside ¼ cup for garnish. Add graham crackers and sugar to food processor; cover and process until finely chopped. Add butter; process until blended. Press onto the bottom and 1 in. up the sides of prepared pan. Place pan on a baking sheet. Bake at 325° for 10 minutes. Cool on a wire rack.
3. In a large bowl, beat the ricotta cheese, cream cheese, sour cream and sugar until well blended. Beat in flour and 2 tablespoons liqueur. Add eggs; beat on low speed just until combined. Pour into crust. Place springform pan in a large baking pan; add 1 in. of hot water to larger pan.
4. Bake at 325° for 1½ hours or until center is just set and top appears dull. Remove springform pan from water bath. Cool on a wire rack for 10 minutes. Carefully run a knife around edge of pan to loosen; cool 1 hour longer. Refrigerate overnight.
5. Toss peaches with remaining liqueur; arrange over top of cheesecake. Sprinkle reserved hazelnuts in the center. Remove sides of pan.

Pineapple Pudding Cake

My mother made this cool and refreshing dessert during the dog days of summer. I love that it calls for low-fat ingredients, so I can indulge my sweet tooth without expanding my waistline!
—**KATHLEEN WORDEN** NORTH ANDOVER, MASSACHUSETTS

PREP: 25 MIN. • **BAKE:** 15 MIN. + CHILLING
MAKES: 20 SERVINGS

- 1 package (9 ounces) yellow cake mix
- 1½ cups cold fat-free milk
- 1 package (1 ounce) sugar-free instant vanilla pudding mix
- 1 package (8 ounces) fat-free cream cheese
- 1 can (20 ounces) unsweetened crushed pineapple, well drained
- 1 carton (8 ounces) frozen fat-free whipped topping, thawed
- ¼ cup chopped walnuts, toasted
- 20 maraschino cherries, well drained

1. Prepare cake mix batter according to package directions; pour into a 13x9-in. baking pan coated with cooking spray.
2. Bake at 350° for 15-20 minutes or until a toothpick inserted near the center comes out clean. Cool completely on a wire rack.
3. In a large bowl, whisk milk and pudding mix for 2 minutes. Let stand for 2 minutes or until soft-set.
4. In a small bowl, beat cream cheese until smooth. Beat in pudding mixture until blended. Spread evenly over cake. Sprinkle with pineapple; spread with whipped topping. Sprinkle with walnuts and garnish with cherries. Refrigerate until serving.

LEFTOVER PINEAPPLE JUICE

Use leftover juice from canned pineapple to make an easy marinade for chicken breasts. Add a little olive oil, soy sauce and garlic, then refrigerate the chicken overnight in the marinade. The next day, it's ready to bake. Or, use the juice to coat apple slices to keep them white—or add it to orange juice for fun flavor!

Strawberry Cake

I garnish the top of this cake with fresh strawberries to give guests a clue as to what delight awaits inside.
—**PAM ANDERSON** BILLINGS, MONTANA

PREP: 25 MIN. • **BAKE:** 25 MIN. + COOLING
MAKES: 12-16 SERVINGS

- 1 package white cake mix (regular size)
- 1 package (3 ounces) strawberry gelatin
- 1 cup water
- ½ cup canola oil
- 4 egg whites
- ½ cup mashed unsweetened strawberries
  Whipped cream or frosting for your choice

1. In a large bowl, combine the dry cake mix, gelatin powder, water and oil. Beat on low speed for 1 minute or until moistened; beat on medium for 4 minutes.
2. In a small bowl with clean beaters, beat egg whites on high speed until stiff peaks form. Fold egg whites and mashed strawberries into cake batter.
3. Pour into three greased and floured 8-in. round baking pans. Bake at 350° for 25-30 minutes or until a toothpick comes out clean. Cool for 10 minutes before removing from pans to wire racks to cool completely.
4. Spread whipped cream or frosting between layers and over top and sides of cake. If frosted with whipped cream, store in the refrigerator.

Cream Cheese Pound Cake

Fresh fruit and a dollop of whipped cream dress up this moist and tender pound cake—it's always a winner with my family and friends.

—RICHARD HOGG
ANDERSON, SOUTH CAROLINA

PREP: 25 MIN.
BAKE: 1¼ HOURS + COOLING
MAKES: 16 SERVINGS

1½ cups butter, softened
1 package (8 ounces) cream cheese, softened
3 cups sugar
6 eggs
2 teaspoons vanilla extract
1 teaspoon lemon extract
3 cups all-purpose flour
½ teaspoon baking powder
¼ teaspoon salt
Confectioners' sugar, sliced fresh strawberries and whipped cream, optional

1. In a large bowl, cream the butter, cream cheese and sugar until light and fluffy. Add eggs, one at a time, beating well after each addition. Beat in extracts. Combine the flour, baking powder and salt; beat into the creamed mixture until blended.

2. Pour into a greased and floured 10-in. fluted tube pan. Bake at 325° for 1¼ to 1½ hours or until a toothpick inserted near the center comes out clean.

3. Cool for 10 minutes before removing from pan to a wire rack to cool completely. Garnish with confectioners' sugar, strawberries and whipped cream if desired.

Red Velvet Cupcakes with Coconut Frosting

There's no better way to celebrate being together than with these fun-loving cupcakes.

—MARIE RIZZIO
INTERLOCHEN, MICHIGAN

PREP: 25 MIN. • **BAKE:** 20 MIN. + COOLING
MAKES: 2 DOZEN

¾ cup butter, softened
1½ cups sugar
2 eggs
1 tablespoon red food coloring
1 teaspoon vanilla extract
1¾ cups all-purpose flour
¼ cup baking cocoa
¾ teaspoon baking soda
¾ teaspoon salt
1 cup buttermilk
1 teaspoon white vinegar
FROSTING
2 packages (8 ounces each) cream cheese, softened
¼ cup butter, softened
1½ cups confectioners' sugar
1 teaspoon vanilla extract
2 cups flaked coconut, divided

1. In a large bowl, cream butter and sugar until light and fluffy. Add eggs, one at a time, beating well after each addition. Stir in food coloring and vanilla. Combine the flour, cocoa, baking soda and salt. Combine buttermilk and vinegar. Add dry ingredients to the creamed mixture alternately with buttermilk mixture, beating well after each addition.

2. Fill foil or paper-lined muffin cups two-thirds full. Bake at 350° for 18-22 minutes or until a toothpick inserted near the center comes out clean. Cool for 10 minutes before removing from pans to wire rack to cool completely.

3. For frosting, in a large bowl, beat cream cheese and butter until fluffy. Add confectioners' sugar and vanilla; beat until smooth. Stir in 1 cup coconut. Frost cupcakes.

4. Toast remaining coconut; sprinkle over cupcakes. Store in the refrigerator.

Strawberry Poke Cake

Strawberry shortcake takes on a wonderful new twist with this super-simple recipe. Pretty red strawberry stripes liven up each slice.

—MARY JO GRIGGS
WEST BEND, WISCONSIN

PREP: 25 MIN. • **BAKE:** 25 MIN. + CHILLING
MAKES: 10-12 SERVINGS

- 1 package white cake mix (regular size)
- 1¼ cups water
- 2 eggs
- ¼ cup canola oil
- 2 packages (10 ounces each) frozen sweetened sliced strawberries, thawed
- 2 packages (3 ounces each) strawberry gelatin
- 1 carton (12 ounces) frozen whipped topping, thawed, divided
  Fresh strawberries, optional

1. In a large bowl, beat the cake mix, water, eggs and oil; beat on low speed for 30 seconds. Beat on medium for 2 minutes.
2. Pour into two greased and floured 9-in. round baking pans.

Bake at 350° for 25-35 minutes or until a toothpick inserted near the center comes out clean. Cool for 10 minutes; remove from pans to wire racks to cool completely.
3. Using a serrated knife, level top of each cake if necessary. Return layers, top side up, to two clean 9-in. round baking pans. Pierce cakes with a meat fork or wooden skewer at ½-in. intervals.
4. Drain juice from strawberries into a 2-cup measuring cup; refrigerate berries. Add water to juice to measure 2 cups; pour into a small saucepan. Bring to a boil; stir in gelatin until dissolved. Chill for 30 minutes. Gently spoon over each cake layer. Chill for 2-3 hours.
5. Dip bottom of one pan in warm water for 10 seconds. Invert cake onto a serving platter. Top with reserved strawberries and 1 cup whipped topping. Place second cake layer over topping.
6. Frost cake with remaining whipped topping. Chill for at least 1 hour. Serve with fresh berries if desired. Refrigerate leftovers.

NOTE *This cake was tested with Pillsbury white cake mix.*

Best Lime Tart

This treat is the ideal balance between tart and sweet, and the almonds in the crust are just wonderful. This is one of my husband's favorite desserts. Enjoy!

—CHARIS O'CONNELL
MOHNTON, PENNSYLVANIA

PREP: 35 MIN. • **BAKE:** 15 MIN. + CHILLING
MAKES: 12 SERVINGS

- 1¼ cups graham cracker crumbs
- 5 tablespoons butter, melted
- ¼ cup ground almonds
- 3 tablespoons sugar

FILLING
- 4 egg yolks
- 1 can (14 ounces) sweetened condensed milk
- ½ cup lime juice
- 2 teaspoons grated lime peel

TOPPING
- ½ cup heavy whipping cream
- 1 tablespoon sugar
- ½ cup sour cream
- 1 teaspoon grated lime peel
  Fresh raspberries and lime wedges

1. In a small bowl, combine cracker crumbs, butter, almonds and sugar. Press onto the bottom and up the sides of a greased 9-in. tart pan. Bake at 325° for 15-18 minutes or until edges are lightly browned.
2. In a large bowl, whisk the egg yolks, milk, lime juice and peel. Pour over crust. Bake for 12-14 minutes or until center is almost set. Cool on a wire rack. Refrigerate for at least 2 hours.
3. In a large bowl, beat cream until it begins to thicken. Add sugar; beat until stiff peaks form. Fold in sour cream and grated lime peel. Spread over tart. Garnish with raspberries and lime wedges.

Chocolate-Dipped Strawberry Cheesecake

Perfect for entertaining, this light and airy cheesecake gets its unique flavor from the chocolate crust. It always brings compliments and adds a touch of elegance to your table.

—KATHY BERGER DRY RIDGE, KENTUCKY

PREP: 45 MIN. + CHILLING • **MAKES:** 12 SERVINGS

1¾ cups chocolate graham cracker crumbs
   (about 9 whole crackers)
¼ cup butter, melted
 1 pound fresh or frozen strawberries,
   thawed
 2 envelopes unflavored gelatin
½ cup cold water
 2 packages (8 ounces each) fat-free cream
   cheese, cubed
 1 cup (8 ounces) fat-free cottage cheese
   Sugar substitute equivalent to ¾ cup sugar
 1 carton (8 ounces) frozen reduced-fat
   whipped topping, thawed, divided
12 medium fresh strawberries
 4 ounces semisweet chocolate, chopped

1. In a small bowl, combine cracker crumbs and butter. Press onto the bottom and 1 in. up the sides of a 9-in. springform pan coated with cooking spray. Place on a baking sheet. Bake at 350° for 10 minutes or until set. Cool on a wire rack.

2. Hull strawberries if necessary; puree in a food processor. Remove and set aside. In a small saucepan, sprinkle gelatin over cold water; let stand for 1 minute. Heat over low heat, stirring until gelatin is completely dissolved. Transfer to the food processor; add the cream cheese, cottage cheese and sugar substitute. Cover and process until smooth.

3. Add strawberry puree; cover and process until blended. Transfer to a large bowl; fold in 2 cups whipped topping. Pour into crust. Cover and refrigerate for 2-3 hours or until set.

4. For garnish, wash strawberries and gently pat with paper towels until completely dry. Cut tops off berries. In a microwave, melt chocolate; stir until smooth. Dip each berry tip until half of the berry is coated, allowing excess to drip off. Place with tips pointing up on a waxed paper-lined baking sheet; refrigerate for at least 30 minutes.

5. Carefully run a knife around edge of springform pan to loosen; remove sides of pan. Garnish cheesecake with chocolate-dipped strawberries and the remaining whipped topping.

NOTE *This recipe was tested with Splenda no-calorie sweetener.*

Classic Carrot Cake

I entered this yummy, moist cake in a Colorado Outfitters Association dessert contest, and it took first place!

—CHERI EBY GUNNISON, COLORADO

PREP: 30 MIN. • **BAKE:** 35 MIN. + COOLING
MAKES: 12 SERVINGS

- 1 can (8 ounces) unsweetened crushed pineapple
- 2 cups shredded carrots
- 4 eggs
- 1 cup sugar
- 1 cup packed brown sugar
- 1 cup canola oil
- 2 cups all-purpose flour
- 2 teaspoons baking soda
- 2 teaspoons ground cinnamon
- ¼ teaspoon salt
- ¾ cup chopped walnuts

FROSTING

- 2 packages (8 ounces each) cream cheese, softened
- ¼ cup butter, softened
- 2 teaspoons vanilla extract
- 1½ cups confectioners' sugar

1. Drain pineapple, reserving 2 tablespoons juice (discard remaining juice or save for another use). In a large bowl, beat the carrots, eggs, sugars, oil, pineapple and reserved juice until well blended. In a small bowl, combine the flour, baking soda, cinnamon and salt; gradually beat into pineapple mixture until blended. Stir in walnuts.

2. Transfer to a greased 13x9-in. baking dish. Bake at 350° for 35-40 minutes or until a toothpick inserted near the center comes out clean. Cool on a wire rack.

3. For frosting, in a large bowl, beat cream cheese and butter until smooth. Beat in vanilla. Gradually beat in confectioners' sugar until smooth. Spread over cake.

Pumpkin Chip Cream Pie

This creamy pie is perfect for any autumn celebration. A store-bought graham cracker crust makes it such a cinch to whip up.

—MARIA REGAKIS SOMERVILLE, MASSACHUSETTS

PREP: 20 MIN. + CHILLING • **MAKES:** 8 SERVINGS

- ¾ cup cold 2% milk
- 1 package (3.4 ounces) instant vanilla pudding mix
- ⅔ cup miniature semisweet chocolate chips
- ½ cup canned pumpkin
- ¾ teaspoon pumpkin pie spice
- 1 carton (8 ounces) frozen whipped topping, thawed, divided
- 1 graham cracker crust (9 inches)
  Slivered almonds and chocolate curls, optional

1. In a large bowl, whisk milk and pudding mix for 2 minutes (mixture will be thick). Stir in the chocolate chips, pumpkin and pie spice. Fold in 2 cups whipped topping. Spoon into crust. Refrigerate for 4 hours or until set.

2. Spread with remaining whipped topping; garnish with almonds and chocolate curls if desired.

FAST FIX Lemon Burst Tartlets

You'll love the taste of lemon and raspberry in these quick and easy bites. They're perfect for a party or as a simple dessert with coffee or tea.

–PAM JAVOR NORTH HUNTINGTON, PA

PREP/TOTAL TIME: 20 MIN. • **MAKES:** 2½ DOZEN

- 1 jar (10 ounces) lemon curd
- 1 carton (8 ounces) frozen whipped topping, thawed
- 5 to 6 drops yellow food coloring, optional
- ⅔ cup raspberry cake and pastry filling
- 2 packages (1.9 ounces each) frozen miniature phyllo tart shells
- 30 fresh raspberries

In a large bowl, combine the lemon curd, whipped topping and food coloring if desired until smooth. Spoon 1 teaspoon raspberry filling into each tart shell. Pipe or spoon lemon mixture over filling. Garnish each with a raspberry. Refrigerate leftovers.

Potluck Banana Cake

I found this recipe over 5 years ago and have been making it for family gatherings ever since. The coffee-flavored frosting complements the moist banana cake.

—KATHY HOFFMAN
TOPTON, PENNSYLVANIA

PREP: 25 MIN. • **BAKE:** 35 MIN. + COOLING
MAKES: 12-15 SERVINGS

- ½ cup butter, softened
- 1 cup sugar
- 2 eggs
- 1 teaspoon vanilla extract
- 2 cups all-purpose flour
- 2 teaspoons baking soda
- ½ teaspoon salt
- 1½ cups mashed ripe bananas (about 3 medium)
- 1 cup (8 ounces) sour cream

COFFEE FROSTING
- ⅓ cup butter, softened
- 2½ cups confectioners' sugar
- 2 teaspoons instant coffee granules
- 2 to 3 tablespoons milk

1. In a large bowl, cream butter and sugar until light and fluffy. Add the eggs, one at a time, beating well after each addition. Stir in the vanilla. Combine the flour, baking soda and salt; add to the creamed mixture alternately with bananas and sour cream, beating well after each addition.

2. Pour batter into a greased 13x9-in. baking dish. Bake at 350° for 35-40 minutes or until a toothpick inserted near the center comes out clean. Cool completely on a wire rack.

3. For frosting, in a small bowl, beat butter and confectioners' sugar until smooth. Dissolve coffee granules in milk; add to butter mixture and beat until smooth. Spread over cake.

Layered Lemon Pies

My sister shared this recipe with me, and it yields a pie that's simply delicious. The secret to the amazing flavor is to use fresh lemon juice.

—NANETTE SORENSEN
TAYLORSVILLE, UTAH

PREP: 55 MIN. + CHILLING
MAKES: 2 PIES (10 SERVINGS EACH)

- Pastry for two single-crust pies (9 inches)
- 1½ cups sugar
- 6 tablespoons cornstarch
- ¼ teaspoon salt
- 2 cups cold water
- 3 egg yolks, lightly beaten
- ⅓ cup lemon juice
- ¼ cup butter, cubed
- 1 teaspoon grated lemon peel
- 1 teaspoon lemon extract
- 3 drops yellow food coloring, optional

SECOND LAYER
- 1 package (8 ounces) cream cheese, softened
- 1 cup confectioners' sugar
- 1½ cups cold 2% milk
- 2 packages (3.4 ounces each) instant lemon pudding mix

TOPPING
- 1 package (8 ounces) cream cheese, softened
- 1 cup confectioners' sugar
- 1 carton (16 ounces) frozen whipped topping, thawed

1. Line two 9-in. pie plates with pastry; trim and flute edges. Line unpricked pastry with a double thickness of heavy-duty foil. Bake at 450° for 8 minutes. Remove foil; bake 5-7 minutes longer or until golden brown. Cool on wire racks.

2. In a large saucepan, combine the sugar, cornstarch and salt. Stir in water until smooth. Cook and stir over medium-high heat until thickened and bubbly. Reduce heat; cook and stir 2 minutes longer. Remove from the heat.

3. Stir a small amount of hot filling into egg yolks; return all to the pan, stirring constantly. Bring to a gentle boil; cook and stir 2 minutes longer. Remove from heat. Gently stir in the lemon juice, butter, lemon peel, extract and food coloring if desired. Cool to room temperature without stirring. Spread lemon mixture into crusts. Refrigerate for 30 minutes or until firm.

4. In a large bowl, beat cream cheese and confectioners' sugar until smooth. Gradually beat in milk. Add pudding mix; beat 2 minutes longer. Let stand for 2 minutes or until soft-set. Gently spread into pies. Refrigerate for 30 minutes or until set.

5. For topping, in a large bowl, beat cream cheese and confectioners' sugar until smooth. Fold in the whipped topping. Spread over tops of pies. Refrigerate until set.

Sour Cream Chocolate Cake

Standing tall with three layers, this classic American cake raises the dessert bar. It makes the perfect grand finale to a Sunday dinner or birthday celebration.

—MARSHA LAWSON
PFLUGERVILLE, TEXAS

PREP: 35 MIN. • **BAKE:** 30 MIN. + COOLING
MAKES: 16 SERVINGS

- 1 cup baking cocoa
- 1 cup boiling water
- 1 cup butter, softened
- 2½ cups sugar
- 4 eggs
- 2 teaspoons vanilla extract
- 3 cups cake flour
- 2 teaspoons baking soda
- ½ teaspoon baking powder
- ½ teaspoon salt
- 1 cup (8 ounces) sour cream

FROSTING
- 2 cups (12 ounces) semisweet chocolate chips
- ½ cup butter, cubed
- 1 cup (8 ounces) sour cream
- 1 teaspoon vanilla extract
- 4½ to 5 cups confectioners' sugar

1. Dissolve cocoa in boiling water; cool. In a large bowl, cream butter and sugar until light and fluffy. Add eggs, one at a time, beating well after each. Beat in vanilla.

Combine the flour, baking soda, baking powder and salt; gradually add to creamed mixture alternately with sour cream, beating well after each addition. Add cocoa mixture and mix well.

2. Pour into three greased and floured 9-in. round baking pans. Bake at 350° for 30-35 minutes or until a toothpick inserted near the center comes out clean. Cool for 10 minutes before removing from pans to wire racks to cool completely.

3. In a microwave, melt chocolate chips and butter; stir until smooth. Cool for 5 minutes. Transfer to a large bowl. Beat in sour cream and vanilla. Add confectioners' sugar; beat until light and fluffy. Spread between layers and over top and sides of cake. Store in refrigerator.

FAST FIX

Lava Chocolate Cakes

True decadence at its best, these petite cakes feature a warm, gooey chocolate center. Whether you enjoy them garnished with a dollop of fresh whipped cream or lightly sprinkled with confectioners' sugar, you'll want to lick the plate clean!

—TASTE OF HOME COOKING SCHOOL

PREP/TOTAL TIME: 30 MIN.
MAKES: 4 SERVINGS

- 4 teaspoons sugar
- ½ cup butter, cubed
- 4 ounces semisweet chocolate, chopped
- 1 cup confectioners' sugar
- 2 eggs
- 2 egg yolks
- 1½ teaspoons instant coffee granules
- ¾ teaspoon vanilla extract
- 6 tablespoons all-purpose flour
- ½ teaspoon salt
  Whipped cream, optional
  Additional confectioners' sugar, optional

1. Grease the bottom and sides of four 6-oz. ramekins; sprinkle each with 1 teaspoon sugar. Place the ramekins on a baking sheet; set aside.

2. In a medium microwave-safe bowl, melt butter and chocolate; stir until smooth. Stir in confectioners' sugar until smooth. Whisk in the eggs, egg yolks, instant coffee and vanilla. Stir in flour and salt; spoon batter into prepared ramekins.

3. Bake at 400° for about 12 minutes or until a thermometer reads 160° and cake sides are set and centers are soft.

4. Remove ramekins to a wire rack to cool for 5 minutes. Carefully run a small knife around cakes to loosen. Invert warm cakes onto serving plates. Lift ramekins off cakes. Serve warm with whipped cream or sprinkle with additional confectioners' sugar if desired.

Chocolate-Peanut Butter Cupcakes

The traditional pairing of peanut butter and chocolate works perfectly in these scrumptious little cakes.

—TASTE OF HOME TEST KITCHEN

PREP: 30 MIN. • **BAKE:** 20 MIN. + COOLING • **MAKES:** 2 DOZEN

- 1 package chocolate cake mix (regular size)
- 1¼ cups water
- ½ cup peanut butter
- ⅓ cup canola oil
- 3 eggs
- 24 miniature peanut butter cups

FROSTING
- 6 ounces semisweet chocolate, chopped
- ⅔ cup heavy whipping cream
- ⅓ cup peanut butter
  - Additional miniature peanut butter cups, chopped

1. In a large bowl, combine the cake mix, water, peanut butter, oil and eggs; beat on low speed for 30 seconds. Beat on medium for 2 minutes or until smooth.

2. Fill paper-lined muffin cups half full. Place a peanut butter cup in the center of each cupcake. Cover each with 1 tablespoonful batter.

3. Bake at 350° for 18-22 minutes or until a toothpick inserted near the center of the cupcake comes out clean. Cool for 10 minutes before removing from pans to wire racks to cool completely.

4. Place chocolate in a small bowl. In a small saucepan, bring cream just to a boil. Pour over chocolate; whisk until smooth. Stir in peanut butter. Cool, stirring occasionally, to room temperature or until mixture reaches a spreading consistency, about 10 minutes.

5. Spread over cupcakes; immediately sprinkle with additional peanut butter cups. Let stand until set.

NOTE *Reduced-fat peanut butter is not recommended for this recipe.*

Old-Fashioned Fudge Cake

This simple one-layer cake has a moist texture and cuts well. The frosting is fast and easy to make.

—MARY SCHILLINGER WOODSTOCK, GEORGIA

PREP: 30 MIN. • **BAKE:** 40 MIN. + COOLING • **MAKES:** 6 SERVINGS

- ¼ cup shortening
- 1 cup sugar
- 1 egg
- 1 egg white
- ½ teaspoon vanilla extract
- 1 cup plus 2 tablespoons all-purpose flour
- 4½ teaspoons baking cocoa
- ½ teaspoon baking soda
- ½ teaspoon salt
- ¼ cup 2% milk
- ½ cup boiling water

FROSTING
- ¾ cup sugar
- ¼ cup half-and-half cream
- 2 tablespoons butter
- ⅓ cup miniature marshmallows
- ¼ cup semisweet chocolate chips

1. In a large bowl, cream shortening and sugar until light and fluffy. Add egg, then egg white, beating well after each addition. Stir in vanilla. Combine the flour, cocoa, baking soda and salt; add to the creamed mixture alternately with milk, beating well after each addition. Stir in water until smooth. Pour into a greased and floured 6-in. round baking pan.

2. Bake at 350° for 40-45 minutes or until a toothpick inserted near the center comes out clean. Cool for 10 minutes before removing from pan to a wire rack to cool completely.

3. In a small saucepan over low heat, combine the sugar, cream and butter. Bring to a boil; cook and stir for 2 minutes. Remove from the heat; stir in marshmallows and chocolate chips until smooth. Spread frosting over top and sides of cake.

FAST FIX Bakery Frosting

This recipe makes it easy to capture the fabulous flavor of cakes from the best bakeries. A big batch of this sweet frosting keeps for 3 months in the refrigerator.
—**BARBARA JONES** TOWER HILL, ILLINOIS

PREP/TOTAL TIME: 10 MIN. • **MAKES:** 8 CUPS

- 2 cups shortening
- ½ cup powdered nondairy creamer
- 1 teaspoon almond extract
- 1 package (32 ounces) confectioners' sugar
- ½ to ¾ cup water
  Food coloring, optional

1. In a large bowl, beat the shortening, creamer and extract until smooth. Gradually beat in confectioners' sugar. Add enough water until frosting reaches desired consistency. If desired, add food coloring.
2. Store in the refrigerator for up to 3 months. Bring to room temperature before spreading.

Bite-Size Apple Pies

Kids can help make these fun handheld bites. Simply wrap strips of pastry around apple wedges and sprinkle on some cinnamon-sugar. Then pop in the oven to bake, and watch them disappear!
—**TASTE OF HOME TEST KITCHEN**

PREP: 20 MIN. • **BAKE:** 15 MIN. • **MAKES:** 16 SERVINGS

- ½ cup sugar
- 2 teaspoons ground cinnamon
- 1 package (14.1 ounces) refrigerated pie pastry
- 3 tablespoons butter, melted, divided
- 2 medium tart apples, each cut into 8 wedges

1. In a small bowl, combine sugar and cinnamon; set aside 1 tablespoon. On a lightly floured surface, unroll pastry. Brush with 2 tablespoons butter; sprinkle with remaining sugar mixture.

2. Cut each sheet into eight 1-in. strips, about 8 inches long. Wrap one strip around each apple wedge, placing sugared side of pastry against the apple.
3. Place on parchment paper-lined baking sheet. Brush tops with remaining butter; sprinkle with reserved sugar mixture. Bake at 425° for 13-15 minutes or until pastry is golden brown. Serve warm.

Chocolate Silk Pie

This quick and creamy chocolate pie not only melts in your mouth, it also melts any and all resistance to dessert!
—**MARY RELYEA** CANASTOTA, NEW YORK

PREP: 30 MIN. + CHILLING • **MAKES:** 6-8 SERVINGS

- 1 unbaked pastry shell (9 inches)
- 1 jar (7 ounces) marshmallow creme
- 1 cup (6 ounces) semisweet chocolate chips
- ¼ cup butter, cubed
- 2 ounces unsweetened chocolate
- 2 tablespoons strong brewed coffee
- 1 cup heavy whipping cream, whipped

TOPPING
- 1 cup heavy whipping cream
- 2 tablespoons confectioners' sugar
  Chocolate curls, optional

1. Line unpricked pastry shell with a double thickness of heavy-duty foil. Bake at 450° for 8 minutes. Remove foil; bake 5 minutes longer. Cool on a wire rack.
2. Meanwhile, in a heavy saucepan, combine the marshmallow creme, chocolate chips, butter, unsweetened chocolate and coffee; cook and stir over low heat until chocolate is melted and mixture is smooth. Cool. Fold in whipped cream; pour into crust.
3. For topping, in a large bowl, beat cream until it begins to thicken. Add confectioners' sugar; beat until stiff peaks form. Spread over filling. Refrigerate for at least 3 hours before serving. Garnish with chocolate curls if desired.

FOR QUICK CHOCOLATE CURLS *Use a vegetable peeler to "peel" curls from a solid block of chocolate. To keep the strips intact, allow them to fall gently onto a plate or a single layer of waxed paper. If you get only shavings, your chocolate may be too hard, so warm it slightly.*

CHERRY COLA CAKE, PAGE 203

SAVORY PARTY BREAD, 202

INDIVIDUAL BEEF WELLINGTONS, 201

FIESTA SWEET POTATO SOUP, 204

EDITORS' FAVORITES

The editors and staff at *Taste of Home*, Taste of Home Cooking School and *Country Woman* magazine read, test and taste hundreds of recipes each year. Here we've gathered their top picks—from crowd-pleasing appetizers and sides to must-have main dishes, desserts and every course in between. These are the recipes they've been asked to share time and again...and they're sure you'll get requests for the recipes, too!

As Chief Food Editor for the *Taste of Home* Brands, I love to find recipes that are simple to make, use easy-to-find ingredients and knock the flavor factor out of the park. So I appreciate that our loyal readers share such great recipes with us and their fellow home cooks. Here are a few favorite gems I like to whip up for my own family.

It's easier than ever to get your daily dose of vegetables when you serve up a beautiful platter of Veggie Nicoise Salad. Lemon & Sage Roasted Chicken bakes up juicy and tender and boasts great citrus flavor. Have room for dessert? Everything about this classic Real Deal Apple Pie makes it a top request at gatherings. The just-right flaky crust cuts beautifully to reveal big chunks of cinnamon apples. How sweet is that?

—KAREN BERNER TASTE OF HOME FOOD EDITOR

Veggie Nicoise Salad

More and more people in my workplace are becoming vegetarians or simply choosing to eat more fresh produce and less meat. This salad combines some of my favorite ingredients in one dish. With the hard-boiled eggs and kidney beans, it delivers enough protein to meet your daily nutritional needs.

–ELIZABETH KELLEY CHICAGO, ILLINOIS

PREP: 40 MIN. • **COOK:** 25 MIN. • **MAKES:** 6 SERVINGS

⅓ cup olive oil
¼ cup lemon juice
2 teaspoons minced fresh oregano
2 teaspoons minced fresh thyme
1 teaspoon Dijon mustard
1 garlic clove, minced
¼ teaspoon coarsely ground pepper
⅛ teaspoon salt

1 pound small red potatoes, halved
1 pound fresh asparagus, trimmed
½ pound fresh green beans, trimmed
1 can (16 ounces) kidney beans, rinsed and drained
1 small red onion, halved and thinly sliced
2 bunches romaine, torn
6 hard-cooked eggs, quartered
1 jar (6½ ounces) marinated quartered artichoke hearts, drained
½ cup Nicoise or kalamata olives

1. In a small bowl, whisk the first eight ingredients; set aside.
2. Place potatoes in a small saucepan and cover with water. Bring to a boil. Reduce heat; cover and simmer for 10-15 minutes or until tender. Drain. Drizzle warm potatoes with 1 tablespoon vinaigrette; toss to coat and set aside.
3. In a large saucepan, bring 4 cups water to a boil. Add asparagus; cook for 2-4 minutes or until crisp-tender. With tongs, remove asparagus and immediately place in ice water. Drain and pat dry.
4. Return water to a boil. Add green beans; cook for 3-4 minutes or until crisp-tender. Remove beans and place in ice water. Drain and pat dry.
5. In a small bowl, combine the kidney beans, onion and 1 tablespoon vinaigrette; toss to coat. Set aside.
6. Just before serving, toss asparagus with 1 tablespoon vinaigrette; toss green beans with 2 teaspoons vinaigrette. Place romaine in a large bowl; drizzle with remaining vinaigrette and toss to coat. Transfer to a serving platter; arrange vegetables, kidney bean mixture, eggs, artichoke hearts and olives over lettuce.

Lemon & Sage Roasted Chicken

Whether it's soaking in marinade or baking in the oven, this easy-to-prepare chicken allows ample hands-free time.
—JAN VALDEZ CHICAGO, ILLINOIS

PREP: 20 MIN. + MARINATING • **BAKE:** 2¼ HOURS + STANDING
MAKES: 6 SERVINGS

¼ cup lemon juice
¼ cup plus 3 tablespoons olive oil, divided

5 garlic cloves, minced
2 tablespoons minced fresh sage
1 roasting chicken (6 to 7 pounds)
2 tablespoons butter, softened
1 medium lemon, cut into wedges
8 medium potatoes, quartered
2 medium onions, quartered
½ teaspoon salt
¼ teaspoon pepper

1. In a 2-gallon resealable plastic bag, combine the lemon juice, ¼ cup oil, garlic and sage. Add the chicken; seal bag and turn to coat. Refrigerate for at least 4 hours. Drain and discard marinade.
2. With fingers, carefully loosen skin from the chicken; rub butter under the skin. Fill cavity with lemon wedges. Place chicken breast side up on a rack in a roasting pan.
3. In a large bowl, combine the potatoes, onions, salt, pepper and remaining oil. Arrange around chicken. Bake, uncovered, at 350° for 2¼ to 2¾ hours or until a thermometer reads 180°. Cover loosely with foil if chicken browns too quickly. Let stand for 15 minutes before carving.

Real Deal Apple Pie

Everyone should know how to make apple pie in the classic style—the real deal! This recipe is a perfect example of why this American icon has been a hit in this country for hundreds of years. It gets its stunning height from 3 pounds of apples. So stock up; you'll need them.
—MARGO FERRICK WESTFORD, MASSACHUSETTS

PREP: 35 MIN. • **BAKE:** 1¼ HOURS + COOLING
MAKES: 8 SERVINGS

2¼ cups all-purpose flour
2 teaspoons sugar
¾ teaspoon kosher salt
1 cup cold unsalted butter, cubed
6 to 8 tablespoons ice water

FILLING
5   medium Braeburn apples (about 1½ pounds), peeled and cut into ¼-in. slices
4 medium Granny Smith apples (about 1½ pounds), peeled and cut into ¼-in. slices
½ cup sugar
3 tablespoons lemon juice
2 tablespoons all-purpose flour
½ teaspoon kosher salt
¾ teaspoon ground cinnamon
    Dash ground nutmeg
3 tablespoons unsalted butter, cut into pieces
1 egg, lightly beaten
1 to 2 tablespoons superfine sugar

1. In a large bowl, mix flour, sugar and salt; cut in butter until crumbly. Gradually add water, tossing with a fork until dough holds together when pressed. Divide dough in two portions so that one is slightly larger than the other; wrap each in plastic wrap. Refrigerate for 1 hour or until easy to handle.
2. Preheat oven to 425°. In a large bowl, combine the apples, sugar, lemon juice, flour, salt, cinnamon and nutmeg.
3. On a lightly floured surface, roll out larger portion of dough to ⅛-in. thick circle. Transfer to a 9-in. pie plate, trimming even with edge. Fill with apple mixture, mounding in the center. Dot apples with butter. Lightly brush rim of pastry with some of the beaten egg.
4. Roll out remaining dough to fit top of pie; place over filling. Trim, seal and flute edges. Cut slits in pastry. Brush top with egg; sprinkle with superfine sugar. Place on a foil-lined 15x10x1-in. baking pan.
5. Bake 20 minutes. Reduce heat to 375°. Bake 50-60 minutes or until crust is golden brown and filling is bubbly. Cool on a wire rack 2 hours before serving.

Food connects people to each other and to moments in time. That's why I love to cook and entertain—to bring people together and share in an appetite for life. As General Manager of the Taste of Home Cooking School, not only do I get to help bring the country's largest food and entertaining magazine to life, but I get to help connect our readers to each other.

Here are a few reader-submitted recipes I'm proud to serve. Wake up tired taste buds with Spicy Breakfast Lasagna. You'll agree this is one egg bake that stands apart! Want to pack in some extra nutrition with dinner? Spinach Bean Salad with Maple Dressing is loaded with good-for-you ingredients. And if you have fancier fare in mind, Individual Beef Wellingtons are guaranteed to please.

—ERIN PUARIEA
TASTE OF HOME COOKING SCHOOL, GENERAL MANAGER

Garlic-Onion Cheese Spread

Whenever there's an event at church, my friends always remind me to bring this cheese spread. Once you add it to crackers, it's hard to stop eating them!
–MICHELLE DEFRIEZ GRAND BLANC, MICHIGAN

PREP/TOTAL TIME: 10 MIN. • **MAKES:** 2¼ CUPS

- 2 packages (8 ounces each) cream cheese, softened
- 2 to 3 tablespoons apricot preserves
- 3 green onions (green portion only), chopped
- 3 tablespoons crumbled cooked bacon
- ½ to 1 teaspoon minced garlic
  Dash pepper
  Assorted crackers

In a small bowl, beat cream cheese and preserves until blended. Stir in the onions, bacon, garlic and pepper. Refrigerate until serving. Serve with crackers.

Spicy Breakfast Lasagna

It's fun to cook up something new for family and friends—especially when it gets rave reviews. When I brought this dish to our breakfast club at work, people said it really woke up their taste buds!
–GUTHRIE TORP JR. HIGHLANDS RANCH, COLORADO

PREP: 20 MIN. + CHILLING • **BAKE:** 35 MIN.
MAKES: 12-16 SERVINGS

- 3 cups (24 ounces) 4% cottage cheese
- ½ cup minced chives
- ¼ cup sliced green onions
- 18 eggs
- ⅓ cup milk
- ½ teaspoon salt
- ¼ teaspoon pepper
- 1 tablespoon butter
- 8 lasagna noodles, cooked and drained
- 4 cups frozen shredded hash browns
- 1 pound bulk pork sausage, cooked and crumbled
- 8 ounces sliced Monterey Jack cheese with jalapeno peppers
- 8 ounces sliced Muenster cheese

1. In a large bowl, combine the cottage cheese, chives and onions; set aside. In a large bowl, whisk the eggs, milk, salt and pepper. In a large skillet, heat butter until hot. Add egg mixture; cook and stir over medium heat until eggs are completely set. Remove from heat; set aside.

2. In a greased 13x9-in. baking dish, place four lasagna noodles. Top with 2 cups hash browns, scrambled eggs, sausage and half of cottage cheese mixture. Cover with Monterey Jack cheese. Repeat layers with the remaining lasagna noodles, hash browns and cottage cheese mixture. Top with Muenster cheese.

3. Cover and refrigerate for 8 hours or overnight. Remove from the refrigerator 30 minutes before baking. Bake, uncovered, at 350° for 35-40 minutes or until a knife inserted near the center comes out clean. Let stand for 5 minutes before cutting.

FAST FIX ▸ Spinach Bean Salad with Maple Dressing

Warm maple dressing slightly wilts the spinach in this salad, giving it a unique texture and memorable flavor. This is quick and easy to make, plus it's healthy and tasty!
–SALLY MALONEY DALLAS, GEORGIA

PREP/TOTAL TIME: 15 MIN. • **MAKES:** 11 SERVINGS

- ¼ cup maple syrup
- 3 tablespoons cider vinegar
- 1 tablespoon olive oil
- 1 tablespoon Dijon mustard
- ¼ teaspoon salt
- ¼ teaspoon coarsely ground pepper
- 1 can (15½ ounces) great northern beans, rinsed and drained
- 2 packages (6 ounces each) fresh baby spinach
- 4 green onions, thinly sliced
- 1 small sweet red pepper, chopped
- 5 bacon strips, cooked and crumbled

1. For dressing, in a small microwave-safe bowl, combine the first six ingredients; set aside. Place beans in another microwave-safe bowl. Microwave, uncovered, for 1-2 minutes or until heated through.
2. In a large salad bowl, combine the spinach, onions, red pepper, bacon and beans. Microwave the dressing, uncovered, for 30-60 seconds or until heated through. Whisk until smooth; drizzle over salad and toss to coat.

Individual Beef Wellingtons

A savory mushroom-wine sauce is perfectly poured over golden pastry in this recipe from our Test Kitchen. This elegant entree is your best bet for Christmas guests.
–TASTE OF HOME TEST KITCHEN

PREP: 30 MIN. • **BAKE:** 25 MIN. • **MAKES:** 6 SERVINGS

- 6 beef tenderloin steaks (1½ to 2 inches thick and 8 ounces each)
- 4 tablespoons butter, divided
- 3 sheets frozen puff pastry, thawed
- 1 egg, lightly beaten
- ½ pound sliced fresh mushrooms
- ¼ cup chopped shallots
- 2 tablespoons all-purpose flour
- 1 can (10½ ounces) condensed beef consomme, undiluted
- 3 tablespoons port wine
- 2 teaspoons minced fresh thyme

1. In a large skillet, brown steaks in 2 tablespoons butter for 2-3 minutes on each side. Remove and keep warm.
2. On a lightly floured surface, roll each puff pastry sheet into a 14x9½-in. rectangle. Cut each into two 7-in. squares (discard scraps). Place a steak in the center of each square. Lightly brush pastry edges with water. Bring opposite corners of pastry over steak; pinch seams to seal tightly. Cut four small slits in top of pastry.
3. Place in a greased 15x10x1-in. baking pan. Brush with egg. Bake at 400° for 25-30 minutes or until pastry is golden brown and meat reaches desired doneness (for medium-rare, a thermometer should read 145°; medium, 160°; well-done, 170°).
4. Meanwhile, in the same skillet, saute mushrooms and shallots in remaining butter for 3-5 minutes or until tender. Combine flour and consomme until smooth; stir into mushroom mixture. Bring to a boil; cook and stir for 2 minutes or until thickened. Stir in wine and thyme. Cook and stir 2 minutes longer. Serve with beef.

Of course I have the best job in the world because I get to taste most of the recipes that go into each issue of *Taste of Home* magazine. And because all of the recipes come from real people who love to cook—and who cook to share their love—you know everything is going to be pretty darn delicious.

Here are a few that I can't seem to stop making at home. Buffalo Chicken Lasagna is the best non-traditional lasagna I've eaten. It's uber spicy, so I tend to cut back on the wing sauce. As for the Savory Party Bread, it's a five-ingredient wonder of melty buttery cheese with warm sourdough bread. And for dessert? Cherry Cola Cake is one of those sweet surprises that contains soda pop and mini marshmallows baked right into the cake. Totally irresistible.

—**JEANNE AMBROSE** TASTE OF HOME EDITOR

Savory Party Bread

It's impossible to stop nibbling on warm pieces of this cheesy, oniony bread. The sliced loaf fans out for a fun presentation.

—**KAY DALY** RALEIGH, NORTH CAROLINA

PREP/TOTAL TIME: 30 MIN. • **MAKES:** 8 SERVINGS

- 1 unsliced round loaf sourdough bread (1 pound)
- 1 pound Monterey Jack cheese
- ½ cup butter, melted
- ½ cup chopped green onions
- 2 to 3 teaspoons poppy seeds

1. Preheat oven to 350°. Cut bread crosswise into 1-in. slices to within ½ in. of bottom of loaf. Repeat cuts in opposite direction. Cut cheese into ¼-in. slices; cut slices into small pieces. Place cheese in cuts.

2. In a small bowl, mix butter, green onions and poppy seeds; drizzle over bread. Wrap in foil; place on a baking sheet. Bake 15 minutes. Unwrap; bake 10 minutes longer or until cheese is melted.

Buffalo Chicken Lasagna

This recipe was inspired by my daughter's favorite food—buffalo wings! It tastes just like it came from a restaurant.

—**MELISSA MILLWOOD** LYMAN, SOUTH CAROLINA

PREP: 1 HOUR 40 MIN. • **BAKE:** 40 MIN. + STANDING
MAKES: 12 SERVINGS

- 1 tablespoon canola oil
- 1½ pounds ground chicken
- 1 small onion, chopped
- 1 celery rib, finely chopped
- 1 large carrot, grated
- 2 garlic cloves, minced
- 1 can (14½ ounces) diced tomatoes, drained
- 1 bottle (12 ounces) buffalo wing sauce
- ½ cup water
- 1½ teaspoons Italian seasoning
- ½ teaspoon salt
- ¼ teaspoon pepper
- 9 lasagna noodles
- 1 carton (15 ounces) ricotta cheese
- 1¾ cups (7 ounces) crumbled blue cheese, divided
- ½ cup minced Italian flat leaf parsley
- 1 egg, lightly beaten
- 3 cups (12 ounces) shredded part-skim mozzarella cheese
- 2 cups (8 ounces) shredded white cheddar cheese

1. In a Dutch oven, heat oil over medium heat. Add the chicken, onion, celery and carrot; cook and stir until meat is no longer pink and vegetables are tender. Add garlic; cook 2 minutes longer. Stir in the tomatoes, wing sauce, water, Italian seasoning, salt and pepper; bring to a boil. Reduce heat; cover and simmer for 1 hour.

2. Meanwhile, cook noodles according to package directions; drain. In a small bowl, mix the ricotta cheese, ¾ cup blue cheese, parsley and egg.

- ¾ **cup butter, softened**
- 1 **cup confectioners' sugar**
- 1 **jar (7 ounces) marshmallow creme**
- 2 **tablespoons frozen cherry-pomegranate juice concentrate, thawed**
  Fresh sweet cherries with stems

1. Preheat oven to 350°. Line bottoms of two greased 9-in. round baking pans with parchment paper; grease paper. Divide marshmallows between pans.

2. In a large bowl, whisk flour, sugar and baking soda. In a small saucepan, combine butter, cola and cocoa; bring just to a boil, stirring occasionally. Add to flour mixture, stirring just until moistened.

3. In a small bowl, whisk eggs, buttermilk and vanilla until blended; add to flour mixture, whisking constantly. Pour into prepared pans, dividing batter evenly. (Marshmallows will float to the top.)

4. Bake 25-30 minutes or until a toothpick inserted in center comes out clean. Cool in pans 10 minutes before removing to wire racks; remove paper. Cool completely.

5. For frosting, in a small bowl, beat butter and confectioners' sugar until smooth. Beat in marshmallow creme and juice concentrate on low speed just until blended.

6. Place one cake layer on a serving plate; spread top with 1 cup frosting. Top with remaining cake layer; spread with remaining frosting. Decorate with cherries.

NOTE *To frost sides as well as top of cake, double amounts for frosting.*

3. Spread 1½ cups sauce into a greased 13x9-in. baking dish. Layer with three noodles, 1½ cups sauce, ⅔ cup ricotta mixture, 1 cup mozzarella cheese, ⅔ cup cheddar cheese and ⅓ cup blue cheese. Repeat the layers twice.

4. Bake, covered, at 350° for 20 minutes. Uncover; bake 20-25 minutes longer or until bubbly and cheese is melted. Let stand for 10 minutes before serving.

Cherry Cola Cake

This heavenly sensation is the royalty of all desserts, thanks to its combination of fluffy cake layers, creamy frosting and cherry topping.

— **CHERI MASON** HARMONY, NORTH CAROLINA

PREP: 30 MIN. • **BAKE:** 25 MIN. + COOLING
MAKES: 12 SERVINGS

- 1½ **cups miniature marshmallows**
- 2 **cups all-purpose flour**
- 2 **cups sugar**
- 1 **teaspoon baking soda**
- 1 **cup butter, cubed**
- 1 **cup cherry-flavored cola**
- 3 **tablespoons baking cocoa**
- 2 **eggs**
- ½ **cup buttermilk**
- 1 **teaspoon vanilla extract**

People always say that we have delicious recipes, and I believe *Country Woman* readers are great cooks. That's why we're proud to share a wealth of recipes that call for fresh, whole foods.

As editor of *Country Woman* magazine, I have many favorites, but here are a few that stand out. Bread & Butter Peppers are a great way to use up a bounty of peppers from the garden or farmer's market. They add zest to ordinary salads and sandwiches. And if you're looking for a slow-cooked sensation with a unique flavor twist, give Mojito Pulled Pork a try. It has a little heat so it's sure to warm up your hungry clan on a cold day. Fiesta Sweet Potato Soup is a family favorite. It's colorful and full of hearty ingredients. And to end dinner on a sweet note, I turn to velvety Butter Pecan Cheesecake. It never disappoints!

—LORI GRZYBOWSKI COUNTRY WOMAN EDITOR

FAST FIX ▶ Fiesta Sweet Potato Soup

Here's a simple soup with plenty of taste and just a little heat. Loaded with sweet potatoes, black beans and sausage, it tastes even better the next day—if you have any left!
—GILDA LESTER MILLSBORO, DELAWARE

PREP/TOTAL TIME: 30 MIN. • **MAKES:** 6 SERVINGS (2¼ QUARTS)

- 1 **package (9 ounces) fully cooked spicy chicken sausage links, chopped**
- 2 **medium sweet potatoes, peeled and cubed**
- 1 **large onion, chopped**
- 1 **small green pepper, diced**
- 2 **tablespoons olive oil**
- 2 **teaspoons ground cumin**
- 2 **cans (14½ ounces each) reduced-sodium chicken broth**
- 1 **can (14½ ounces) diced tomatoes with mild green chilies, undrained**
- 1 **can (15 ounces) black beans, rinsed and drained**
- 2 **tablespoons minced fresh cilantro**
  Sour cream and thinly sliced green onions

1. In a large saucepan, saute the sausage, sweet potatoes, onion and pepper in oil until onion is tender. Add cumin; cook 1 minute longer. Stir in the broth, tomatoes and beans. Bring to a boil. Reduce heat; cover and simmer for 10 minutes or until potatoes are tender. Stir in cilantro.

2. Garnish servings with sour cream and green onions.

Bread & Butter Peppers

If your pepper plants are as prolific as mine, this recipe will come in handy. The crunchy mix of sliced peppers gives a kick to salads, side dishes and sandwich toppings.
—STARR MILAM SHELDON, WISCONSIN

PREP: 20 MIN. + STANDING • **COOK:** 5 MIN. + CHILLING
MAKES: 1 QUART

- 2½ **cups seeded sliced banana peppers (about 7 peppers)**
- 1 **medium green pepper, julienned or 1 medium green tomato, halved and sliced**
- 1 **jalapeno pepper, seeded and sliced**
- 1 **small onion, sliced**
- ¼ **cup canning salt**
- 12 to 15 **ice cubes**
- 2 **cups sugar**
- 1 **cup white vinegar**
- 1 **tablespoon mustard seed**
- ½ **teaspoon celery seed**

1. In a large bowl, combine the peppers, onion and salt; top with ice. Let stand for 2 hours. Rinse and drain well.

2. In a large saucepan, combine the sugar, vinegar, mustard seed and celery seed. Bring to a boil; cook and stir just until sugar is dissolved. Pour over pepper mixture; cool. Cover tightly and refrigerate for at least 24 hours. Store in the refrigerator for up to 3 months.
NOTE *Wear disposable gloves when cutting hot peppers; the oils can burn skin. Avoid touching your face.*

SLOW COOKER Mojito Pulled Pork

This fork-tender pulled pork tastes fabulous on a bun, on toasted bread or wrapped in a tortilla. My kids like to eat it spooned over rice in its citrus-flavored juices.
—**MINDY OSWALT** WINNETKA, CALIFORNIA

PREP: 20 MIN. • **COOK:** 7 HOURS • **MAKES:** 16 SERVINGS

- 1 boneless pork shoulder roast (4 to 5 pounds)
- 2 teaspoons salt
- 2 teaspoons dried oregano
- 2 teaspoons each ground cumin, paprika and pepper
- 1 bunch fresh cilantro, divided
- 2 medium onions, halved and sliced
- ¼ cup canned chopped green chilies
- 4 garlic cloves, minced
- 2 cans (14½ ounces each) reduced-sodium chicken broth
- ⅔ cup orange juice
- ½ cup lime juice
- 16 sandwich buns, split
  Barbecue sauce

1. Cut roast in half. Combine the salt, oregano, cumin, paprika and pepper; rub over pork. Place in a 4- or 5-qt. slow cooker.
2. Mince cilantro to measure ¼ cup; set aside. Trim remaining cilantro, discarding stems. Add the whole cilantro leaves, onions, chilies and garlic to the slow cooker. Combine the broth, orange juice and lime juice; pour over roast. Cover and cook on low for 7-9 hours or until meat is tender.
3. Remove roast; cool slightly. Skim fat from cooking juices; set aside 3 cups juices. Discard remaining juices. Shred pork with two forks and return to slow cooker. Stir in minced cilantro and reserved cooking juices; heat through. Spoon ½ cup meat onto each bun. Serve with barbecue sauce.

Butter Pecan Cheesecake

Fall always makes me yearn for this pecan cheesecake, but it's delicious any time of year. You'll want to put it on your list of favorite holiday desserts.
—**LAURA SYLVESTER** MECHANICSVILLE, VIRGINIA

PREP: 30 MIN. • **BAKE:** 70 MIN. + CHILLING • **MAKES:** 16 SERVINGS

- 1½ cups graham cracker crumbs
- ½ cup finely chopped pecans
- ⅓ cup sugar
- ⅓ cup butter, melted

FILLING
- 3 packages (8 ounces each) cream cheese, softened
- 1½ cups sugar
- 2 cups (16 ounces) sour cream
- 1 teaspoon vanilla extract
- ½ teaspoon butter flavoring
- 3 eggs, lightly beaten
- 1 cup finely chopped pecans

1. In a large bowl, combine the cracker crumbs, pecans, sugar and butter; set aside ⅓ cup for topping. Press remaining crumb mixture onto the bottom and 1 in. up the sides of a greased 9-in. springform pan.
2. Place springform pan on a double thickness of heavy-duty foil (about 18 in. square). Securely wrap foil around pan.
3. In a large bowl, beat cream cheese and sugar until smooth. Beat in the sour cream, vanilla and butter flavoring. Add eggs; beat on low speed just until combined. Fold in pecans. Pour into crust; sprinkle with reserved crumb mixture. Place springform pan in a large baking pan; add 1 in. of hot water to larger pan.
4. Bake at 325° for 70-80 minutes or until center is almost set. Remove springform pan from water bath. Cool on a wire rack for 10 minutes. Carefully run a knife around edge of pan to loosen; cool 1 hour longer. Refrigerate overnight. Remove sides of pan.

ALL-AMERICAN BACON CHEESEBURGERS, PAGE 209

PATRIOTIC ICE CREAM CUPCAKES, 208

OGRE EYES HOT COCOA, 213

SWEET & SALTY SNOWMEN, 222

SEASONAL SPECIALTIES

Christmas, Thanksgiving, the Fourth of July...special occasions call for special food. Family cooks know that holidays and the changing of the seasons offer an opportunity to experiment with new ingredients and flavors and get creative in the kitchen! In this chapter, you'll find some of their most popular recipes sure to impress guests during festive celebrations. From summer's flame-broiled fare to winter's cozy comfort foods, the perfect dish is always at your fingertips.

Frozen Ice Cream Delight

For summer picnics and potlucks, you can't go wrong with this refreshing frozen treat. It's also handy—you can make it days in advance.

—SUSAN BRACKEN APEX, NORTH CAROLINA

PREP: 30 MIN. + FREEZING • **MAKES:** 12-16 SERVINGS

- 2½ cups cream-filled chocolate sandwich cookie crumbs, divided
- ½ cup butter, melted
- ½ cup sugar
- ½ gallon chocolate, coffee or vanilla ice cream, softened
- 2 cups confectioners' sugar
- ⅔ cup semisweet chocolate chips
- ½ cup butter, cubed
- 1 can (12 ounces) evaporated milk
- 1 teaspoon vanilla extract
- 1½ cups salted peanuts
- 1 carton (8 ounces) frozen whipped topping, thawed

1. Combine 2 cups cookie crumbs with butter and sugar. Press onto the bottom of a 13x9-in. dish. Freeze for 15 minutes.

2. Spread ice cream over crumbs; freeze until firm, about 3 hours.

3. In a small saucepan, combine the confectioners' sugar, chocolate chips, butter and evaporated milk. Bring to a boil; boil for 8 minutes. Remove from the heat; stir in vanilla. Cool to room temperature.

4. Spoon sauce over ice cream layer; sprinkle with peanuts. Freeze until firm. Spread whipped topping over the top; sprinkle with remaining cookie crumbs. Freeze for at least 3 hours before serving.

Patriotic Ice Cream Cupcakes

Create flavor fireworks with these ice cream cupcakes. The hand-held treats feature red velvet cake, blue moon ice cream and creamy, white frozen topping.

—TASTE OF HOME TEST KITCHEN

PREP: 30 MIN. + FREEZING • **BAKE:** 15 MIN. + COOLING
MAKES: 3 DOZEN

- 1 package red velvet cake mix (regular size)
- 1 quart blue moon ice cream, softened
- 3 cups heavy whipping cream
- 1½ cups marshmallow creme
  Red, white and blue sprinkles
  Blue colored sugar

1. Prepare cake mix batter according to package directions for cupcakes.

2. Fill paper-lined muffin cups half full. Bake at 350° for 11-14 minutes or until a toothpick inserted near the center comes out clean. Cool for 10 minutes before removing from pans to wire racks to cool completely.

3. Working quickly, spread ice cream over cupcakes. Freeze for at least 1 hour.

4. In a large bowl, combine cream and marshmallow creme; beat until stiff peaks form. Pipe over cupcakes; decorate with sprinkles and colored sugar. Freeze for 4 hours or until firm.

EDITOR'S *Note: As a substitute for blue moon ice cream, tint softened vanilla ice cream with blue food coloring.*

FAST FIX **All-American Bacon Cheeseburgers**

Looking for all-star recipe to serve your clan this Fourth of July? You won't need to call them to the table twice when they see these giant, juicy burgers on the menu.

—JACKIE BURNS KETTLE FALLS, WASHINGTON

PREP/TOTAL TIME: 30 MIN. • **MAKES:** 4 SERVINGS

- 2 **tablespoons finely chopped onion**
- 2 **tablespoons ketchup**
- 1 **garlic clove, minced**
- 1 **teaspoon sugar**
- 1 **teaspoon Worcestershire sauce**
- 1 **teaspoon steak sauce**
- ¼ **teaspoon cider vinegar**
- 1 **pound ground beef**
- 4 **slices sharp cheddar cheese**
- 4 **hamburger buns, split and toasted**
- 8 **cooked bacon strips**
  Optional toppings: lettuce leaves and tomato, onion and pickle slices

1. In a large bowl, combine the first seven ingredients. Crumble beef over mixture and mix well. Shape into four patties.

2. Grill burgers, covered, over medium heat or broil 3 in. from the heat for 4-7 minutes on each side or until a thermometer reads 160° and juices run clear. Top with cheese. Grill 1 minute longer or until the cheese is melted. Serve on buns with bacon and toppings of your choice.

Grilled Vegetable Medley

This is my favorite way to fix fresh summer vegetables. Cleanup is a breeze because the veggies cook in foil. It goes from garden to table in under an hour.

—**LORI DANIELS** BEVERLY, WEST VIRGINIA

PREP: 15 MIN. • **GRILL:** 20 MIN. • **MAKES:** 8 SERVINGS

- ¼ cup olive oil
- 1 teaspoon salt
- 1 teaspoon dried parsley flakes
- 1 teaspoon dried basil
- 3 large ears fresh corn on the cob, cut into 3-inch pieces
- 2 medium zucchini, cut into ¼-inch slices
- 1 medium yellow summer squash, cut into ¼-inch slices
- 1 medium sweet onion, sliced
- 1 large green pepper, diced
- 10 cherry tomatoes
- 1 jar (4½ ounces) whole mushrooms, drained
- ¼ cup butter

1. In a large bowl, combine the oil, salt, parsley and basil. Add vegetables and toss to coat. Place on a double thickness of heavy-duty foil (about 28x18 in.). Dot with butter. Fold foil around vegetables and seal tightly.

2. Grill, covered, over medium heat for 20-25 minutes or until corn is tender, turning once. Open carefully to allow steam to escape.

Delicious Tomato Pie

How about pie for dinner? This savory staple is a wonderful way to accentuate summer's abundance of tomatoes from the garden or farm stand.

—**EDIE DESPAIN** LOGAN, UTAH

PREP: 15 MIN. • **BAKE:** 30 MIN. • **MAKES:** 8 SERVINGS

- 1¼ pounds tomatoes (5 large), cut into ½-inch slices, seeded
- 1 pastry shell (9 inches), baked
- ½ cup thinly sliced green onions
- 2 tablespoons minced fresh basil
- ¼ teaspoon salt
- ¼ teaspoon pepper
- ½ cup reduced-fat mayonnaise
- ½ cup shredded reduced-fat cheddar cheese
- 2 bacon strips, cooked and crumbled
- 2 tablespoons shredded Parmesan cheese

1. Place half of the tomatoes in pastry shell. Top with onions and remaining tomatoes. Sprinkle with the basil, salt and pepper. Combine mayonnaise and cheddar cheese; spread over the tomatoes, leaving 1½ in. around the edge. Sprinkle with the bacon and Parmesan cheese.

2. Bake at 350° for 30-35 minutes or until tomatoes are tender.

SEEDING A TOMATO

To seed a tomato, cut in half horizontally and remove the stem. Holding a tomato half over a bowl or sink, scrape out seeds with a small spoon or squeeze the tomato to force out the seeds. Then slice or dice as directed in the recipe.

FAST FIX ▶ Pot of S'mores

Mom's easy Dutch oven version of the popular camping treat is so good and gooey. The hardest part is waiting for the treats to cool so you can devour them. Yum!

—**JUNE DRESS** MERIDIAN, IDAHO

PREP/TOTAL TIME: 25 MIN. • **MAKES:** 12 SERVINGS

- 1 package (14½ ounces) whole graham crackers, crushed
- ½ cup butter, melted
- 1 can (14 ounces) sweetened condensed milk
- 2 cups (12 ounces) semisweet chocolate chips
- 1 cup butterscotch chips
- 2 cups miniature marshmallows

1. Prepare grill or campfire for low heat, using 16-18 charcoal briquettes or large wood chips.
2. Line a Dutch oven with heavy-duty aluminum foil. Combine cracker crumbs and butter; press onto the bottom of the pan. Pour milk over crust and sprinkle with chocolate and butterscotch chips. Top with marshmallows.
3. Cover Dutch oven. When briquettes or wood chips are covered with white ash, place Dutch oven directly on top of six of them. Using long-handled tongs, place remaining briquettes on pan cover.
4. Cook for 15 minutes or until chips are melted. To check for doneness, use the tongs to carefully lift the cover.

Strawberry Lover's Pie

The second question people ask when I serve them this pie is, "What's your recipe?" It comes right after their first question—"May I have another slice?"

—**LAURETHA ROWE** SCRANTON, KANSAS

PREP: 25 MIN. + CHILLING • **MAKES:** 6-8 SERVINGS

- 3 ounces semisweet chocolate, divided
- 1 tablespoon butter
- 1 pastry shell (9 inches), baked
- 2 packages (3 ounces each) cream cheese, softened
- ½ cup sour cream
- 3 tablespoons sugar
- ½ teaspoon vanilla extract
- 3 to 4 cups fresh strawberries, hulled
- ⅓ cup strawberry jam, melted

1. In a large saucepan, melt 2 oz. chocolate and butter over low heat, stirring constantly; spread or brush over the bottom and up the sides of pastry shell. Chill.
2. Meanwhile, in a large bowl, beat the cream cheese, sour cream, sugar and vanilla until smooth. Spread over chocolate layer; cover and chill for 2 hours.
3. Arrange strawberries over the filling; brush with jam. Melt the remaining chocolate and drizzle over the top.

> ❝This pie is super-easy to make and looks beautiful when it's done. My friends were bidding on who could take the last slice.❞

—**NEWGARDENERSC** FROM TASTEOFHOME.COM

Halloween Layered Fudge

Here's an easy and foolproof fudge recipe that screams "Halloween!" thanks to the two-tone color scheme. You can also make the fudge with mango extract for a citrusy twist.

—TASTE OF HOME TEST KITCHEN

PREP: 15 MIN. + CHILLING
MAKES: ABOUT 2 POUNDS

- 1 teaspoon butter
- 2 cups (12 ounces) semisweet chocolate chips
- 1 can (14 ounces) sweetened condensed milk, divided
- 8 ounces white candy coating
- ¼ teaspoon orange extract
- 2 to 4 drops orange paste food coloring

1. Line an 8-in. square pan with foil; butter foil and set aside.
2. In a microwave-safe bowl, heat chocolate chips and 1 cup milk on high for 30 seconds; stir. Repeat until mixture is smooth. Pour into prepared pan. Chill for 10 minutes.
3. Meanwhile, in a microwave-safe bowl, melt candy coating with remaining milk; stir until smooth. Stir in extract and food coloring. Spread over chocolate layer.
4. Chill for 1 hour or until firm. Using foil, remove fudge from pan. Cut into 1-in. squares.

EDITOR'S Note: This recipe was tested in a 1,100-watt microwave.

Pumpkin Torte

This beautiful layered cake has a creamy filling with a mild pumpkin flavor and a little spice. It's quick to prep and always turns out moist and tender. The nuts and caramel topping add a pretty finishing touch.
—TRIXIE FISHER PIQUA, OHIO

PREP: 30 MIN.
BAKE: 25 MIN. + COOLING
MAKES: 10-12 SERVINGS

- 1 package yellow cake mix (regular size)
- 1 can (15 ounces) solid-pack pumpkin, divided
- ½ cup milk
- 4 eggs
- ⅓ cup canola oil
- 1½ teaspoons pumpkin pie spice, divided
- 1 package (8 ounces) cream cheese, softened
- 1 cup confectioners' sugar
- 1 carton (16 ounces) frozen whipped topping, thawed
- ¼ cup caramel ice cream topping
- ⅓ cup chopped pecans, toasted

1. In a large bowl, combine the cake mix, 1 cup pumpkin, milk, eggs, oil and 1 teaspoon pumpkin pie spice; beat on low speed for 30 seconds. Beat on medium for 2 minutes. Pour into two greased and floured 9-in. round baking pans.
2. Bake at 350° for 25-30 minutes or until a toothpick inserted near the centers comes out clean. Cool cakes for 10 minutes before removing from pans to wire racks to cool completely.
3. In a large bowl, beat the cream cheese until light and fluffy. Add the confectioners' sugar and remaining pumpkin and pumpkin pie spice; beat until smooth. Fold in whipped topping.
4. Cut each cake horizontally into two layers. Place bottom layer on a serving plate; spread with a fourth of the filling. Repeat layers three times. Drizzle with caramel topping; sprinkle with pecans. Store in the refrigerator.

Melted Witch Puddles

The doomed wicked witch from *The Wizard of Oz* was the inspiration behind these delicious treats that use a variety of convenience foods.

—TASTE OF HOME TEST KITCHEN

PREP: 1 HOUR + CHILLING
MAKES: 3 DOZEN

- 1 teaspoon water
- 4 drops yellow food coloring
- 1½ cups flaked coconut
- 2 cups (12 ounces) semisweet chocolate chips
- 6 tablespoons shortening, divided
- 36 chocolate cream-filled chocolate sandwich cookies
- 36 Bugles
- 4 cups vanilla or white chips
- 36 pretzel sticks

1. In a large resealable plastic bag, combine water and food coloring; add coconut. Seal bag and shake to tint coconut; set aside. In a microwave, melt chocolate chips and 2 tablespoons shortening; stir until smooth.

2. For witches' hats, place about ⅓ cup chocolate mixture in a resealable plastic bag; cut a small hole in a corner of bag. Pipe a small amount of chocolate on a cookie. Dip a Bugle in some of the remaining chocolate; allow excess to drip off. Position over chocolate on cookie, forming a witch's hat. Set on waxed paper to dry. Repeat with remaining chocolate, Bugles and cookies.

3. For puddles, melt vanilla chips and the remaining shortening; stir until smooth. Place mixture in a large heavy-duty resealable plastic bag; cut a small hole in a corner of bag. Pipe mixture into the shape of a puddle onto waxed paper-lined baking sheets.

4. Immediately place a witch's hat on the puddle. Place a pretzel stick alongside the hat; sprinkle reserved tinted coconut at the end of the pretzel stick. Repeat with remaining puddles, hats and brooms. Chill for 15 minutes or until set. Store in an airtight container.

FAST FIX ▶ Ogre Eyes Hot Cocoa

Here's looking at you! Halloween guests of all ages will get a kick out of this eerie vision staring back at them. It's a snap to make thanks to the quick and easy recipe.

—JEANNIE KLUGH
LANCASTER, PENNSYLVANIA

PREP/TOTAL TIME: 25 MIN.
MAKES: 8 SERVINGS

- 8 cups milk, divided
- 1 cup mint chocolate chips
- 1 cup instant hot cocoa mix
- 16 large marshmallows
- 16 Crows candies
- 16 lollipop sticks

1. In a large saucepan, combine 1 cup milk, chocolate chips and cocoa mix. Cook and stir over low heat until chips are melted. Stir in remaining milk; heat through.

2. Meanwhile, cut a slit in top of each marshmallow; insert a candy. Carefully insert a lollipop stick through the bottom of each marshmallow and into each candy.

3. Pour hot cocoa into mugs or cups; place two prepared marshmallows in each cup. Serve immediately.

NOTE *If mint chocolate chips are not available, place 2 cups (12 ounces) semisweet chocolate chips and ¼ teaspoon peppermint extract in a plastic bag; seal and toss to coat. Allow chips to stand for 24-48 hours.*

FAST FIX ▶ Dracula Cookies

Come late October, my friends and family can "count" on me to reintroduce them to my famous Dracula cookies. For a fun variation, use peanut butter balls dipped in candy coating or powdered doughnut balls in place of the hazelnut truffles. You won't have any trouble getting little goblins to gobble these up!

—CHRISTY HINRICHS PARKVILLE, MISSOURI

PREP/TOTAL TIME: 30 MIN. • **MAKES:** 6 COOKIES

- 6 **hazelnut truffles**
- 5 **ounces white candy coating, chopped**
- 1 **green or red Fruit Roll-Up**
- 6 **Oreo cookies**
- 1 **can (6.4 ounces) black decorating icing**
- 6 **slivered almonds, cut in half**

1. Place truffles on a waxed paper-lined pan. Freeze for 10 minutes or until chilled. Meanwhile, in a microwave bowl, melt candy coating; stir until smooth. Dip truffles in coating to cover completely; allow excess to drip off. Return to prepared pan. Refrigerate until hardened.

2. Cut Fruit Roll-Up into 2½x1½-in. strips. Reheat candy coating if necessary. Dip truffles in candy coating again; allow excess to drip off. Place one on each cookie. Wrap a fruit strip around base of truffle for cape. Let stand until set.

3. Using decorating icing and a round tip, pipe hair, eyes and mouth on each. Insert almonds for fangs. Store in an airtight container.

NOTE *This recipe was tested with Ferrero Rocher hazelnut truffles.*

❝I made this for my daughter's birthday treat at school since her birthday is close to Halloween. In place of the truffles, I used a package of crushed Oreos mixed with a package of cream cheese.❞

—SLPSLP FROM TASTEOFHOME.COM

🍲 SLOW COOKER Beef Stew with Ghoulish Mashed Potatoes

Guests will be delighted with the seasonal flavors of this hearty beef stew, including mushrooms and parsnips. Rich mashed potato ghosts are piped onto each bowl. You will love the convenient slow cooker preparation.
—TASTE OF HOME TEST KITCHEN

PREP: 30 MIN. • **COOK:** 8 HOURS • **MAKES:** 6 SERVINGS

- 2 **pounds beef stew meat, cut into 1-inch cubes**
- 1 **pound fresh mushrooms, halved**
- 2 **cups fresh baby carrots**
- 2 **medium parsnips, peeled, halved lengthwise and sliced**
- 2 **medium onions, chopped**
- 1½ **cups beef broth**
- 3 **tablespoons tomato paste**
- 1 **tablespoon Worcestershire sauce**
- 2 **garlic cloves, minced**
- ½ **teaspoon ground cloves**
- ¼ **teaspoon pepper**
- 8 **medium potatoes (2⅓ pounds), peeled and cubed**
- ⅔ **cup sour cream**
- 6 **tablespoons butter, cubed**
- 1 **teaspoon salt, divided**
- 1 **cup frozen peas**
- 2 **tablespoons all-purpose flour**
- 2 **tablespoons water**

1. In a 5-qt. slow cooker, combine the first 11 ingredients. Cover and cook on low for 8-9 hours or until beef and vegetables are tender.
2. About 30 minutes before serving, place potatoes in a large saucepan and cover with water. Bring to a boil. Reduce heat; cover and simmer for 15-20 minutes or until tender. Drain. Return potatoes to pan; add the sour cream, butter and ½ teaspoon salt. Mash the potatoes until smooth.

3. Set aside 12 peas for garnish. Add remaining peas to the slow cooker. Increase heat to high. In a bowl, whisk the flour, water and remaining salt until smooth; stir into stew. Cover and cook for 5 minutes or until thickened.
4. Divide stew among six bowls. Place mashed potatoes in large resealable plastic bag; cut a 2-in. hole in one corner. Pipe ghost potatoes onto stew; garnish with reserved peas.

Grinch Punch

This frothy beverage works for Halloween, Christmas or St. Patty's Day. It always satisfies a crowd.
—JANICE HODGE CUSTER, SOUTH DAKOTA

PREP: 20 MIN. + CHILLING • **MAKES:** 4 QUARTS

- ⅓ **cup sugar**
- 6 **tablespoons plus 1½ teaspoons water**
- ⅓ **cup evaporated milk**
- ½ **teaspoon almond extract**
- 12 **drops neon green food coloring**
- 1 **bottle (2 liters) lemon-lime soda, chilled**
- 2 **pints vanilla ice cream**

1. In a large saucepan, combine sugar and water. Cook and stir over medium heat until sugar is dissolved; remove from the heat. Stir in milk and extract. Transfer to a bowl; cool to room temperature. Cover and refrigerate until chilled.
2. Just before serving, transfer milk mixture to a punch bowl. Stir in the food coloring and soda. Top with scoops of ice cream.

FAST FIX

Pumpkin Mousse

My family loves this cool and creamy pumpkin-flavored mousse. I love it because it's a cinch to make.

—LISA MCCLOSKEY DWIGHT, ILLINOIS

PREP/TOTAL TIME: 10 MIN.
MAKES: 6 SERVINGS

- 1 **carton (4 ounces) whipped cream cheese with cinnamon and brown sugar**
- 1 **cup pumpkin pie filling**
- ½ **cup whipped topping**
- 6 **individual graham cracker tart shells**
  Additional whipped topping and ground cinnamon

In a small bowl, combine the cream cheese and pumpkin until blended. Fold in whipped topping. Fill tart shells. Garnish each with additional whipped topping and sprinkle with cinnamon. Store in the refrigerator.

Halloween Layer Cake

My husband and kids look forward to me making this fun layered cake every Halloween. You can also use the orange and chocolate batters to make marble cupcakes.

—KAREN WIRTH TAVISTOCK, ONTARIO

PREP: 20 MIN. • **BAKE:** 30 MIN.
MAKES: 12-16 SERVINGS

- 1 **cup butter, softened**
- 2 **cups sugar**
- 4 **eggs**
- 3 **cups all-purpose flour**
- 1 **tablespoon baking powder**
- ½ **teaspoon salt**
- 1 **cup milk**
- ¼ **cup baking cocoa**

- ¼ **cup water**
- ½ **teaspoon vanilla extract**
- ½ **teaspoon orange extract**
- 1 **tablespoon grated orange peel**
- 10 **drops yellow food coloring**
- 6 **drops red food coloring**

FROSTING
- 3 **packages (3 ounces each) cream cheese, softened**
- 5¾ **cups confectioners' sugar**
- 2 **tablespoons milk**
- 8 **drops yellow food coloring**
- 6 **drops red food coloring**

GLAZE
- 3 **ounces semisweet chocolate**
- ⅓ **cup heavy whipping cream**
  Candy corn for garnish

1. In a bowl, cream butter and sugar until light and fluffy. Add eggs, one at a time, beating well after each. Combine flour, baking powder and salt; add alternately with milk to creamed mixture. Mix well. Combine cocoa, water and vanilla; stir in 2 cups cake batter.

2. Pour into a greased and floured 9-in. round baking pan. Add orange extract, peel and food coloring to remaining batter. Pour into two greased and floured 9-in. round baking pans. Bake at 350° for 30 minutes or until cake tests done. Cool for 10 minutes before removing from pans to wire racks.

3. In a bowl, beat all frosting ingredients until smooth. Place one orange cake layer on a cake plate; spread with ½ cup frosting. Top with chocolate layer; spread with ½ cup frosting. Top with second orange layer. Frost the sides and top of each.

4. Microwave chocolate and cream on high 1½ minutes or, stirring once. Stir until smooth; let cool 2 minutes. Slowly pour over cake, letting glaze drizzle down sides. Garnish with candy corn.

Deluxe Pumpkin Cheesecake

Here's the ultimate pumpkin dessert. It has a unique gingersnap crust and rich, luscious swirls of cheesecake and pumpkin. If you want something extra special for the holidays, you must try this recipe!

—SHARON SKILDUM
MAPLE GROVE, MINNESOTA

PREP: 35 MIN. • **BAKE:** 50 MIN. + CHILLING
MAKES: 12 SERVINGS

- 1 **cup crushed gingersnap cookies (about 20 cookies)**
- ⅓ **cup finely chopped pecans**
- ¼ **cup butter, melted**
- 4 **packages (8 ounces each) cream cheese, softened, divided**
- 1½ **cups sugar, divided**
- 2 **tablespoons cornstarch**
- 2 **teaspoons vanilla extract**
- 4 **eggs**
- 1 **cup canned pumpkin**
- 2 **teaspoons ground cinnamon**
- 1½ **teaspoons ground nutmeg**

GARNISH
　　Chocolate syrup, caramel ice cream topping, whipped topping and additional crushed gingersnap cookies, optional

1. Place a greased 9-in. springform pan on a double thickness of heavy-duty foil (about 18 in. square). Securely wrap foil around pan.
2. In a small bowl, combine the cookie crumbs, pecans and butter. Press onto the bottom of prepared pan. Place on a baking sheet. Bake at 350° for 8-10 minutes or until set. Cool on a wire rack.
3. For filling, in a large bowl, beat 1 package of cream cheese, ½ cup sugar and cornstarch until smooth, about 2 minutes. Beat in remaining cream cheese, one package at a time until smooth. Add remaining sugar and vanilla. Add eggs; beat on low speed just until combined.
4. Place 2 cups filling in a small bowl; stir in the pumpkin, cinnamon, and nutmeg. Remove ¾ cup pumpkin filling; set aside. Pour remaining pumpkin filling over crust; top with remaining plain filling. Cut through with a knife to swirl. Drop reserved pumpkin filling by spoonfuls over cheesecake; cut through with a knife to swirl.
5. Place springform pan in a large baking pan; add 1 in. of hot water to larger pan. Bake at 350° for 55-65 minutes or until center is just set and top appears dull. Remove

springform pan from water bath. Cool on a wire rack for 10 minutes. Carefully run a knife around edge of pan to loosen; cool 1 hour longer. Refrigerate overnight.
6. Garnish with chocolate syrup, caramel sauce, whipped topping and additional crushed gingersnaps if desired.

Pilgrim Hat Cookies

We dreamed up this combination for a yummy treat to take into school before our Thanksgiving break. Both kids and teachers loved them!

—MEGAN AND MITCHELL VOGEL
JEFFERSON, WISCONSIN

PREP: 1 HOUR • **MAKES:** 32 COOKIES

- 1 **cup vanilla frosting**
- 7 **drops yellow food coloring**
- 32 **miniature peanut butter cups**
- 1 **package (11½ ounces) fudge-striped cookies**
- 32 **pieces orange mini Chiclets gum**

1. In a small shallow bowl, combine frosting and food coloring. Remove paper liners from peanut butter cups.
2. Holding the bottom of a peanut butter cup, dip top of cup in yellow frosting. Position over center hole on the bottom of cookie, forming the hatband and crown. Add a buckle of Chiclets gum. Repeat with remaining cups and cookies.

Creamy Make Ahead Mashed Potatoes

Smooth mashed potatoes get even better when topped with a savory trio of cheese, onions and bacon. Prep them the day before an event and you'll enjoy them even more!
—**JOANN KOERKENMEIER** DAMIANSVILLE, ILLINOIS

PREP: 25 MIN. • **BAKE:** 40 MIN. • **MAKES:** 10 SERVINGS

- 3 pounds potatoes (about 9 medium), peeled and cubed
- 1 package (8 ounces) cream cheese, softened
- ½ cup sour cream
- ½ cup butter, cubed
- ¼ cup 2% milk
- 1½ teaspoons onion powder
- 1 teaspoon salt
- 1 teaspoon garlic powder
- ½ teaspoon pepper
- 6 bacon strips, chopped
- 1 cup (4 ounces) shredded cheddar cheese
- 3 green onions, chopped

1. Place potatoes in a Dutch oven and cover with water. Bring to a boil. Reduce heat; cover and cook for 10-15 minutes or until tender. Drain; mash potatoes with cream cheese, sour cream and butter. Stir in the milk and seasonings.

2. In a small skillet, cook bacon over medium heat until crisp. Remove to paper towels with a slotted spoon; drain.

3. Transfer potato mixture to a greased 13x9-in. baking dish; sprinkle with cheese, onions and bacon. Cover and refrigerate until ready to use.

4. Remove from the refrigerator 30 minutes before baking. Bake, uncovered, at 350° for 40-50 minutes or until heated through.

Crunchy Sweet Potato Casserole

Cinnamon and nutmeg and a crunchy cornflake-walnut topping make this comforting spud dish a delight to eat.
—**VIRGINIA SLATER** WEST SUNBURY, PENNSYLVANIA

PREP: 15 MIN. • **BAKE:** 25 MIN. • **MAKES:** 6 SERVINGS

- 2 cups mashed sweet potatoes
- ½ cup butter, melted
- ¼ cup sugar
- ¼ cup packed brown sugar
- 2 eggs, lightly beaten
- ½ cup 2% milk
- 1 teaspoon ground cinnamon
- ½ teaspoon ground nutmeg

TOPPING

- 1 cup crushed cornflakes
- ½ cup chopped walnuts
- ¼ cup packed brown sugar
- ¼ cup butter, cubed

1. In a large bowl, combine the first eight ingredients. Spoon into a greased 1½-qt. baking dish. Bake, uncovered, at 375° for 20 minutes or until a thermometer reads 160°.

2. Combine topping ingredients; sprinkle over potatoes. Bake 5-10 minutes longer or until the topping is lightly browned.

SWEET POTATOES 101

Select firm sweet potatoes with no cracks or bruises. If stored in a cool, dark, well-ventilated place, they'll remain fresh for about 2 weeks. If the temperature is above 60°, they'll sprout sooner or become woody. Once cooked, sweet potatoes can be stored for up to 1 week in the refrigerator.

Champagne-Basted Turkey

I've prepared this recipe every Thanksgiving for years, and we all love it. The secret? Use lots of fresh parsley and keep basting. You'll end up with a tender turkey, and a new favorite recipe.
—**SHARON HAWK** EDWARDSVILLE, ILLINOIS

PREP: 20 MIN. • **BAKE:** 3½ HOURS + STANDING
MAKES: 14 SERVINGS (1⅔ CUPS GRAVY)

- 1 **turkey (14 to 16 pounds)**
- ¼ **cup butter, softened**
- 1 **teaspoon salt**
- 1 **teaspoon celery salt**
- ¾ **teaspoon pepper**
  Fresh sage and parsley sprigs, optional
- 2 **cups champagne or other sparkling wine**
- 2 **medium onions, chopped**
- 1½ **cups minced fresh parsley**
- 1 **cup condensed beef consomme, undiluted**
- ½ **teaspoon dried thyme**
- ½ **teaspoon dried marjoram**

GRAVY
- 1 **tablespoon butter**
- 1 **tablespoon all-purpose flour**

1. Pat turkey dry. Combine the butter, salt, celery salt and pepper; rub over the outside and inside of turkey. Place sage and parsley sprigs in cavity if desired. Tuck wings under turkey; tie drumsticks together. Place breast side up on a rack in a roasting pan.

2. Bake, uncovered, at 325° for 30 minutes. In a large bowl, combine the champagne, onions, parsley, consomme, thyme and marjoram; pour into pan. Bake for 3 to 3½ hours longer or until a thermometer reads 180°, basting occasionally with champagne mixture. Cover loosely with foil if turkey browns too quickly. Cover and let stand for 20 minutes before slicing.

3. For gravy, strain drippings into a small bowl. In a small saucepan, melt butter. Stir in flour until smooth; gradually add drippings. Bring to a boil; cook and stir for 2 minutes or until thickened. Serve with turkey.

Coconut Cashew Brittle

This rich, buttery brittle has always been part of our holiday candy collection. A bonanza of flaked coconut and cashews make it extra scrumptious.

—DARLENE BRENDEN
SALEM, OREGON

PREP: 25 MIN. • **BAKE:** 10 MIN.
MAKES: ABOUT 3 POUNDS

- 2 tablespoons plus 1 cup butter, divided
- 2 cups cashew halves
- 2 cups flaked coconut
- 2 cups sugar
- 1 cup light corn syrup
- ½ cup plus 1 teaspoon water, divided
- 2 teaspoons vanilla extract
- 1½ teaspoons baking soda

1. Butter two 15x10x1-in. pans with 1 tablespoon butter each; set pans aside.

2. Combine cashews and coconut on a third 15x10x1-in. baking pan. Bake at 350° for 8-10 minutes or until golden brown, stirring occasionally.

3. In a large heavy saucepan, combine the sugar, corn syrup and ½ cup water. Cook and stir over medium heat until mixture comes to a boil. Add remaining butter; cook and stir until butter is melted. Continue cooking, without stirring, until a candy thermometer reads 300° (hard-crack stage).

4. Meanwhile, combine the vanilla, baking soda and remaining water.

Remove saucepan from the heat; add cashews and coconut. Add baking soda mixture; stir until light and foamy. Quickly pour onto prepared baking sheets. Spread with a buttered metal spatula to ¼-in. thickness. Cool before breaking into pieces. Store in an airtight container.

NOTE *We recommend that you test your candy thermometer before each use by bringing water to a boil; the thermometer should read 212°. Adjust your recipe temperature up or down based on your test.*

Holiday Cheesecake

This showstopper celebrates cheesecake in all its lusciousness. Each slice is overloaded with fun, festive candy toppings.

—TASTE OF HOME COOKING SCHOOL

PREP: 30 MIN.
BAKE: 1½ HOURS + CHILLING
MAKES: 16 SERVINGS

- 1½ cups graham cracker crumbs
- ½ cup pecans, toasted and finely chopped
- 2 tablespoons light brown sugar
- 6 tablespoons butter, melted

FILLING
- 4 packages (8 ounces each) cream cheese, softened
- 1 cup sugar
- 3 teaspoons vanilla extract
- 4 eggs, lightly beaten
- 1 cup (6 ounces) miniature semisweet chocolate chips

TOPPING
- 2 cups (16 ounces) sour cream
- ¼ cup sugar
- Assorted candies

1. Place an ungreased 9-in. springform pan on a double thickness of heavy-duty foil (about 18 in. square). Securely wrap foil around pan.

2. In a small bowl, combine the cracker crumbs, pecans and brown sugar; stir in butter. Press onto bottom and 1½ in. up the sides of prepared pan. Place on a baking sheet. Bake at 350° for 5 minutes. Cool on a wire rack.

3. In a large bowl, beat the cream cheese, sugar and vanilla until smooth. Add eggs; beat on low speed just until combined. Fold in chocolate chips. Pour into crust. Place in a larger baking pan; add 1 in. of hot water to larger pan.

4. Bake at 325° for 1½ hours or until center is just set and top appears dull. In a small bowl, combine sour cream and sugar until smooth; spoon over hot cheesecake and spread to cover. Bake for 5 minutes longer or until topping is just set.

5. Remove springform pan from water bath. Cool on a wire rack for 10 minutes. Carefully run a knife around edge of pan to loosen; cool 1 hour longer. Refrigerate overnight. Remove sides of pan. Garnish the cheesecake with candies.

Peppermint Ribbon Cake

With its pretty red layer and fabulous mint flavor, this dessert is just right for the holidays. Because I work full-time, I like that it calls for a convenient cake mix to keep prep easy.

—LISA VARNER EL PASO, TEXAS

PREP: 20 MIN. • **BAKE:** 35 MIN. + COOLING
MAKES: 12 SERVINGS

- 1 package white cake mix (regular size)
- ½ teaspoon peppermint extract
- ½ teaspoon red food coloring
- ½ cup plus 2 tablespoons crushed peppermint candies, divided
- 1 cup confectioners' sugar
- 1 tablespoon 2% milk

1. Prepare cake batter according to package directions. Transfer 1 cup to a small bowl; stir in the extract, food coloring and ½ cup crushed peppermint candies.

2. Spoon 2 cups of the remaining batter into a greased and floured 10-in. fluted tube pan. Carefully top with the peppermint batter; do not swirl. Top with the remaining plain batter.

3. Bake at 350° for 35-45 minutes or until a toothpick inserted near the center comes out clean. Cool for 10 minutes before removing cake from pan to a wire rack to cool completely.

4. Combine confectioners' sugar and milk; drizzle over cake. Sprinkle with remaining crushed peppermint candies.

FAST FIX ▶ Traditional Popcorn Balls

Kids of all ages enjoy these colorful old-fashioned treats. One batch goes a long way.

—CATHY KARGES
HAZEN, NORTH DAKOTA

PREP/TOTAL TIME: 20 MIN.
MAKES: 20 SERVINGS

- 7 quarts popped popcorn
- 1 cup sugar
- 1 cup light corn syrup
- ¼ cup water
- ¼ teaspoon salt
- 3 tablespoons butter
- 1 teaspoon vanilla extract
   Food coloring, optional

1. Place popcorn in a large baking pan; keep warm in a 200° oven.

2. In a heavy saucepan, combine the sugar, corn syrup, water and salt. Cook over medium heat until a candy thermometer reads 235° (soft-ball stage).

3. Remove from the heat. Add the butter, vanilla and food coloring if desired; stir until butter is melted. Immediately pour over popcorn and stir until evenly coated.

4. When mixture is cool enough to handle, quickly shape into 3-in. balls, dipping hands in cold water to prevent sticking.

NOTE *We recommend that you test your candy thermometer before each use by bringing water to a boil; the thermometer should read 212°. Adjust your recipe temperature up or down based on your test.*

FAST FIX Snickerdoodles

The history of this whimsically named treat is widely disputed, but the popularity of the classic cinnamon-sugar-coated cookie is undeniable! Add this version from our Test Kitchen staff to your holiday cookie collection.

—TASTE OF HOME TEST KITCHEN

PREP/TOTAL TIME: 25 MIN. • **MAKES:** 2½ DOZEN

- ½ cup butter, softened
- 1 cup plus 2 tablespoons sugar, divided
- 1 egg
- ½ teaspoon vanilla extract
- 1½ cups all-purpose flour
- ¼ teaspoon baking soda
- ¼ teaspoon cream of tartar
- 1 teaspoon ground cinnamon

1. In a large bowl, cream butter and 1 cup sugar until light and fluffy. Beat in egg and vanilla. Combine the flour, baking soda and cream of tartar; gradually add to the creamed mixture and mix well. In a small bowl, combine cinnamon and remaining sugar.

2. Shape dough into 1-in. balls; roll in cinnamon-sugar. Place 2 in. apart on ungreased baking sheets. Bake at 375° for 10-12 minutes or until lightly browned. Remove to wire racks to cool.

Chocolate-Coated Pretzels

These pretty pretzels are easy to prepare and make fun gifts. They're a great way to get your sweet-and-salty fix without loading up on a lot of calories.

—VIRGINIA CHRONIC ROBINSON, ILLINOIS

PREP: 15 MIN. + STANDING • **MAKES:** 5-6 DOZEN

- 1 to 1¼ pounds white and/or milk chocolate candy coating, coarsely chopped
- 1 package (8 ounces) miniature pretzels
  Nonpariels, colored jimmies and colored sugar, optional

In a microwave, melt half of candy coating at a time; stir until smooth. Dip pretzels in candy coating; allow excess to drip off. Place on waxed paper; let stand until almost set. Garnish as desired; let stand until set.

FAST FIX Sweet & Salty Snowmen

Kids have a blast creating different looks for their pretzel snowmen with candy scarves, buttons and top hats. If any are left over, the sticks make adorable table decorations posed in glasses filled with shredded coconut or mini marshmallows for snow.

—CAROL BERNDT AVON, SOUTH DAKOTA

PREP/TOTAL TIME: 25 MIN. • **MAKES:** 8 SNOWMEN

- 8 pretzel rods
- 6 ounces white baking chocolate, melted
  Assorted candies: M&M's miniature baking bits, miniature chocolate chips, small gumdrops, jelly rings, Fruit by the Foot fruit rolls

1. Dip pretzel rods two-thirds of the way into melted white chocolate, or drizzle chocolate over pretzels with a spoon. Attach baking bits for buttons and noses and chocolate chips for eyes.

2. For hats, dip the bottom of a small gumdrop into chocolate and press onto a jelly ring; attach to the top of each pretzel.

3. Carefully stand snowmen by placing them upright in a tall glass or pressing the bottom of the pretzel rods into a 2-in.-thick piece of Styrofoam. For scarves, cut fruit rolls into thin strips; tie around snowmen.

NOTE *This recipe was tested with Chuckles jelly rings.*

Peppermint Lollipops

These splendid suckers from our Test Kitchen are a festive Christmas confection. There are endless color and design options, so let your creative juices flow.

—TASTE OF HOME TEST KITCHEN

PREP: 5 MIN. • **COOK:** 30 MIN. + STANDING
MAKES: 10 LOLLIPOPS

- 1½ cups sugar
- ¾ cup water
- ⅔ cup light corn syrup
- ½ teaspoon cream of tartar
- ½ teaspoon peppermint oil
  Red and/or green paste food coloring
- 10 lollipop sticks
  Crushed peppermint candies, optional

1. Butter 10 assorted metal cookie cutters and place on a parchment paper-lined baking sheet; set aside. In a large heavy saucepan, combine the sugar, water, corn syrup and cream of tartar. Cook and stir over medium heat until sugar is dissolved. Bring to a boil. Cook, without stirring, until a candy thermometer reads 300° (hard-crack stage).

2. Remove from the heat. Stir in oil, keeping face away from mixture as odor is very strong. For each color of candy swirls, pour ¼ cup sugar mixture into a ramekin or custard cup; tint red or green.

3. Immediately pour remaining sugar mixture into prepared cookie cutters. Drizzle with colored mixtures as desired; cut through with a toothpick to swirl. Remove cutters just before lollipops are set; firmly press a lollipop stick into each. Sprinkle peppermint candies over tops if desired.

Shortbread Ornament Cookies

These buttery shortbread cookies are almost too pretty to eat! Use holiday ornament cookie cutters or any other shapes you like.

—TASTE OF HOME TEST KITCHEN

PREP: 1½ HOURS + CHILLING • **BAKE:** 15 MIN./BATCH + COOLING
MAKES: ABOUT 3 DOZEN

- 3 cups all-purpose flour
- ¾ cup sugar
- ¼ teaspoon salt
- 1½ cups cold butter, cubed
- 2 tablespoons cold water
- ½ teaspoon rum extract
- ½ teaspoon almond extract

ICING

- 2 cups confectioners' sugar
- 2 tablespoons plus 2 teaspoons 2% milk
  Food coloring of your choice, optional
  Colored edible glitter and nonpareils

1. In a large bowl, combine the flour, sugar and salt; cut in butter until mixture resembles coarse crumbs. Stir in water and extracts until mixture forms a ball.

2. On a lightly floured surface, roll dough to ¼-in. thickness. Cut with floured cookie cutters. Place 1 in. apart on ungreased baking sheets. Cover and refrigerate for 30 minutes.

3. Bake at 325° for 15-18 minutes or until edges are lightly browned. Cool for 2 minutes before removing to wire racks to cool completely.

4. For icing, in a large bowl, whisk the confectioners' sugar and milk. Divide into small bowls; tint with food coloring if desired. Gently spread over cookies. Decorate as desired.

FAST FIX ▶

Holiday Lettuce Salad

My family always requests that I make this salad for get-togethers. It's light and very good; everyone goes back for seconds.

—BRYAN BRAACK ELDRIDGE, IOWA

PREP/TOTAL TIME: 20 MIN.
MAKES: 14 SERVINGS

- 10 cups torn romaine
- 2 medium red apples, cubed
- 2 medium pears, cubed
- 1 cup (4 ounces) shredded Swiss cheese
- ½ cup dried cranberries
- 6 tablespoons lemon juice
- 3 tablespoons canola oil
- 3 tablespoons light corn syrup
- 1½ teaspoons grated onion
- 1½ teaspoons Dijon mustard
- ½ teaspoon salt
- ½ cup chopped lightly salted cashews

1. In a salad bowl, combine the first five ingredients.
2. For dressing, in a small bowl, whisk the lemon juice, oil, corn syrup, onion, mustard and salt. Pour over romaine mixture; toss to coat. Sprinkle with cashews.

Cinnamon Chocolate Minties

These cookies are also great with white chocolate instead of semisweet. For a simple topping, you can also use powdered sugar with crushed peppermint candies.

—BARBARA ESTABROOK RHINELANDER, WISCONSIN

PREP: 45 MIN.
BAKE: 10 MIN./BATCH + COOLING
MAKES: ABOUT 4 DOZEN

- ½ cup butter, softened
- ½ cup sugar
- ½ cup packed brown sugar
- 1 egg
- 1 teaspoon vanilla extract
- 1½ cups all-purpose flour
- ⅓ cup baking cocoa
- 1 teaspoon ground cinnamon
- ¼ teaspoon baking soda
- ⅓ cup coarsely crushed soft peppermint candies
- ⅓ cup dark chocolate chips

DRIZZLE
- ½ cup semisweet chocolate chips
- ½ teaspoon canola oil
- 2 teaspoons finely crushed soft peppermint candies

1. In a small bowl, cream butter and sugars until light and fluffy. Beat in egg and vanilla. Combine the flour, cocoa, cinnamon and baking soda; gradually add to creamed mixture and mix well. Fold in the candies and dark chocolate chips.
2. Shape into 1-in. balls; place 1 in. apart on greased baking sheets. Flatten slightly. Bake at 350° for 6-8 minutes or until set. Remove to wire racks to cool completely.
3. In a small bowl, melt semisweet chips with oil; stir until smooth. Drizzle over cookies. Sprinkle with candies. Let stand until set. Store in an airtight container.
NOTE *This recipe was tested with Bob's Sweet Stripes peppermint candies.*

Gingerbread Cookies

The aroma of these cookies brings back fond memories of my Grandma's house. My boys always linger around the kitchen when I make them, and my husband usually takes a batch to work to share with his co-workers.
—**CHRISTY THELEN** KELLOGG, IOWA

PREP: 30 MIN. + CHILLING
BAKE: 10 MIN./BATCH + COOLING
MAKES: 5 DOZEN

- ¾ cup butter, softened
- 1 cup packed brown sugar
- 1 egg
- ¾ cup molasses
- 4 cups all-purpose flour
- 2 teaspoons ground ginger
- 1½ teaspoons baking soda
- 1½ teaspoons ground cinnamon
- ¾ teaspoon ground cloves
- ¼ teaspoon salt
  Vanilla frosting of your choice
  Red and green paste food coloring

1. In a large bowl, cream butter and brown sugar until light and fluffy. Add egg and molasses.

Combine the flour, ginger, baking soda, cinnamon, cloves and salt; gradually add to creamed mixture and mix well. Cover and refrigerate for 4 hours or overnight or until easy to handle.

2. On a lightly floured surface, roll dough to ⅛-in. thickness. Cut with floured 2½-in. cookie cutters. Place 1 in. apart on ungreased baking sheets.

3. Bake at 350° for 8-10 minutes or until edges are firm. Remove to wire racks to cool. Tint some of the frosting red and some green. Decorate cookies.

Layered Christmas Gelatin

As soon as the merriest month of the year arrives, I know it's time to pull this treasured recipe out of my box. The traditional colors in this salad make my spread look so pretty.
—**DIANE SCHEFELKER** IRETON, IOWA

PREP: 30 MIN. + CHILLING
MAKES: 10 SERVINGS

- 1 package (3 ounces) lime gelatin
- 1 cup boiling water
- ⅓ cup unsweetened pineapple juice
- 1 cup crushed pineapple, drained

CREAM CHEESE LAYER
- 1 teaspoon unflavored gelatin
- 2 tablespoons cold water
- 1 package (8 ounces) cream cheese, softened
- ⅓ cup milk

BERRY LAYER
- 2 packages (3 ounces each) strawberry gelatin
- 2 cups boiling water
- 1 can (14 ounces) whole-berry cranberry sauce
  Whipped topping, optional

1. Dissolve lime gelatin in boiling water; stir in pineapple juice. Stir in pineapple. Pour into an 11x7-in. dish; refrigerate until set.

2. In a small saucepan, sprinkle unflavored gelatin over cold water; let stand for 1 minute. Heat over low heat, stirring until gelatin is completely dissolved. Transfer to a small bowl. Beat in cream cheese and milk until smooth. Spread over lime layer; refrigerate until set.

3. Dissolve strawberry gelatin in boiling water; stir in cranberry sauce. Cool for 10 minutes. Carefully spoon over cream cheese layer. Refrigerate until set.

4. Cut into squares. Garnish with whipped topping if desired.

GENERAL INDEX

This handy index lists every recipe by food category, major ingredient and/or cooking method, so you can easily locate recipes to suit your needs.

p. 59

p. 88

p. 37

p. 83

p. 154

p. 109

p. 162

p. 62

p. 96

p. 39

p. 111

p. 132

p. 89

p. 65

ALPHABETICAL RECIPE INDEX

This handy index lists every recipe in alphabetical order so you can easily find your favorite recipes.

p. 209

p. 182

p. 133

p. 217

D

p. 33

E

F

G

H

I

J

L

p. 85

p. 213

p. 92

p. 188

p. 21

p. 176

Ingredient Substitutions

WHEN YOU NEED:	IN THIS AMOUNT:	SUBSTITUTE:
Baking Powder	1 teaspoon	½ teaspoon cream of tartar plus ¼ teaspoon baking soda
Broth	1 cup	1 cup hot water plus 1 teaspoon bouillon granules *or* 1 bouillon cube
Buttermilk	1 cup	1 tablespoon lemon juice *or* white vinegar plus enough milk to measure 1 cup; let stand 5 minutes. *Or* 1 cup plain yogurt.
Cajun Seasoning	1 teaspoon	¼ teaspoon cayenne pepper, ½ teaspoon dried thyme, ¼ teaspoon dried basil and 1 minced garlic clove
Chocolate, Semisweet	1 square (1 ounce)	1 square (1 ounce) unsweetened chocolate plus 1 tablespoon sugar *or* 3 tablespoons semisweet chocolate chips
Chocolate	1 square (1 ounce)	3 tablespoons baking cocoa plus 1 tablespoon shortening *or* canola oil
Cornstarch	1 tablespoon	2 tablespoons all-purpose flour (for thickening)
Corn Syrup, Dark	1 cup	¾ cup light corn syrup plus ¼ cup molasses
Corn Syrup, Light	1 cup	1 cup sugar plus ¼ cup water
Cracker Crumbs	1 cup	1 cup dry bread crumbs
Cream, Half-and-Half	1 cup	1 tablespoon melted butter plus enough whole milk to measure 1 cup
Egg	1 whole	2 egg whites *or* 2 egg yolks *or* ¼ cup egg substitute
Flour, Cake	1 cup	1 cup minus 2 tablespoons (⅞ cup) all-purpose flour
Flour, Self-Rising	1 cup	1½ teaspoons baking powder, ½ teaspoon salt and enough all-purpose flour to measure 1 cup
Garlic, Fresh	1 clove	⅛ teaspoon garlic powder
Gingerroot, Fresh	1 teaspoon	¼ teaspoon ground ginger
Honey	1 cup	1¼ cups sugar plus ¼ cup water
Lemon Juice	1 teaspoon	¼ teaspoon cider vinegar
Lemon Peel	1 teaspoon	½ teaspoon lemon extract
Milk, Whole	1 cup	½ cup evaporated milk plus ½ cup water *or* 1 cup water plus ⅓ cup nonfat dry milk powder
Molasses	1 cup	1 cup honey
Mustard, Prepared	1 tablespoon	½ teaspoon ground mustard plus 2 teaspoons cider *or* white vinegar
Onion	1 small onion	1 teaspoon onion powder *or* 1 tablespoon dried minced onion (⅓ cup chopped)
Poultry Seasoning	1 teaspoon	¾ teaspoon rubbed sage plus ¼ teaspoon dried thyme
Sour Cream	1 cup	1 cup plain yogurt
Sugar	1 cup	1 cup packed brown sugar *or* 2 cups sifted confectioners' sugar
Tomato Juice	1 cup	½ cup tomato sauce plus ½ cup water
Tomato Sauce	2 cups	¾ cup tomato paste plus 1 cup water
Yeast	1 package (¼ ounce) active dry	1 cake (⅝ ounce) compressed yeast

Get Cooking with a Well-Stocked Kitchen

In a perfect world, you would plan out weekly or even monthly menus and have all the ingredients on hand to make each night's dinner. The reality, however, is you likely haven't thought about dinner until you've walked through the door.

With a reasonably stocked pantry, refrigerator and freezer, you'll still be able to serve a satisfying meal in short order. Consider these tips:

QUICK-COOKING MEATS like boneless chicken breasts, chicken thighs, pork tenderloin, pork chops, ground meats, Italian sausage, sirloin and flank steaks, fish fillets and shrimp should be stocked in the freezer. Wrap them individually (except shrimp), so you can remove only the amount you need. For the quickest defrosting, wrap meats for freezing in small, thin packages.

FROZEN VEGETABLES prepackaged in plastic bags are a real time-saver. Simply pour out the amount needed. No preparation is required!

PASTAS, RICE, RICE MIXES AND COUSCOUS are great staples to have in the pantry—and they generally have a long shelf life. Remember, thinner pastas, such as angel hair, cook faster than thicker pastas. Fresh (refrigerated) pasta cooks faster than dried.

DAIRY PRODUCTS like milk, sour cream, cheeses (shredded, cubed or crumbled), eggs, yogurt and butter or margarine are perishable, so check the use-by date on the packages and replace as needed.

CONDIMENTS such as ketchup, mustard, mayonnaise, salad dressings, salsa, taco sauce, soy sauce, stir-fry sauce, lemon juice, etc. add flavor to many dishes. Personalize the list to suit your family's needs.

FRESH FRUIT AND VEGETABLES can make a satisfying predinner snack. Oranges and apples are not as perishable as bananas. Ready-to-use salad greens are great for an instant salad.

DRIED HERBS, SPICES, VINEGARS and seasoning mixes add lots of flavor and keep for months.

PASTA SAUCES, OLIVES, BEANS, broths, canned tomatoes, canned vegetables, and canned or dried soups are great to have on hand for a quick meal...and many of these items are common recipe ingredients.

GET YOUR FAMILY INTO THE HABIT of posting a grocery list. When an item is used up or is almost gone, just add it to your list for the next shopping trip. This way you won't completely run out of an item, and you'll also save time when writing your grocery list.

Make the Most of Your Time Every Night

With recipes in hand and your kitchen stocked, you're well on your way to a relaxing family meal. Here are some pointers to help you get dinner on the table fast:

PREHEAT THE OVEN OR GRILL before starting on the recipe.

PULL OUT ALL THE INGREDIENTS, mixing tools and cooking tools before beginning any prep work.

USE CONVENIENCE ITEMS whenever possible, such as pre-chopped garlic, onion and peppers, shredded or cubed cheese, seasoning mixes, jarred sauces, etc.

MULTITASK! While the meat is simmering for a main dish, toss a salad, cook a side dish or start on dessert.

ENCOURAGE HELPERS. Have younger children set the table. Older ones can help with ingredient preparation or even assemble simple recipes themselves.

TAKE CARE OF TWO MEALS IN ONE NIGHT by planning main dish leftovers or making a double batch of favorite sides.

Tricks to Tame Hunger When it Strikes

Are the kids begging for a pre-supper snack? Calm rumbling tummies with some nutritious, not-too-filling noshes.

START WITH A SMALL TOSSED SALAD. Try a ready-to-serve salad mix and add their favorite salad dressing and a little protein, like cubed cheese or julienned slices of deli meat.

CUT UP AN APPLE and smear a little peanut butter on each slice. Or offer other fruits such as seedless grapes, cantaloupe, oranges or bananas. For variety, give kids a vanilla yogurt or reduced-fat ranch dressing as a dipper for the fruit, or combine a little reduced-fat sour cream with a sprinkling of brown sugar. Too tired to cut up the fruit? A fruit snack cup will do the trick, too.

DURING THE COLD MONTHS, serve up a small mug of soup with a few oyster crackers to hit the spot.

RAW VEGGIES such as carrots, cucumbers, mushrooms, broccoli and cauliflower are tasty treats, especially when served with a little hummus for dipping. Many of these vegetables can be purchased precut.

GIVE KIDS A SMALL SERVING of cheese and crackers. Look for presliced cheese and cut the slices into smaller squares to fit the crackers. Choose a cracker that's made from whole wheat, such as an all-natural, seven-grain cracker.